TOTAL Guitar
PLAY BETTER NOW!

— *Presents* —

HOW TO PLAY

Guitar

ACOUSTIC AND ELECTRIC- LEARN TO PLAY LIKE A ROCK HERO

CARLTON BOOKS

CONTENTS

ANATOMY OF AN
ELECTRIC GUITAR

1 TOP Electric guitars have been made from an astonishing array of materials over the years. The most common woods are ash, alder, mahogany, rosewood, maple and ebony, but some intrepid makers have used steel, plastics, hemp, and even bits of Muddy Waters' house. Bodies can be solid, hollow, or a blend of the two. What's yours made of? Have a listen to guitars made of other materials and with different body shapes, and note the differences in tone and the way they feel to hold.

2 BRIDGE/TAILPIECE This secures your strings to the body of the guitar, and provides a stable 'base' for the strings to vibrate and make sound. There are many kinds, ranging from simple steel bars to complex vibrato systems with 'whammy' bars which you waggle to change pitch. As you learn, be careful not to lean too hard on your bridge – this can send the strings 'sharp' and make them sound out of tune.

3 CUTAWAYS The main purpose of a cutaway is to make sure your left hand can more easily access the upper frets on the fingerboard. Without them high notes would be too much of a finger stretch. Cutaways also reduce bodyweight, and this affects tone, particularly on acoustic guitars. Not all cutaways are created equal – some offer more access, some less. The first few times you play notes past the 12th fret, pay attention to how your left-hand thumb is positioned as it supports your hand.

4 Neck Guitar neck materials vary, but most are made from maple or mahogany. The way they join the body affects sustain and tone (most are bolted on, glued in, or extended through the guitar's body). Neck 'profile' refers to the thickness and shape of the neck: even if

Guitar necks vary in shape, size and feel

"TOO HIGH AND YOU'LL HAVE TO WORK MUCH HARDER TO PRESS AND HOLD THE STRINGS AGAINST THE FRETS WHEN PLAYING"

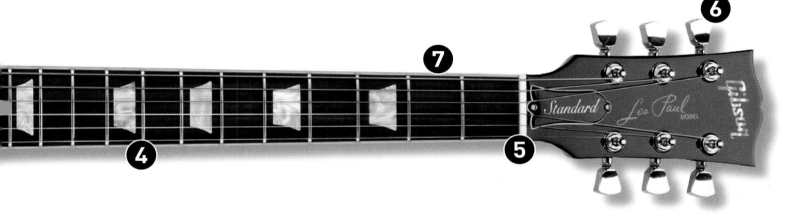

you have particularly small or large hands, there'll be a guitar to suit you. Notice the dots on the upper edge – these are position markers, and you unconsciously use these to put your fingers in the right place.

5 TOP NUT This doesn't look like it's going to change much for your playing or tone but it's hugely important as it governs both string spacing and the height of the strings above the fretboard – this is referred to as the 'action' of a guitar – literally the height above the fretboard that the strings are. Too high and you'll have to work hard to press and hold the strings on the frets when playing, resulting in much less speed and ease. This is a common problem with cheaper 'learner' guitars, but any guitar repairer will be able to remedy this – go in and ask to have your guitar 'set up'.

6 MACHINEHEADS These geared pegs hold your strings in place and are used to tune your string to pitch (hence their nickname, 'tuners'). They come in various shapes and

sizes, and some designs are very sophisticated, but all do the same job. If your guitar keeps going out of tune, try tightening the screws that hold these on to the body.

7 FINGERBOARD The 'big three' fingerboard woods are ebony, rosewood and maple. Each has a different tonal character, with light-coloured maple described as 'bright' and browner rosewood as 'warm'. Ebony, the most luxurious option, is generally black, and combines characteristics of both. Most fingerboards have inlays to improve looks and provide a visual reference. Guitar fingerboards vary in how rounded or flat they are, a property called the 'radius', and frets come in different thicknesses: both have a subtle effect on the way a guitar feels, particularly when you're bending the strings.

8 PICKUPS The pickups are the soul of an electric guitar. Nothing can alter the tone of an axe more than fitting a different set. There are four main types. Single coils are brighter-

sounding but produce hum; humbuckers were devised to cancel this hum and have a warmer, darker tone; P-90s are a type of single coil which provide a more rounded, 'fatter' sound. Finally, active pickups employ battery-powered circuitry to provide a boosted sound for rock and metal styles. All of them perform the same function – they pick up the vibration of the string via a magnetic field, and send this signal to your amplifier. Some acoustics are fitted with an acoustic-specific pickup system so they can be plugged into an amplifier or PA.

9 CONTROLS AND PICKUP SELECTOR Most electric guitars have tone and volume controls. If your guitar has more than one pickup, the pickup selector switch can be used to choose either a combination of pickups, or to have the sound come from just one. This allows one guitar to make many different tones. As a rule, pickups nearer the neck are bassier and used for 'rhythm' sounds, and those nearer the bridge have more treble and are favoured for the lead guitar sound.

ANATOMY OF AN
ACOUSTIC GUITAR

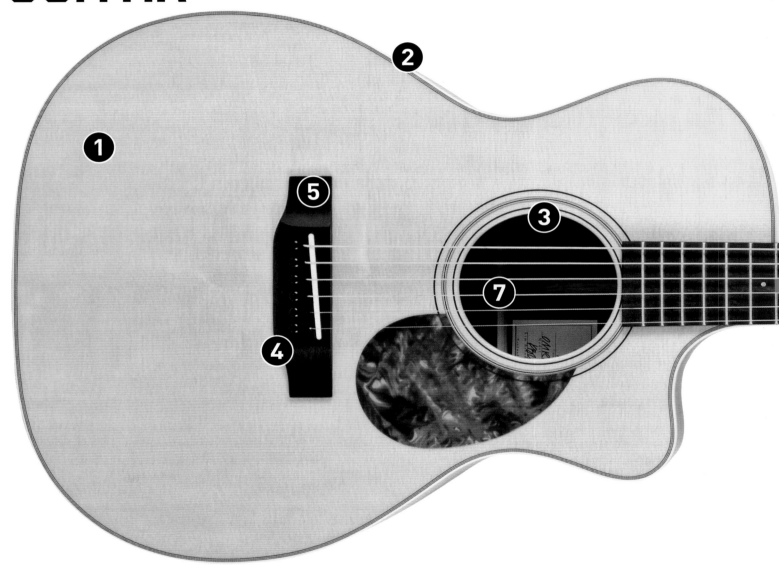

1 TOP The soundboard, or 'top' of an acoustic guitar is a key component in the way it responds. Construction of the soundboard is either laminate (multiple plies glued together), or solid (a single layer of wood), and popular choices include spruce, cedar, mahogany and maple. And different woods will give your guitar a different sound. So choose one you like! When you strum, the soundboard vibrates to help amplify the instrument and create the familiar sound of a resonant steel-string acoustic guitar.

2 BACK & SIDES The back and sides of an acoustic guitar are just as important, and like the soundboard, are available in laminate or solid construction. The wood choice for the back and sides is often a more rigid one than the top – they project the sound back towards the soundboard rather than absorbing it, adding to the resonance and sustain. Rosewood and mahogany are popular wood choices for back and sides.

3 SOUNDHOLE The 'mouth' of your acoustic guitar is not the only, or even the main place that acoustic guitar sound comes from. It emanates from the vibrating top and other surfaces, and the soundhole helps this to happen focusing the projection of the sound.

4 BRIDGE PINS Your acoustic's strings are held in place at the bridge by the bridge pins. These are commonly made of plastic, although bone and synthetic bone material

Acoustic pickup systems aren't transparent – they have their own tonal characteristics

"DIFFERENT WOODS WILL GIVE YOUR GUITAR DIFFERENT SOUNDS SO CHOOSE ONE THAT YOU LIKE!"

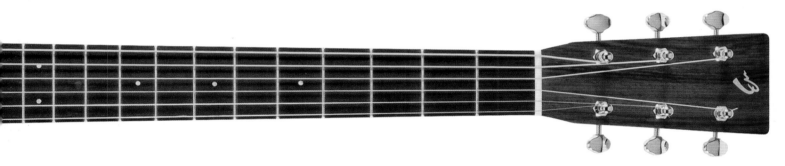

ones are also available. They can be tricky to remove, but stringwinders often feature a 'pin puller' to help get them out without damaging the guitar.

5 SADDLE As with the other plastic parts on your acoustic (namely, the top nut and bridge pins) the saddle is available in a variety of tone-enhancing materials. Once again, each material changes the sound. The saddle on your acoustic is responsible for the string height at the bridge, and is another key component in the transfer of vibration of the strings to the top of the acoustic. Compensated

saddles are available to give correct intonation, while the height and thickness can be adjusted by filing.

6 ELECTRONICS Many acoustic guitars also feature a pickup and preamp section so that that you can plug into an amp or PA system. The most common type of pickup is a piezo transducer, which sits under the saddle and converts the vibrations into a signal, however there are systems available which include microphones, magnetic pickups or a blend. The signal is then run through a preamp which offers EQ, volume controls and often

handy features such as a tuner and feedback-busting switches.

7 BRACING The strings on your acoustic put a large amount of tension on the neck and top of the guitar, effectively pulling the top end of the guitar towards the bottom in an attempt to bend the whole thing. So acoustic guitars are braced inside to help strengthen the top and sides. The braces also add to the tone of the guitar, and the most common method is called 'X bracing' (due to the fact that it forms and 'X' shape along the underside of the top) which was first developed by Martin Guitars.

ICONS
FENDER STRATOCASTER

Used everywhere from Woodstock to Wayne's World, we salute the double-horned, triple-pickup'd icon of rock 'n' roll

When it was launched in 1954, the Fender Stratocaster looked so far ahead of its time it could have fallen from a flying saucer. That futuristic design was thanks in part to Western swing guitarist, Bill Carson. Frustrated by what he regarded as shortcomings on the earlier Telecaster, Bill pestered Leo Fender to improve the guitar with body contouring, more pickups and a vibrato unit. Instead, Leo and his team went back to the drawing board.

Like the Telecaster, Leo's new guitar had an ash body (alder was introduced in 1956) and a bolt-on maple neck. There the similarity ends. The double cutaway body, lifted from the '51 Precision Bass, was contoured for comfort ("It fits better to your body like a well tailored shirt," said Carson) then loaded with three singlecoil pickups and an innovative vibrato, albeit misnamed as a 'synchronised tremolo'.

The Strat unites guitarists as diverse as Buddy Holly, Eric Clapton and Bon Jovi's Richie Sambora. Stevie Ray Vaughan called his battered '63 model 'Number One'. In Wayne's World, a white '64 Strat is Wayne Campbell's 'Excalibur'.

The Strat is Jimi Hendrix mangling The Star-Spangled Banner at Woodstock in 1969 and Mark Knopfler's '61 ringing out on Sultans Of Swing. It's also Hank Marvin of The Shadows playing the first UK-imported Stratocaster on echo-drenched classics such as Wonderful Land (1961).

The Strat has been tweaked over the years: a rosewood fingerboard in 1958; a big headstock in '66; a five-way switch in '77 (after players began jamming the three-way switch to 'in between positions'); locking vibratos and humbuckers, thanks to Eddie Van Halen's influence; and more recently, a nine-and-a-half-inch or even 12-inch fingerboard radius for easier string bending.

STRAT TIMELINE

1954
Leo Fender launches his Iconic strat. It's a timeless classic

1966
The big-headstock Stratocaster makes its debut

1977
A five-way pickup switch becomes standard

2011
Fender currently produces 59 Stratocaster models

This 57-year-old design could have been born yesterday

WORDS: ED MITCHELL

WHAT TO LOOK FOR STRAT ANATOMY

Leo Fender's design remains the most iconic electric guitar ever. Here are the key S-type features...

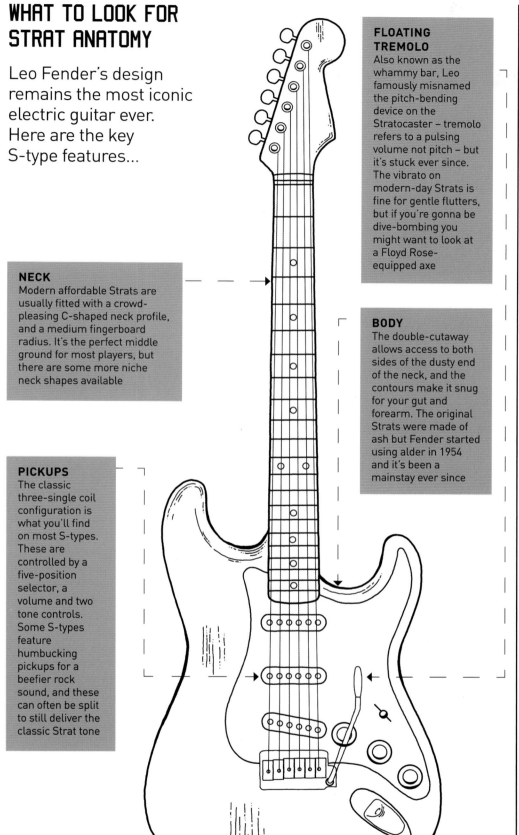

NECK
Modern affordable Strats are usually fitted with a crowd-pleasing C-shaped neck profile, and a medium fingerboard radius. It's the perfect middle ground for most players, but there are some more niche neck shapes available

PICKUPS
The classic three-single coil configuration is what you'll find on most S-types. These are controlled by a five-position selector, a volume and two tone controls. Some S-types feature humbucking pickups for a beefier rock sound, and these can often be split to still deliver the classic Strat tone

FLOATING TREMOLO
Also known as the whammy bar, Leo famously misnamed the pitch-bending device on the Stratocaster – tremolo refers to a pulsing volume not pitch – but it's stuck ever since. The vibrato on modern-day Strats is fine for gentle flutters, but if you're gonna be dive-bombing you might want to look at a Floyd Rose-equipped axe

BODY
The double-cutaway allows access to both sides of the dusty end of the neck, and the contours make it snug for your gut and forearm. The original Strats were made of ash but Fender started using alder in 1954 and it's been a mainstay ever since

ESSENTIAL LISTENING

The Strat has been at the forefront of guitar tone since its inception. Here are five examples of the killer S-type sound that we all love

THE JIMI HENDRIX EXPERIENCE
Little Wing
Arguably the most iconic Strat player ever gives us one of the most imitated Strat tones ever. Jimi's most famous ballad is a work of languid beauty, seeing him coax pure gold out of a 60s Strat through a Leslie speaker.

DEREK AND THE DOMINOS
Layla
Eric Clapton used his famous 'Brownie' Strat to sublime effect in this air-guitar staple, trading muscular, chunky licks and wailing solos with Duane Allman.

RED HOT CHILI PEPPERS
Under The Bridge
Frusciante's a Hendrix disciple, and from the crystal clear intro riff to the just-breaking-up chordal riffs and chorus, this is pure Strat.

BIFFY CLYRO
Mountains
Simon Neil has the ability to make a Strat sound massive, and that skill is shown to great effect on this song.

DAFT PUNK
Get Lucky
Need funky guitar? Call Nile Rodgers! Daft Punk did and the disco legend rocked up to the studio with his 'Hitmaker' Strat and a right hand blessed by the gods of groove themselves – the result: a modern pop classic.

ILLUSTRATION: STEPHEN KELLY

GIBSON LES PAUL STANDARD

In 1958, Gibson unveiled the guitar that would set the standard for ultimate rock tone and sustain. Just ask Eric...

A
lthough the Gibson Les Paul guitar was originally launched in 1952, it wasn't until July 58 that the company perfected a slab of tonal brilliance, christened the Standard. Blessed with stunning tone, sustain and playability, the Standard became even more desirable in 59 when choice examples left Gibson's original Kalamazoo, Michigan factory with highly figured flame or Tiger Stripe maple tops. The boosted eye candy completed the package but incredibly the guitar was extinct by 1961. It was replaced by a double cutaway, all-mahogany Les Paul branded model that would eventually be renamed the SG.

The Les Paul Standard is associated with Jimmy Page, Peter Green, Billy Gibbons, Paul Kossoff of Free and, of course, Slash. But the iconic six-string might have gone the way of the dinosaurs if it weren't for Eric Clapton and US blues guitarist, Mike Bloomfield. In 1966, Eric stunned us with his incredible tone on John Mayall's Beano album (Blues Breakers With Eric Clapton). Thanks to Eric's tone and intensity, demand for the Standard was such that it was relaunched as a Goldtop in 1968. Mike Bloomfield exerted a similar influence with his incendiary '59 Standard-fuelled licks on the 1968 album Super Session.

Fifty years after it was originally launched, Gibson unveiled its pimped '2008' model Les Paul Standard. The hardware was upgraded with TonePros parts, locking Grover machineheads and Burstbucker Pro pickups, and the setup was improved by the use of a Plek machine. In 2010, Gibson announced the Les Paul Standard Limited, which includes the company's Robot self-tuning technology. Nevertheless the essence of the original remains.

LES PAUL TIMELINE

1958
Gibson Guitars' ultimate tone machine is born

1961
The singlecut Standard is discontinued. Say what?!

1968
Thanks to Clapton, the Standard is back

2008
The Standard is tweaked for righteous playability

The rock elite have an undying love for this legendary singlecut

WORDS: ED MITCHELL

WHAT TO LOOK FOR LES PAUL ANATOMY

From blues to metal, the dual-humbucker single-cut is a rock-guitar staple

NECK
Like the body, a single-cut's neck is usually mahogany, and often glued (set), rather than bolted. The classic scale length for 22-fret single-cuts is Gibson's 24.75 inches – less than typical Fender scale lengths. To compensate for the string tension, they're often strung with heavier-gauge wires

PICKUPS
Early Les Pauls were fitted with P-90 single coils, giving a beefed-up sound compared to those found in a Strat. But come 1956, the Les Paul became known for the fat, hum-free sound of Seth Lover's PAF (Patent Applied For) humbucking pickup. Modern single-cuts often include a coil split switch, giving you the versatility of single coils and humbuckers in the same guitar

BRIDGE
LP-style guitars often sport the trusty tune-o-matic bridge and stop tailpiece. The six saddles can be adjusted individually for intonation, but not for height, as on a Strat bridge

BODY
The classic single-cut comprises a mahogany body, and often a maple cap to add some brightness to the sound, while giving some extra visual bling. Les Paul's original body design was a solid slab of wood, but many modern LP-style single-cuts feature weight-relief chambering

CONTROLS
The two humbuckers are switched by a three-way toggle switch and different single-cuts offer different control layouts. Most common is two volume/two tone controls, however, some single-cuts feature two volumes/one tone, one volume/one tone, or sometimes just one master volume control

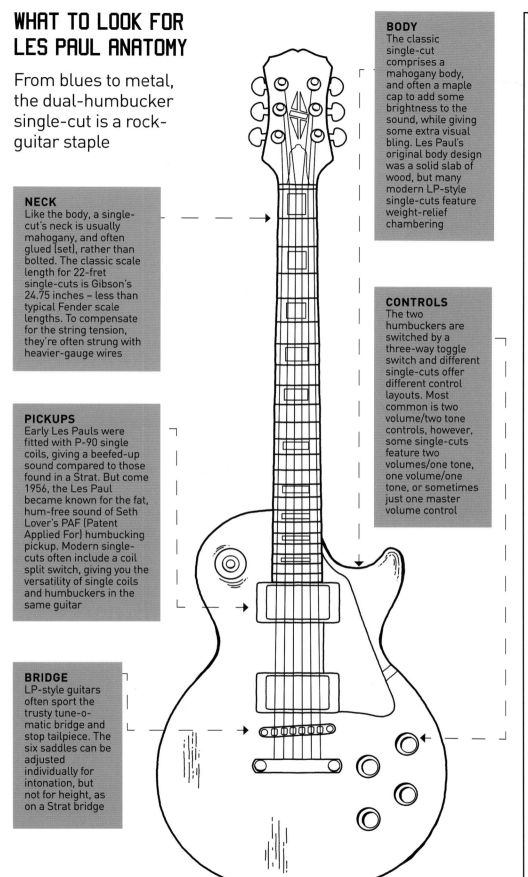

ILLUSTRATION: STEPHEN KELLY

ESSENTIAL LISTENING

The most famous rock guitar of all time has got a few belters in its catalogue...

THE ROLLING STONES
(I Can't Get No) Satisfaction
Keith Richards recorded this riff with his Les Paul trying to sketch out a horn part. Thank the rock gods his bandmates convinced him to stick with the guitar riff...

FLEETWOOD MAC
Oh Well
Peter Green's '59 Les Paul was wired incorrectly, creating the unique 'out of phase' sound. Cue leagues of guitarists replicating the 'mistake'

LED ZEPPELIN
Whole Lotta Love
For Zep's second album, Jimmy Page turned to a '59 LP he'd bought off Joe Walsh. He stuck it through a Marshall stack, cranked it up, and played the legendary riff...

GUNS N' ROSES
Welcome To The Jungle
Is Slash playing a Kris Derrig LP copy here? Who knows, but that slab of wood matched with a modded Marshall head fired Appetite For Destruction into the stratosphere.

OZZY OSBOURNE
Crazy Train
Randy Rhoads' saturated, crushing riff on Ozzy's statement solo hit was conjured using his trusty '72 Les Paul Custom.

ICONS
FENDER TELECASTER

Designed to be near indestructible and ideal if you like it loud. We honour the ingenious solidbody that started it all

When the Tele first arrived, its solid body was a huge innovation – it limited feedback and enabled higher-volume playing, while the no-nonsense construction made for easy mass production. Leo Fender had already brought the single-pickup Esquire to market in 1950, but he quickly found he needed to compete with two and three-pickup electrics. Fender soon began producing two-pickup Esquires – now with truss rods – dubbing them Broadcasters.

The name only lasted three months, after Gretsch politely pointed out its similarity to its Broadkaster drum line. Fender simply cut the headstock decals, leaving only the Fender name – these valuable models are known as 'Nocasters', and were only produced for half of 1951. Manager Don Randall thought up Telecaster, and soon the model became the blueprint for the modern electric.

The Tele has appeared in many guises over the years – including the semi-hollow Thinline, neck-humbucker Custom and double-humbucker Deluxe – and fuelled genres from country (Brad Paisley) to rock (Keith Richards) and metal (Jim Root), proving there's plenty of life in the ol' plank yet.

TELE TIMELINE

1950
Fender launches the Broadcaster, adding a truss rod and extra pickup to the Esquire

1951
Fender is forced to drop the Broadcaster name due to Gretsch's Broadkaster drum range

1951
The company officially renames the Broadcaster as the Telecaster

1968
The Telecaster Thinline is introduced, followed by Custom and Deluxe variations

WORDS: MICHAEL BROWN PHOTOGRAPHY: NEIL GODWIN

WHAT TO LOOK FOR
TELE ANATOMY

Leo Fender's original is the best there is for many players. Here's the T-type lowdown.

SLAB BODY
The Telecaster's slab body is most commonly cut from ash, alder or pine. It's a simple shape that has stuck ever since its introduction thanks to its agile weight and easy access. Unlike the Stratocaster, the Telecaster body doesn't usually feature arm or belly carves

BRIDGE
'Classic' examples of the Tele bridge usually offer three saddles (two-per string), whereas modern versions give you six individual saddles. The obvious benefit of this is that you can adjust the height and intonation of each string independently, however, traditionalists swear by the resonant qualities of the classic three-saddle design

PICKUPS
Telecasters are known for their versatility. The bright twang from the bridge single coil can be clear, aggressive or chime-y depending on how you manipulate it. The neck pickup is where you'll find those classic woody Fender sounds, and it sounds brilliant for playing lead stuff too

ILLUSTRATION: STEPHEN KELLY

ESSENTIAL LISTENING
The Tele has been used on thousands of hits – here's just a few of them...

LED ZEPPELIN
Good Times, Bad Times
He later became one of the Les Paul's most famous users, but despite that Jimmy Page invented hard rock with a Telecaster, which he used for almost every part on the first Zep album.

QUEEN
Crazy Little Thing Called Love
Brian May borrowed Roger Taylor's Tele to record the classic rockabilly-style solo on Queen's 1980 megahit.

RAGE AGAINST THE MACHINE
Killing In The Name
When it was drop D time, Tom Morello turned to his trusty Standard Tele 'Sendero Luminoso'.

JEFF BUCKLEY
Hallelujah
With delicate chords, played on a Tele with buckets of reverb from an Alesis Quadraverb rackmount unit, Buckley's timeless rendition is an exercise in fragile simplicity.

RADIOHEAD
My Iron Lung
Johnny Greenwood put his trusty 1990 Tele Plus (modded with Lace Sensor pickups and a kill switch) through a DigiTech Whammy to create the otherworldly arpeggios in the verses.

GIBSON ES 335

We raise a glass to perhaps Gibson's second greatest creation: the semi-acoustic that thinks that it's a solid...

Beloved by jazzmen and rockers alike. The 335 does it all

I came up with the idea of putting a solid block of maple in an acoustic model," so said Ted McCarty, Gibson company president and pioneer of guitar design during their hallowed 'golden period' of the 1950s. "It would get some of the same tone as a regular solidbody, plus the instrument's hollow wings would vibrate and we'd get an electric solidbody plus a hollowbody."

The result of McCarty's brainstorming is the Gibson ES-335. Launched in 1958, this revolutionary semi-acoustic guitar has seen service with the likes of Eric Clapton, Alex Lifeson and Chris Cornell, who recently got his own signature model.

The genius of the ES-335 is that it offers big-bodied hollowbody tone and sustain in a slim 44.45mm (1.75-inch) thick body. Sustain is boosted by McCarty's solid block of maple, which runs through the body, providing the anchoring point for the bridge, tailpiece and twin humbuckers. The block also helps to prevent the feedback that often troubles fully hollow electrics such as the Epiphone ES-230TD Casino and Gibson ES-330. Alvin Lee of the band Ten Years After proved just how well an ES-335 can perform at high gain when he pulled incendiary runs from 'Big Red' (pimped with a single coil in the middle position) at Woodstock.

While Gibson produced a number of variations on the ES-335 theme over the years (including the top-line Varitone-loaded ES-355, the chassis for blues legend BB King's Lucille signature model), the fat-necked '58 to '60 'Dots' are considered the greatest ever made.

GIBSON ES-335 TIMELINE

1958
The classic 'dot' neck ES-335 is launched

1962
Block fingerboard inlays replace the dots

1965
Stop tailpiece dropped in favour of a trapeze unit

1981
ES-335 discontinued, then quickly reissued as the 'Dot'

WORDS: ED MITCHELL

WHAT TO LOOK FOR
355 ANATOMY

They aren't just for
bluesers – semis have
got sonics for all!

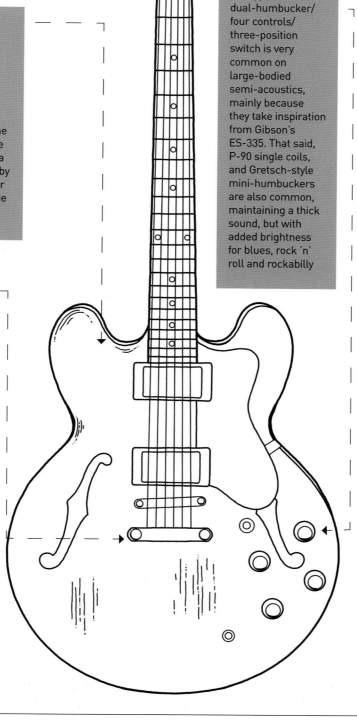

BODY
Let's get this straight; a
semi-acoustic is an electric
guitar, it's not an amp'd-up
acoustic (that's an electro-
acoustic). However, they do
add some 'acoustic'
properties to the electric
guitar; and it comes from the
body. We're focussing on the
larger type, which features a
solid 'centre block' flanked by
hollow wings. They're louder
unplugged, and the air inside
creates resonance and a
smooth high-end

BRIDGE
As with a LP, a fixed
tune-o-matic is a
common feature
here, but more
traditional models
(such as the
Epiphone Casino) are
adorned with trapeze
tailpieces, and for
some, a Bigsby
vibrato is an essential
add-on for a
semi-acoustic. These
retro vibratos add a
more subtle, gentle
flutter to your
whammy than
Fender-style
vibratos, and many
players swear by the
added sustain
created by bolting the
large mechanical
Bigsby to their
guitar's bodies

ELECTRONICS
The typical Gibson
dual-humbucker/
four controls/
three-position
switch is very
common on
large-bodied
semi-acoustics,
mainly because
they take inspiration
from Gibson's
ES-335. That said,
P-90 single coils,
and Gretsch-style
mini-humbuckers
are also common,
maintaining a thick
sound, but with
added brightness
for blues, rock 'n'
roll and rockabilly

ILLUSTRATION: STEPHEN KELLY

ESSENTIAL LISTENING
Semis have been bringing air
to hit records for decades…

BB KING
The Thrill
Is Gone
BB King was
never far away
from a Gibson
ES-style semi,
each one dubbed
Lucille. The great man's tone
and touch here typifies one of
the most lyrical players ever.

THE SMITHS
Stop Me If You've
Heard This One
Before
Johnny Marr
turned to a rare
12-string Gibson
ES-335 to record The Smiths'
final record, Strangeways
Here We Come.

ERIC JOHNSON
Cliffs Of Dover
Guitar god
Johnson's most
famous bit of
guitar virtuosity
was recorded
using an ES-335. Semis can
shred, too!

OASIS
Champagne
Supernova
Noel Gallagher is
famously vague
about the specific
gear used on What's The Story
(Morning Glory), but his trusty
Epiphone Riviera, with
mini-humbuckers, is all over
this album, and most likely
used for the rhythm part here.

FOO FIGHTERS
Breakout

Grohl describes
his Gibson Trini
Lopez as "the
sound of the Foo
Fighters" – he's
used it on every Foos album,
and it's centre stage in this
1999 hit.

IBANEZ RG SERIES

One of the greatest metal guitar ranges of all time was launched more than 30 years ago, with more than a little help from Steve Vai

I n 1987, Ibanez launched a pair of revolutionary guitars that are now recognised as shred icons: the JEM777 Steve Vai signature model and its more affordable sibling the RG550. While Vai's guitar came loaded with love 'em or loath 'em features like his monkey grip handle, the HSH (humbucker/singlecoil/humbucker) powered RG550 was basically an edited down JEM model. What remained was an affordable guitar, honed to make it as player friendly as possible.

For instance, the RG550's lightweight basswood body had a deep treble side cutaway and an angled neck heel to promote unhindered highest fret access. Its ultra-slim maple neck, the thinnest and flattest available at the time, came well-endowed with 24 jumbo frets. The legendary tuning stability provided by the 'Edge' licensed Floyd Rose vibrato and its Top Lok III locking top nut practically begged overzealous shredders to whammy the hell out of the new model. Plus, at a time when most metal guitars could only handle dive-bombing duties, the 550's recessed vibrato cavity offered over seven semitones of pull-back. Ibanez even designed its vibrato to have more mass than a Floyd to enhance the guitar's tone and sustain.

Such was the brilliance of the RG550 that it was quickly adopted as the chassis for a succession of new models. The HSS format RG560 soon followed, but that was only the tip of the pointy headstock. In 1994, Ibanez introduced the rounded 'All Access Neck Joint' on its ever-evolving RG models. The high spec, Japanese-made Prestige series made its debut in 1997 with the very green RG3070GN model. In 2004, the RG series received the ultimate tweak when Ibanez unveiled its neck-thru RGT guitar range. The versatility of the RG chassis was further enhanced in 2007 with the release of the eight string RG2228.

IBANEZ RG TIMELINE

1987
The classic Ibanez RG550 model is launched

1994
'All access joint' introduced on all rg models

1996
Prestige series debuts with the RG3070 GN

2002
Neck-thru construction RGT series guitars launched

The Ibanez RG Premium RG870QMZ is part of an iconic shred guitar stable

WHAT TO LOOK FOR RG ANATOMY

Want to shred? The double-cut rock axe is a staple of the guitar world...

NECK
Shredders favour thin, sleek neck profiles, usually with 24 frets on the board. The enhancements don't stop there – the fretboard radius will be wider to help bigger string bends maintain their sustain, and some guitars also have a 'compound radius', where the neck is rounder at the nut and flatter at the neck

BRIDGE
Extreme whammy bar techniques are made stable on shred guitars thanks to double-locking vibratos. The Floyd Rose is the most famous example (although Ibanez uses the Edge vibrato), but tuning stability comes at a price – changing strings and intonating the guitar can be a right pain in the behind...

BODY
The bodies of double-cut shred machines are built to offer comfort, tone, access and speed, while drawing basic inspiration from the classic Strat shape. Unlike the Strat, though these guitars are often mahogany, basswood or alder. The exaggerated cutaways let you reach the highest notes, and they're often lighter, yet still capable of delivering heavy tones

PICKUPS
Let's not mess about, these guitars are for melting faces. As such, they come loaded with high-output pickups for punchy notes and ringing sustain. Active pickups, up the ante, featuring a battery-powered gain and volume-boosting preamp. At £500 the pickups are normally own-brand, but not always, as you'll see...

SWITCHING
Versatility is key, and you'll often find guitars with a HSS or HSH, configuration with multiple switching options. The humbuckers are often splittable (for single-coil sounds), but the tone and volume controls are most commonly limited to one of each

ESSENTIAL LISTENING

Shred machines have been the bedrock of virtuoso guitar for decades. As you'll see here...

VAN HALEN
Eruption
With whammy bar histrionics and lightning fast tapping, many say that Eruption is the genesis of shred. EVH's built-from-parts 'Frankenstein' set the template for a generation of hot-rodded S-type guitars.

DEF LEPPARD
Pour Some Sugar On Me
Def Leppard were massive in America during the 80s thanks, in part, to their LA rock sound. Phil Collen recorded their biggest hit using his 'Crackle Jack' Jackson Soloist.

EXTREME
Get The Funk Out
Nuno Bettencourt debuted his N4 on Extreme's 1990 album Pornograffiti and he's rarely played anything else since!

METALLICA
The Unforgiven
Kirk Hammett has used ESP guitars since the 80s and the solo to this classic power ballad was recorded with his signature ESP KH-1.

STEVE VAI
Tender Surrender
In the 90s, aspiring shredders the world over hankered after the Ibanez/Vai designed JEM model. This track showcases the guitar's versatility, as Vai takes us on a tour of the JEM's pickup settings.

ESSENTIAL GUITAR ACCESSORIES

1 CABLES
Jack cables are pretty straightforward, and while you can spend a fortune on plugging in, we'd suggest going for a solid option to start with. Look for one with a metal casing that's user-servicable and get a length that's appropriate for the environment that you'll be using it in. If you're chaining a lot of effects pedals together, you can buy short patch cable jack leads to keep the clutter down, and your tone up!

2 PICKS
There are no rules as to which type of pick you should use, it comes down to preference. However, you might find that the 'give' in a thinner plectrum is better for strumming multiple strings (playing acoustic chords wheras a thicker pick will maintain accuracy on single notes and solos. Our advice? Spend a little bit of money on different shaped, size and material picks.

3 STRAP
Electric guitars come fitted with two strap 'buttons' for you to attach the strap to, while acoustics sometimes only have one. If this is the case, you'll need to opt for a strap with a bootlace to tie around your headstock (behind the nut, under the strings). Opt for a strap that is comfortable and adjust the height so that it as at a similar position to when you're sat down.

4 STAND
Lean your guitar against a wall/desk/chair at your peril! Guitar stands are one of the less interesting but very necessary purchases you can make. Fortunately, they are affordable, and come in various guises: from low-profile a-frames to space-saving wall hangers to multi-guitar racks.

5 TUNER
An electronic tuner is a must-have. There are many options available, from desktop boxes, guitar pedals or clip-on tuners that attach to the headstock of your guitar. It's important to get into the habit of tuning every time you pick up the guitar, not only will you train your ear, but your friends and family will thank you for it!

6 STRAPLOCKS
These little add-ons will make sure that your strap stays firmly attached to your guitar. New straps often have a tight fit to the strap button, but once they wear a bit, you might want to consider locking them down and there are plenty of options available.

7 GIGBAG

Some guitars come with a hardcase included, but a gigbag is lightweight, while still offering enough protection. We'd advise going for a bag with some padding – 10mm is usually the minimum – and at least one extra pocket for storing picks, tab books, cables etc. Some gigbags also include a velcro neck strap inside to stop the guitar from bouncing around too much.

8 METRONOME

A far cry from the wooden triangles of yore (although these are still available and just as reliable!), a digital metronome will fit in your guitar case's pocket and ensure you're always playing to a solid pulse. Many offer different count subdivisions, a range of bleep, tock and percussive sounds (we've even come across a barking dog noise) and an all-important headphone output.

9 STRING WINDER

This attachment will speed up turning a tuning peg, meaning that you can wind your strings more evenly and quicker than by hand. They range from basic plastic one, to battery-powered versions. We'd opt for a sensible one with different spaced grooves (so you can use it on different tuning pegs if needed). Some, like the one pictured include snips on the end or cutting off the excess bits of string.

10 STRINGS

The thicker the string, the more tension required to create the same pitch at a given scale length (the length of the string when it's on your guitar). So heavier strings are more resistant when it comes to fretting and bending notes. Some prefer the tone a thicker string makes, and if you're playing in low tunings, the tension of a thicker string helps keep the tuning stable.

11 PRACTICE AMPS

These days, small digital amps are well-equipped with effects and emulations of classic amplifiers that will respond at the lower volumes needed at home. Many also include features like Bluetooth for jamming along to music from your device and USB ports for recording.

12 CAPO

A capo clamps around your guitar neck fretting all of the strings at once. This allows you to play the tunes you already know in different keys, while maintaining the rich sound of open chord shapes. They help you transform mundane progressions into something more interesting, and they're a godsend if you want to sing along without stretching your voice!

ALTERED TUNINGS

There's so much music to be discovered simply by retuning your guitar. Here's a guide to some great open and alternate tunings – some common, others less so – and a handful of chords to get you started with each one, plus some pointers on where to hear it on record

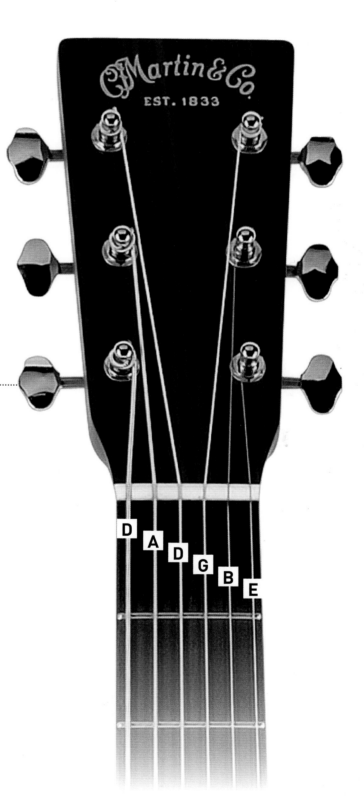

DROP D

The simple act of lowering the pitch of the sixth string by a single tone from E to D is an easy way of adding weight to the bass end, while also freeing up your fretting hand to focus on melody. Drop D tuning enables instant one-finger power chords, and makes your trusty open D chord sound huge. When tackling an altered tuning find out where the basic major and minor triads are, and how you might play a I-IV-V chord progression. Try the starter chords we've added with each tuning. Or just throw caution to the wind and jump right in!

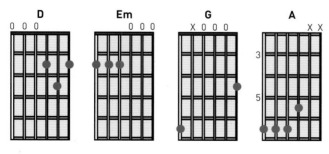

Hear it here
Mr Tambourine Man by Bob Dylan
(*Bringing It All Back Home*, 1965)

OPEN D

The Open D tuning is a widely used tuning in folk and blues styles. Its open nature makes it a particular favourite with slide-guitar players, and the tuning also pushes the guitar's range closer to that of a piano, for greater expressiveness. Experiment with harmonics in this tuning, barring your finger across the 5th, 7th and 12th fret for some heavenly chordal strums.

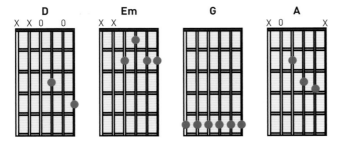

Hear it here
Babel by Mumford & Sons
(*Babel*, 2012)

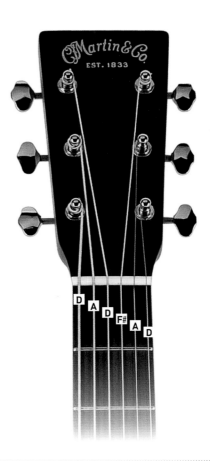

OPEN D MINOR

Trying the common drop D or DADGAD tunings for the first time, players are struck by the realisation that favourite licks sound fresh and new, simply because the notes have moved. Open D minor tuning – surely the saddest of all tunings – is less often used than many others on this list, but its minor tonality proves very atmospheric – and major chords are easy to find, making composition a rewarding experience.

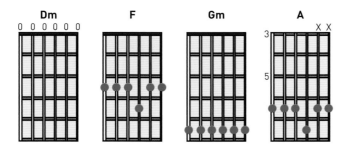

Hear it here
Hard Time Killing Floor Blues by Chris Thomas King
(*O Brother, Where Art Thou? Soundtrack*, 2000)

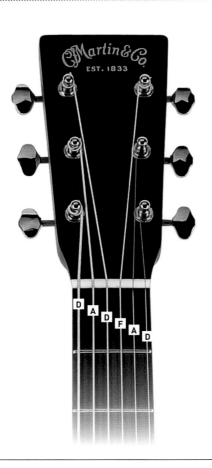

OPEN E

Open E tuning is essentially Open D tuning, two frets higher, and so licks in one of course translate readily to the other – but it deserves attention in our roundup here because of its appeal to slide guitar players. As with Open D tuning, barre major chords are readily available all the way up the fretboard. Open E's increased string tension and the prevalence of songs in the key of E in blues styles makes the tuning a must-try for aspiring bottleneck players.

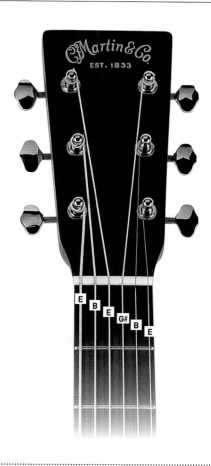

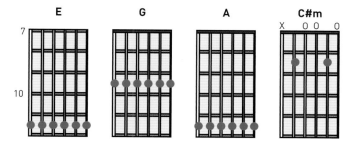

Hear it here
She Talks To Angels by The Black Crowes
(*Shake Your Money Maker*, 1990)

OPEN G

Many styles use open G tuning, from the Delta blues to folk and rock. But it has become virtually synonymous with Keith Richards – and for very good reason, since its discovery was a songwriting revelation for the legendary guitarist, and many of the band's biggest hits are played using it, including Gimme Shelter, Brown Sugar and Start Me Up. Richards removes the sixth string completely, making it easier to strum the five-string major chord. As a one-finger barre is all that's required to play a major chord, the other fingers are then free to create melody notes.

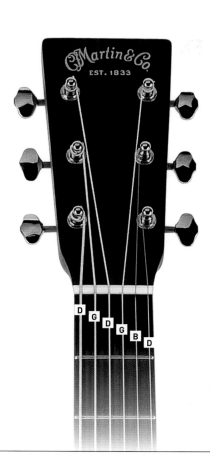

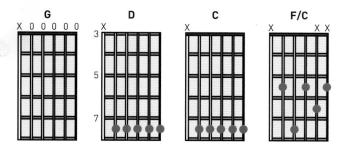

Hear it here
Wild Horses by The Rolling Stones
(*Sticky Fingers*, 1971)

OPEN CSUS2

This is the rich and beautiful open Csus2, comprising CGCGCD, low to high. But for the ease with which DADGAD can be pronounced as a word, we struggle to see why Csus2 tuning can't share the popularity that its cousin has enjoyed. It provides excellent scope for playing drone-like strumming accompaniment, open-string runs and deep, resonant bass notes. Well-known exponents of the tuning include English folk legends Nic Jones and Martin Simpson.

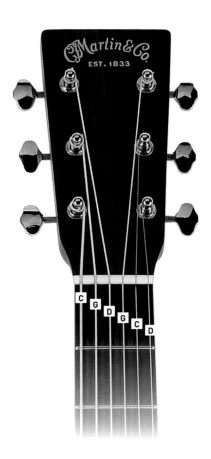

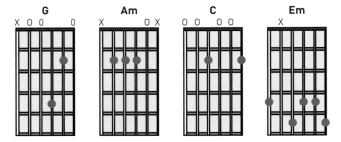

Hear it here
The Cocks Are Crowing by John Doyle
(*Wayward Son*, 2005)

DADGAD

DADGAD tuning is regarded as the discovery of the English folk guitarist Davey Graham, and is a revelation for many. Enjoying the distinction of being one of the few tunings you can pronounce, it's unrivalled in its ease of use – all those D and A strings are brimming with drone and melodic potential. It's classed as a 'modal' tuning, implying that it's neither major nor minor in tonality, allowing easy adaptability to various moods. Noodling in DADGAD can sound flattering, and instantly rewarding.

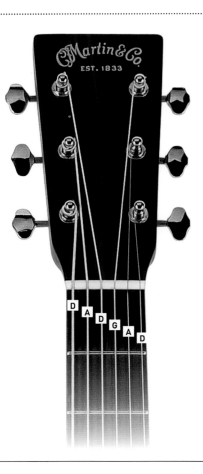

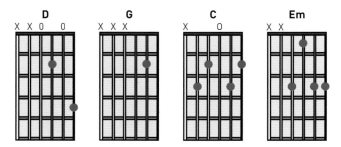

Hear it here
Black Mountain Side by Led Zeppelin
(*Led Zeppelin*, 1969)

OPEN C

Another great tuning for slide, certainly, but there's more to open C than that. Ditch the slide, add a capo and there's some interesting fingerpicking and harmonics to be had here, with ringing notes that can create a layered drone effect to widen your sound.It could make you an instant open-tuning convert. It certainly lured the likes of Ben Howard and John Butler in with its alternate charms.

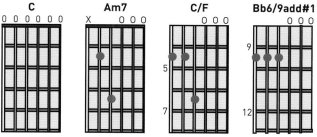

Hear it here
Ocean by John Butler
(*John Butler*, 1998)

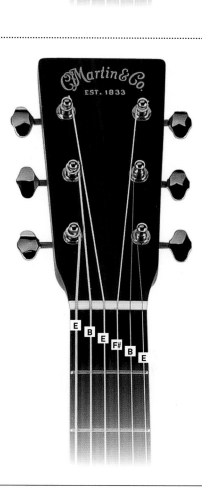

MODAL E

A real hidden gem that John Mayer has put to good use on a couple of his songs, Modal E tuning is like DADGAD's more exotic, brighter-sounding brother, and provides a lush melancholic mix of picked melodies and strumming shapes. This one pairs up well with a second guitar being played in standard tuning for a rich, multi-layered sound.

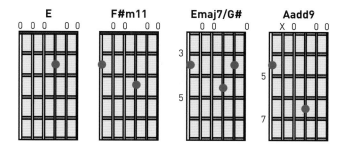

Hear it here
In Your Atmosphere (LA Song) by John Mayer
Where The Light Is (2008)

LESSONS

Learning to play the guitar doesn't have to be difficult! In this section, we cut out the boring stuff that slows you down, and get straight to the point – playing the guitar and sounding great! Even if you've never strummed a note before, we'll be showing you how to play your first chords and scales, then once you've got the basics down, you can move on to our rhythm and lead guitar workouts. Take your time, start slow, and you'll be playing in no time!

TAB GUIDE

Get to grips with this easy-to-follow guide to
musical terms and more

WHAT IS TAB?

This is where the key signature and time signatures are shown

♩=72 ← This is the beats per minute (BPM)

2nd string 2nd string 3rd string 4th string
3rd fret 1st fret 2nd fret Open

0:51

CD time (where the part occurs on the original CD)

Tab is short for tablature, a notational system used to give detailed information as to where notes should be played on the fretboard. Tab appears underneath conventional music notation as six horizontal lines that represent the strings of the guitar, from the sixth (thick) string at the bottom to the first (thin) string at the top. On these lines, numbers represent which frets you place your fingers. For example, an A note on the 2nd fret, third string, will be shown as a number '2' on the third line down on the tab. Unfretted strings are shown with a '0'. The key and time signatures are shown in the notation.

FRET BOXES: CHORDS, SCALES AND CAPO NOTATION

HAND LABELLING

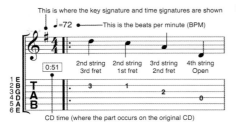

Here are the abbreviations used for each finger. Fretting hand: 1, 2, 3, 4, (T) Picking hand: p (thumb), i (index), m (middle), a (annular), c (little finger).

NUT AND FRETBOARD

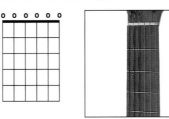

This fretbox diagram represents the guitar's fretboard exactly, as seen in the photograph.

CHORD EXAMPLE

G

This diagram represents a G chord. The 'o's are open strings, and a circled number is a fretting hand finger. A black 'o' or circled number is the root note (here, G).

CAPO EXAMPLE

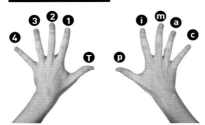

A (G)

The text denotes a capo – for this A chord, place it at the 2nd fret. Capos change the fret number ordering. Here, the original 5th fret now becomes the 3rd fret and so on.

CAPO NOTATION

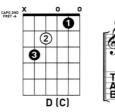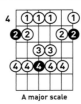

D (C)

D (C) Capo 2nd fret

The chord looks like a C in the tab, but the capo on the 2nd fret raises the pitch to make it a D. The 2nd fret capo'd notes are shown with a '0' in the tab as if they were open strings.

SCALE EXAMPLE

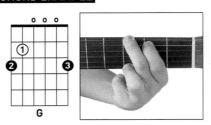

A major scale

This illustrates the fret hand fingering for the A major scale using black dots for root notes and white dots for other scale tones. The photo shows part of the scale on the fourth string.

GUITAR TECHNIQUES: PICKING

DOWN AND UP-PICKING

The symbols under the tab tell you the first note is to be down-picked and the second note is to be up-picked.

TREMOLO PICKING

Each of the four notes are to be alternate-picked (down and up-picked) very rapidly and continuously.

PALM MUTING

PM

Palm-mute by resting the edge of your picking hand palm on the strings near the bridge saddles.

PICK RAKE

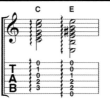

rake

Drag the pick across the strings shown with a single sweep. This is often used to augment a rake's last note.

APPREGGIATED CHORD

C   E

Play the notes of the chord by strumming across the relevant strings in the direction of the arrow head.

FRETTING HAND

HAMMER-ON & PULL-OFF

Pick the first note then hammer down on the string for the second note. Pick the third note and pull-off for the fourth note.

NOTE TRILLS

After picking the first note, rapidly alternate between the two notes shown in brackets using hammer-ons and pull-offs.

SLIDES (GLISSANDO)

Pick the first note and then slide to the next. For the last two notes pick the first, slide to the next and then re-pick it (RP).

FRET-HAND TAPPING

Sound the notes marked with a square by hammering-on/tapping with your fret hand fingers, instead of picking.

FRET-HAND MUTING
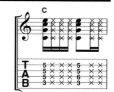

X markings represent notes and strings that are muted by your fret hand when struck by your picking hand.

BENDING AND VIBRATO

BEND AND RELEASE

Fret the first note (here, the 5th fret) and bend up to the pitch of the bracketed note, before releasing.

RE-PICKED BEND

Bend up to the pitch shown in the brackets, then re-pick the note while holding the bent note at the pitch shown.

PRE-BEND

Silently bend the string up from the 5th fret (PB5) to the pitch of the 7th fret note, pick it and release to the 5th fret note.

QUARTER-TONE BEND

Pick the note then bend up a quarter-tone (a very small amount). This is sometimes referred to as a 'blues curl'.

VIBRATO

Your fretting hand vibrates the string by small bend-ups and releases. Exaggerate this effect to create a 'wide' vibrato.

HARMONICS

NATURAL HARMONICS

Pick the note while lightly touching the string directly over the fret indicated. A chiming harmonic results.

ARTIFICIAL HARMONICS

Fret the note as shown, then lightly place your index finger directly over 'x' fret (AH'x') and pick (with a pick, p or a).

PINCHED HARMONICS

After fretting the note in the triangle, dig into the string with the side of your thumb as you sound it with the pick.

TAPPED HARMONICS

Place your finger on the note as shown, but sound it with a quick pick hand tap at the fret shown (TH17) for a harmonic.

TOUCHED HARMONICS

A previously sounded note is touched above the fret marked TCH (eg, TCH 9) for it to sound a harmonic.

VIBRATO BAR / WHAMMY BAR

WHAMMY BAR BENDS

The note is picked as shown, then the vibrato bar is raised and lowered to the pitches shown in brackets.

SCOOP AND DOOP

Scoop: depress the bar just before striking the note and release. Doop: lower the bar slightly after picking.

SUSTAINED NOTE AND DIVEBOMB

A note is sustained then the vibrato bar is depressed to slack. The square bracket indicates a further articulation.

GARGLE

Sound the note and 'flick' the vibrato bar with your picking hand so it 'quivers'. This results in a 'gargling' sound!

WHAMMY BAR VIBRATO

Gently rock the whammy bar to repeatedly bend the pitch up and down. This sounds similar to fret hand vibrato.

OTHERS

PICK SCRAPE

The edge of the pick is dragged either down or up along the lower strings to produce a scraped sound.

VIOLINING

Turn the volume control down, sound the note(s) and then turn the volume up for a smooth fade in.

FINGER NUMBERING

The numbers in the traditional notation refer to the fingers required to play each note.

PIMA DIRECTIONS

Any kind of fingerpicking requirements are shown at the bottom of the tab notation.

PICK HAND TAPPING

Tap (hammer-on) with a finger of your picking hand onto the fret marked with a circle. Usually with 'i' or 'm'.

ESSENTIAL OPEN CHORDS

New to the guitar? We show you the ropes with eight essential beginner chords to practise with

The most basic guitar chords are also known as open chords. A chord is a group of notes played together. Open chords simply include unfretted open strings. We recommend beginners learn the eight chords shown in Examples 1 and 2. You can play lots of songs using just these simple chords alone, so get to know them well.

When you play them, make sure the strings ring out clearly. Place your fingers on the strings close to the frets and arch them so that you don't touch another string. Keep your thumb in the middle of the back of the neck so you can arch your fingers.

Next, try changing from chord to chord. Try to use an 'anchor' finger to make these changes easier. For instance, in Example 3 the C and A minor chords share two notes (on the second and fourth strings), so you can hold down these notes as you change chord. The digits holding the notes are your anchor fingers. Aim to keep your finger movement minimal.

Finally, practising examples 5 and 6 will help you to establish what you've learned from the lessons on these pages. Don't be afraid to spend a lot of time practising with these pages.

EXAMPLE 1: MAJOR CHORDS

C

A

G

E

D

These diagrams will help you to memorise your first guitar chords. Simply press down on the strings behind the frets – the numbers tell you which fingers to use. The black dots represent root notes. For example, A is the root note of both A major and A minor chords.

EXAMPLE 2: MINOR CHORDS

A minor

E minor

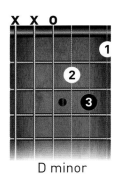

D minor

The main difference between major and minor chords is that the minor versions sound sad and moody compared to the bright-sounding major variants. Practise Examples 1 and 2, then try making up your own sequence of chords. Use major chords for a happy sound and minor chords for a darker sound.

EXAMPLE 3: ANCHOR FINGERS

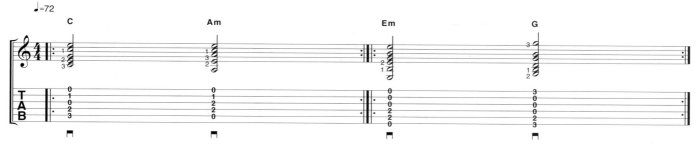

C and A minor share notes on the second and fourth strings, so keep your first and second fingers 'anchored' in place as you change between them. This makes the change easier. If you play E minor with your first and second fingers (instead of your second and third), you can 'anchor' your first to help with changing to a G chord.

EXAMPLE 4: BLOCK SHIFTS

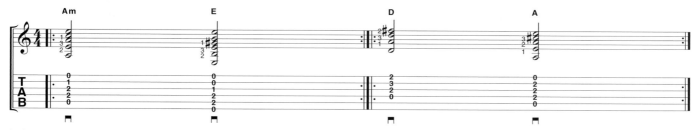

Another way to make chord changes easier is to move your fingers together as a block. A minor to E is the best example – the two chords are the same shape, but on different strings. You can adapt this method for other shapes too. So although D and A are different shapes, you can still start by moving all three fingers as a block.

EXAMPLE 5: C TO E

There's no opportunity to use an anchor finger here. However, you can make the change from C to E easier by focusing on your first and second fingers. Simply hold them in the C chord shape as you change to E. Once you've landed on the third and fifth strings, move your third finger onto the fourth string.

EXAMPLE 6: G TO D

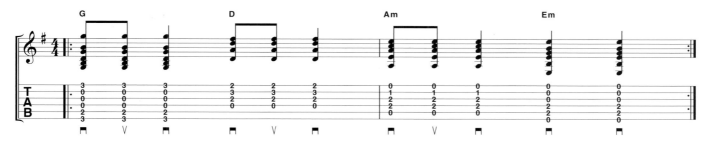

The change from G to D in bar 1 is a challenging open chord shift, because you have to completely reorganise your fingers. A minor to E minor is easier – simply shift your second and third fingers down a string and take your first finger off altogether.

ESSENTIAL STRUMMING

A few simple chords and beginner rhythm techniques go a long way.
Master the essential basics with this simple guide to strumming

With some basic chord shapes down, it's time to master strumming. Combining chords and strumming opens up a world of guitar playing for beginners.

Most guitarists start by strumming downstrokes. That's a simple strum in the direction of the ground. At this stage, your goal should be to play evenly and in time. Count to four with a repetitive, even pulse and strum in time with your count.

Choose an easy chord – this is a rhythm exercise, so don't give yourself tricky chords or changes. We've demonstrated downstrokes using an E

chord in Example 2 below. The next step is to add some upstrokes. Keep your four count and downstrokes going and then simply add an upstroke in between each downstroke, as illustrated in Example 3.

You can create more interesting rhythm parts by simply leaving out certain strums. We've given you a tricky rhythm pattern to try in Example 4, plus a top tip in Example 5. Finally, check out Example 6. Practise the chords shown below and spend some time playing rhythms that include downstrokes and upstrokes.

EXAMPLE 1: CHORDS

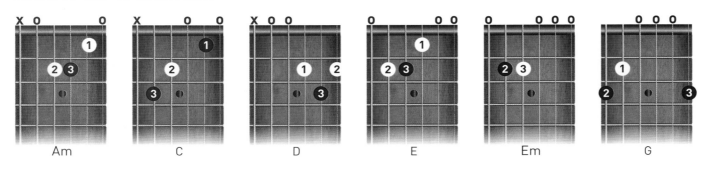

These six chords should be on every beginner guitarist's to-do list. The dots tell you where on the neck to place your fingers. Black dots are root notes. These are the notes that the chord takes its name from. For example, the root note for both the E and E minor chords is aan E.

EXAMPLE 2: DOWNSTROKES

Once you've got a few chords under your belt, try strumming this simple rhythm. We've used an E chord here, but you can choose anything that suits you.
Simply strum down towards the ground on each chord shown here. Count to four and strum in time with your count.

EXAMPLE 3: DOWNSTROKES AND UPSTROKES

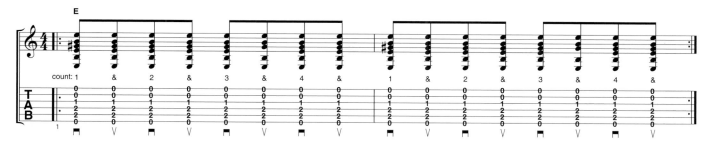

Most strummed guitar parts are a combination of downstrokes and upstrokes. Your aim here is to generate a smooth, even rhythm. Count to four, as you did in Example 2, strumming downstrokes on the numbered beats and adding upstrokes in between. Alternatively, you can count '1 & 2 & 3 & 4 &', placing the upstrokes on each '&'.

EXAMPLE 4: RHYTHM

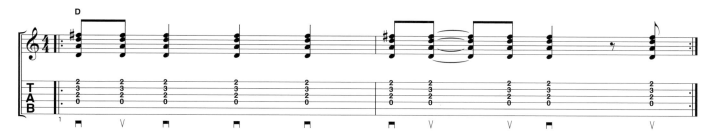

You can create lots of different rhythms based on alternating downstrokes and upstrokes. What makes the music sound interesting is the strokes you leave out, because this creates rhythm and groove. Each bar is still based on eight strums (four downstrokes and four upstrokes) – simply avoid the strings on certain hits.

EXAMPLE 5: TARGETING STRINGS

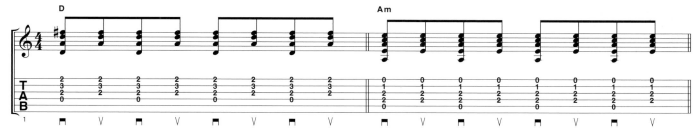

It can be tricky to strike the right strings with chords like A minor and D. Try targeting the lowest string in the chord on your downstroke and strum fewer strings on the upstroke so that your pick doesn't collide with the bass strings. We've shown D and A minor here, but practise C minor as well if you're familiar with it.

EXAMPLE 6: BRINGING IT ALL TOGETHER

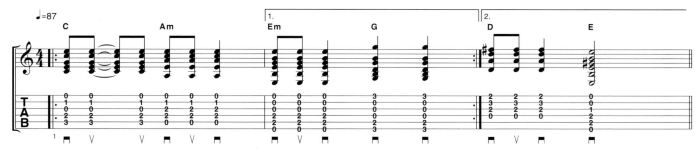

This backing track combines downstroke and upstroke rhythm playing with some of the chords we've looked at. Try practising the strumming patterns using just one chord, so that you can focus on learning the rhythm. Similarly, try practising the chord changes without the strumming until you get to grips with both movements.

ESSENTIAL BARRE CHORDS

Don't be put off by their fearsome reputation – just two simple barre chords can expand your rhythm playing across the whole fretboard.

Barre chords have a reputation as a finger-busting technique because of the strength required to play them. The idea is that you use your first finger to fret several strings. It does take practise and perseverance, but there are many benefits to mastering the technique..

You can start playing rhythm parts across the whole fretboard using two barre chords. Example 1 shows how to move an open position E chord around the neck as a barre chord. In Example 2, you can do the same thing with an open A chord; you can use the minor variants of both shapes, too.

Stick with these shapes to begin with and try to spot relationships between the chords in the other examples. Example 3 shows how to transpose a sequence of barre chords into another key – the trick is visualising the whole chord progression on the neck.

Examples 4 and 5 focus on playing across a wider range of the fretboard, using ascending chord progressions and partial barres. Example 6 demonstrates how a tricky key signature can be made easier if you use barre chords.

EXAMPLE 1: BARRE CHORDS ACROSS THE NECK

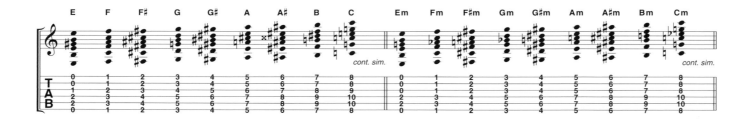

These barre chords are based on two easy open chords: E and E minor. We've moved the shape fret by fret as far as 8th position, but you can continue with C#, D, D#, E, etc.
If you start in open position and work your way up to D# in 11th position, you'll have learnt 12 major and 12 minor chords.

EXAMPLE 2: CHORD CHANGE EXERCISE

When it comes to barre chords, E and A are the most important shapes, so spend time working on these changes – it'll help you build the all-important strength and co-ordination required for barre chords. Play all the open chords with your second, third and fourth fingers so that you can barre with your first finger.

EXAMPLE 3: TRANSPOSABLE CHORD SEQUENCES

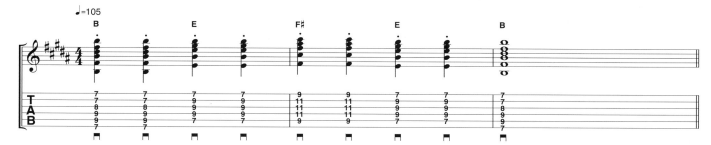

You can easily transpose entire chord progressions if you use barre chords. The tab above shows a chord progression in the key of B, but you can simply move all the chords down two frets to transpose from B to A.

EXAMPLE 4: ASCENDING CHORD SEQUENCES

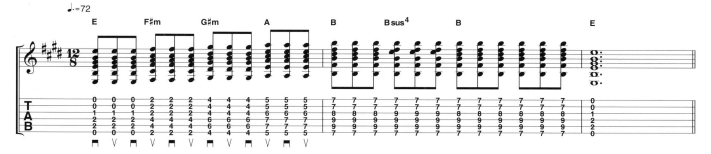

With open chords, the range of notes available is limited to one area of the neck. With barre chords, you can play as far up the neck as you like. This chord sequence ascends to 7th position. Experiment by playing even further up the neck, or try a descending chord progression.

EXAMPLE 5: ARPEGGIOS/PARTIAL BARRES

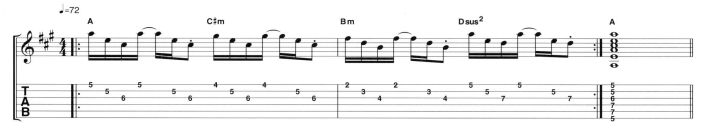

It's true that you can play arpeggios using open chords, but barre chords extend the range of notes available to you. In this example, we've played the arpeggios on the first, second and third strings only. This makes the chords easier to play because you don't have to barre across all six strings. This is known as a partial barre.

EXAMPLE 6: DIFFICULT KEY SIGNATURES

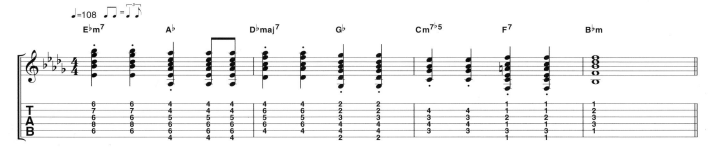

These chords come from the key of Bb minor – one that's totally unsuited to open chords. You can easily play in any key using barre chords, though. Have a go at transposing the sequence one or two semitones higher. It's no harder (or easier) to play, because the shapes always stay the same.

ESSENTIAL
PENTATONIC LICKS

Get to grips with the most important guitar scale you'll ever learn with these different examples

The minor pentatonic scale is essential. Don't take our word for it – Eric Clapton, Slash and Joe Bonamassa all make heavy use of this vital scale. From heavy metal to jazz, the minor pentatonic scale is found in all guitar music.

Start by familiarising yourself with the basic scale pattern. We've tabbed it in the key of A minor in Example 1 below. A few minutes spent practising this pattern every day will prepare you for the licks that follow in this lesson and give you a framework with which to start improvising your own licks. Examples 2 to 6 are simple minor pentatonic licks, and each one has a different idea for you to explore. In Example 2, it's the picking, or specifically, choosing where to

use downstrokes or upstrokes. Our suggested picking directions underneath the tab help you play accurately and in time.

Examples 3 and 4 repeat short groups of notes from the scale, an idea known as sequencing. This is useful when you're ready to start experimenting. Both licks ascend the scale, but you can try a descending pattern, or grouping different numbers of notes together – two, three, four, five and even six-note groupings can sound great.

Example 5 demonstrates how to use string bends to change from note to note. Finally, in Example 6, we give you a more challenging blues lick where you can focus on your vibrato and phrasing.

EXAMPLE 1: A MINOR PENTATONIC SCALE

The notes in the scale are A, C, D, E and G. Once you get to G, the notes just start on A again. We've coloured all the A notes in red so you know which notes are home notes (called root notes). Use your first finger for the 5th fret notes, your third finger for the 7th fret notes and your fourth finger for the 8th fret notes.

EXAMPLE 2: SIMPLE LICK

The key to mastering this simple lick is the picking: play 'down, up, up' in both bars. Other picking patterns work, too, but the idea here is that you sync your picking in time with the music. Your downstrokes should fall on the main pulse of the music and your upstrokes in between.

EXAMPLE 3: ASCENDING LICK

This lick is based on groups of three notes taken from the scale. Follow the fretting instructions from Example 1 and stick to them. Pick each three-note phrase with a 'down, up, down' pattern. The final note isn't in the scale pattern, but it's an A root note in a different position, so it still sounds fine.

EXAMPLE 4: SEQUENCED LICK

Sequencing is when you take a simple melody and repeat it, but higher or lower in pitch. This lick takes a four-note phrase and then repeats it higher in the scale. Alternate between a downstroke and an upstroke with every note until the last two notes, which you should play with downstrokes.

EXAMPLE 5: STRING BEND LICK

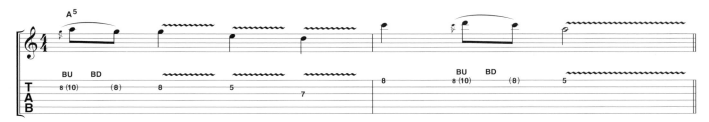

The trick with string bends is making sure that you bend up to a note in the correct scale. There are two string bends here: one from G to A and one from C to D. Remember the notes in the A minor pentatonic scale? They're A, C, D, E and G, so you can see we've kept our bends within the A minor pentatonic scale.

EXAMPLE 6: BLUES LICK

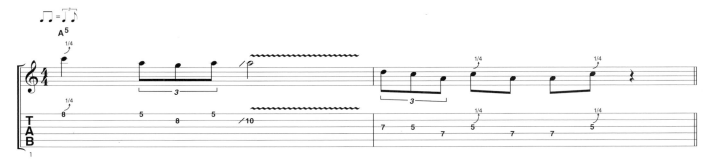

This more challenging blues lick uses the minor pentatonic scale with a swung rhythm. Practise just playing the notes, mastering the fingering and the rhythm before you turn your attention to the finer points, like vibrato and the tricky quarter-tone bends.

RHYTHM GUITAR WORKOUT

Many of us strive for technical prowess in our lead playing, forgetting that 99 percent of the time we'll be playing rhythm. If you're struggling with timing, getting stuck with tricky rhythmic groupings and troublesome chord shapes, or just trying to get your pick-hand speed beyond an annoying tempo 'ceiling', then this section of the Handbook is just for you. Over the next 10 pages, we break rhythm playing down into various technical elements, focusing on picking, rhythm patterns, chords and creative playing ideas. As always, make sure you practise along with a metronome at a variety of tempos. This promotes good general practice but will also hone your inner 'clock' and ultimately make you a better guitarist. Let's get started!

CHORD PLAYING

Are your fingers struggling to stretch? Landing on the wrong strings?
Fret buzzes? It's time to make your fret hand a finely-tuned athlete

For this section we've provided some rhythm exercises that focus on a few of the more common difficulties associated with the fret hand. Typically, a lack of strength and/or coordination and 'wandering finger syndrome'. These can all be improved with practice.

As a general rule when you're playing guitar, try to keep your fret hand 'square' to the fretboard, with your fingers pointing in roughly the same direction as the frets. This means keeping the thumb positioned loosely behind the neck in a neutral position (somewhere behind the first and second fingers). Follow these simple rules and you'll be performing miracles in no time!

EXAMPLE 1

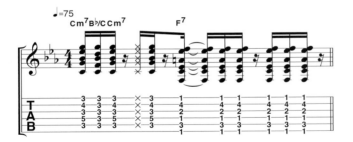

This riff is designed to develop strength in your barred first finger, as well as improve strength and accuracy in the sometimes 'wandering' fourth finger.

EXAMPLE 2

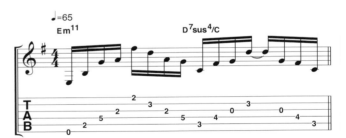

This arpeggio idea will help your first finger barre even further, while helping to develop the desired 'in line with the neck' fret-hand position.

EXAMPLE 3

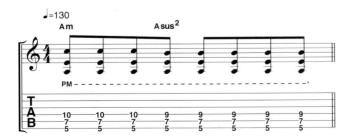

The tricky stretch between third and fourth fingers is the key lesson here. Moving to the 9th fret will naturally promote a better thumb position behind the neck.

EXAMPLE 4

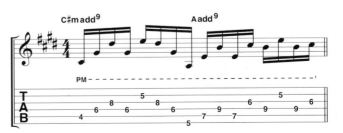

The third-to-fourth-finger stretch is developed in this Andy Summers-style riff. This time including all the fingers.

EXAMPLE 5

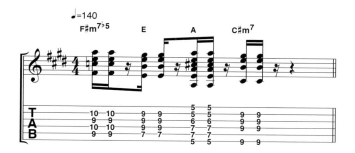

All four chord shapes are very different, thus helping to improve your speed between changes. Aim for a 'block movement', where all fingers move simultaneously.

EXAMPLE 6

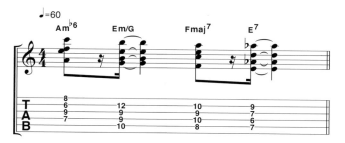

These chord shapes are even more difficult, combining fast changes with wider stretches. This is a great conditioning and coordination exercise for the fret hand.

EXAMPLE 7

A lot of fast fretting boils down to 'muscle memory'. Here, the first and third fingers alternately swap positions; repeat the phrase at a slow tempo to memorise it.

EXAMPLE 8

More fast fret-hand shifts are combined with a fourth-finger driven idea here. The wide stretches will help to improve fourth-finger dexterity and strength.

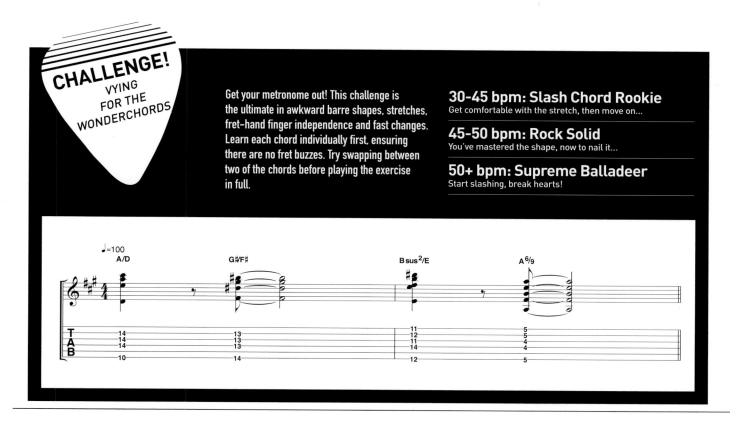

CHALLENGE! VYING FOR THE WONDERCHORDS

Get your metronome out! This challenge is the ultimate in awkward barre shapes, stretches, fret-hand finger independence and fast changes. Learn each chord individually first, ensuring there are no fret buzzes. Try swapping between two of the chords before playing the exercise in full.

30-45 bpm: Slash Chord Rookie
Get comfortable with the stretch, then move on...

45-50 bpm: Rock Solid
You've mastered the shape, now to nail it...

50+ bpm: Supreme Balladeer
Start slashing, break hearts!

CHORD VARIATION

Increase your chord vocabulary the easy way with our creative approach to learning new shapes

One way to improve your rhythm playing is using new chords. To avoid spending days with our noses buried in impenetrable chord dictionaries, we're taking a more creative approach to learning new shapes. Starting with a simple 'A shape' barre chord, in this lesson, we've identified 10 common variations on the basic shape as used in many pop and rock songs by countless guitarists. Every shape can be moved around the fretboard into new key signatures.

Relating shapes to a simple root chord is a great way to memorise new chords. Try playing through the new shapes and then see how the fingerings relate to the main barre chord shape.

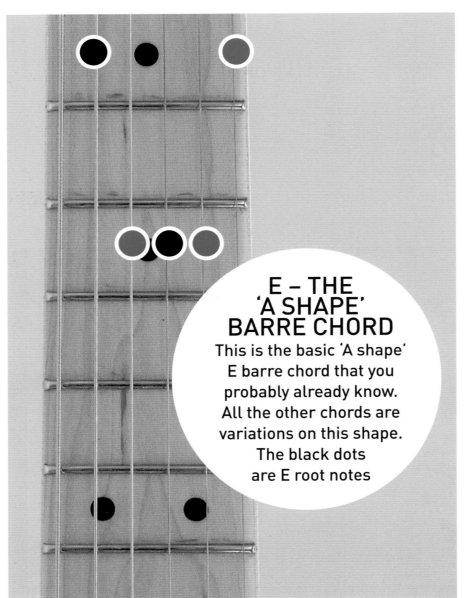

E – THE 'A SHAPE' BARRE CHORD
This is the basic 'A shape' E barre chord that you probably already know. All the other chords are variations on this shape. The black dots are E root notes

E-E/G# WITH HAMMER-ON

Hear this Hendrix-influenced chord embellishment in the opening notes of the Pearl Jam song Yellow Ledbetter. It's a simple hammer-on to the 11th fret on the fifth string.

E-A/C#

This change from E to A/C# is one of Keith Richards' regular guitar tricks, as heard (in different keys) in Brown Sugar and Start Me Up. Notice that the variation is based on an open C chord shape.

E-C#M

This move isn't associated with a specific player but if you play the A shape using just your first finger (leaving out the barre), C#m is just a simple fingering move away. A useful change!

EADD9

Andy Summers uses major and minor variants of this chord in Message In A Bottle and Every Breath You Take. It's a stretch, but it's a simple variation on our basic barre chord.

B7 (D SHAPE)

The opening chords to Jimi's Red House use this shape. Placed before the E barre chord, this forms the staple V-I progression; possibly the most important change in music.

E (G SHAPE)

The root chord in Jeff Buckley's version of Hallelujah looks like an open G, but it's also related to our basic shape. You'll need a capo on the 5th fret to play along in C major with Jeff.

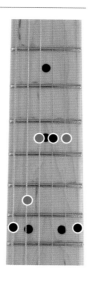

EAUG

This chord opens Chuck Berry's No Particular Place To Go and School Days. It's a 'symmetrical' chord, so any note can be the root.

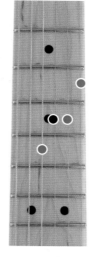

"RELATING SHAPES TO A SIMPLE ROOT CHORD IS A GREAT WAY TO MEMORISE NEW CHORDS"

E5

This is a powerchord on top of a powerchord. You don't have to play the whole shape, but it is still useful to know it: pick any two adjacent strings and you are playing a powerchord.

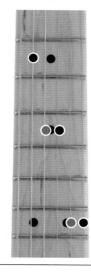

E-ESUS2-ESUS4

These sus chords are common variations on our shape, both in open position and as barre chords. Check out John Lennon's Happy Xmas (War Is Over) for an example.

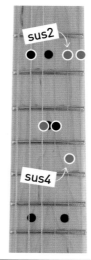

sus2

sus4

EM11

This jazz chord shape is played by Larry Carlton in his cover of Miles Davis's So What. Three of the four intervals are perfect 4ths, giving an unusual, nebulous sound compared to chords built strictly with 3rds.

EXPANDING BASIC CHORD PROGRESSION

Discover how some simple chord variations can help bring new life to one of the most common chord progressions

The I-V-VI-IV is one of the most common chord progressions in rock and pop music. Thousands of songs have been written using this chord sequence. Search 'Axis Of Awesome: Four Chords' on YouTube to hear a bunch of them.

Just because a progression has been used before it doesn't mean you can't play it in a creative way, adding your own unique style. To illustrate this point we've outlined the progression in the key of A major here. We've started with simple strummed chords and then tabbed out three more ways you can play the chord sequence. Try out our tabbed parts and then experiment to find more of your own rhythm ideas.

BASIC CHORD PROGRESSION

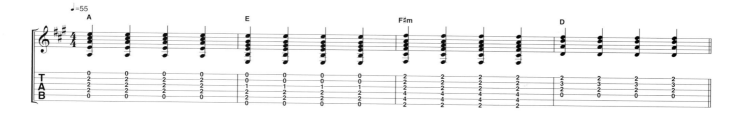

This is as simple as our progression gets with open chords and just one barre chord all strummed on the beat. At the moment, what we've got here isn't particularly interesting but when you're given a chord sequence to learn, these shapes are inevitably the first ones you'll think of.

VARIATION 1

We're outlining the same progression here, but this time we're based in the 4th and 5th fret positions and peppering the basic progression with all sorts of embellishments. We've used staccato chords, single notes and partial chords to mix things up.

VARIATION 2

Moving up the fretboard again, this time to 9th position, you can see that there's a new set of shapes you can use to outline the basic chord progression.

VARIATION 3

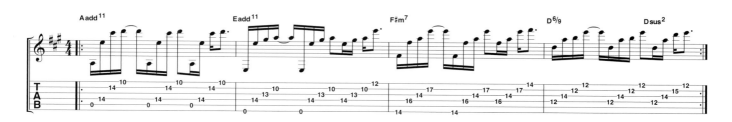

You can still play accompaniment parts above the 12th fret. Here, we've once again outlined the basic chord progression this time using arpeggios around the 10th to 16th frets. There's a stretch or two here but persevere because these arpeggios sound great.

RIFFING

Syncopated riffing with all four fretting-hand fingers is a vital part of a rhythm guitarist's arsenal.
Hone your accompaniment skills here!

A ny guitarist with experience agree that an important part of any guitarist's rhythm playing box of tricks is riffing around single notes.

In these examples, we're going to explore some of the difficulties guitar players may encounter when playing non-chord based accompaniments. These hurdles include overcoming tricky stretches and an over-reliance on the first finger.

The following four riffs are all designed to address both of these very common issues and to prepare you for those frequent situations that you might come across when playing live.

EXAMPLE 1

This classic rock idea combines wide stretches and syncopation. Follow the picking directions very carefully and keep note of which notes fall on the beat.

EXAMPLE 2

The subtle shift to the 16th-note offbeat completely changes the feel of this riff and the picking directions – great for balancing out your picking skills.

EXAMPLE 3

This riff is designed to avoid the first finger as far as possible, making the hand feel slightly off balance at first. The hammer-ons require strength and stamina, so practise slowly and gradually build speed as the exercise starts to feel easier.

EXAMPLE 4

Here we start with the often under-used fourth finger and avoid the overused first finger to help promote the strength in your other digit; 3/4 is an unusual time signature in rock and metal so remember to count to three to keep time.

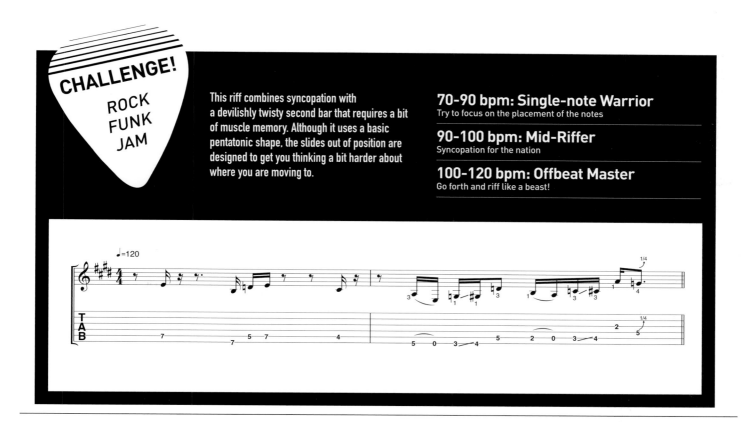

CHALLENGE!
ROCK FUNK JAM

This riff combines syncopation with a devilishly twisty second bar that requires a bit of muscle memory. Although it uses a basic pentatonic shape, the slides out of position are designed to get you thinking a bit harder about where you are moving to.

70-90 bpm: Single-note Warrior
Try to focus on the placement of the notes

90-100 bpm: Mid-Riffer
Syncopation for the nation

100-120 bpm: Offbeat Master
Go forth and riff like a beast!

20 INSPIRING CHORDS

Tired of always reaching for the same boring chord shapes? Read on as we show you some of our favourite chord shapes that are guaranteed to take your playing to new heights

MELANCHOLIC CHORDS

The minor tonality of these chords creates a sombre vibe that's perfect for sad songs.

If you compare an A major chord to A minor you will hear that the former sounds bright and cheerful, whereas the other is sad and mournful. This is thanks to the change from a major 3rd to a minor 3rd. These shapes all exploit that minor 3rd to create a dark, moody atmosphere. The open

strings enable you to reach notes that can't necessarily be fretted and have a sad, droning sound.

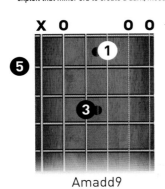

Amadd9

Emadd9

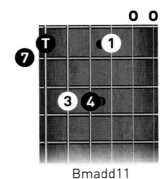

Bmadd11

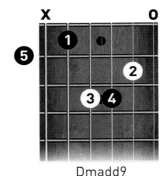

Dmadd9

MELLOW CHORDS

Try out these shapes for a warm, comforting effect that's suitable for ballads or mellow jazz tunes.

The C#m9 and Am11 shapes shown here are very common jazz guitar chords as used by players such as George Benson or Wes Montgomery. The Eadd9 and Fmaj7 chords have an open, airy sound that's perfect for folky acoustic material.

We've played the Fmaj7 chord 'thumb over the neck'-style, but if this is too much of a challenge, you can simply omit the lowest two strings all together.

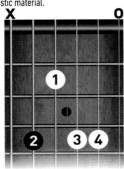

C#m9

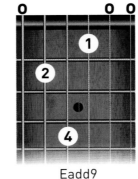

Eadd9

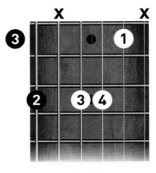

Am11

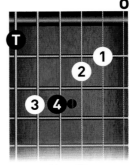

Fmaj7

MYSTERIOUS CHORDS

The close intervals in these chords give off an uneasy, haunting air that will give your playing an edge.

Two notes that are a tone or semitone apart are naturally dissonant as the frequencies fight each other. This is not necessarily a bad thing, as demonstrated by these chords, which utilise those close intervals in order to put the listener on edge. The Am9/E chord is tricky to finger at first, so try positioning your second and fourth fingers before adding your first and third.

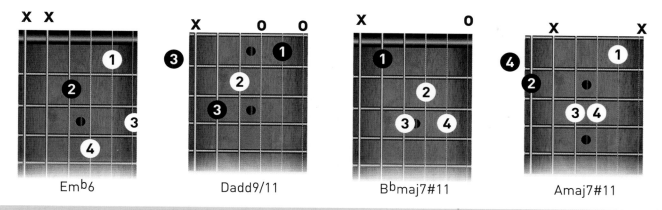

Em♭6   Dadd9/11   B♭maj7#11   Amaj7#11

TENSE CHORDS

Try out these shapes for an angular, clashing sound that will take your listener by surprise.

Tension in music works best in small doses so, rather than using these chords for a whole song or section, use them fleetingly. For example, if you have a song in the key of A, going to an E chord has a natural, predictable feel. You can enhance things by switching to the tense sounding E7#9 chord. The Caug chord works in a similar way in the key of F major.

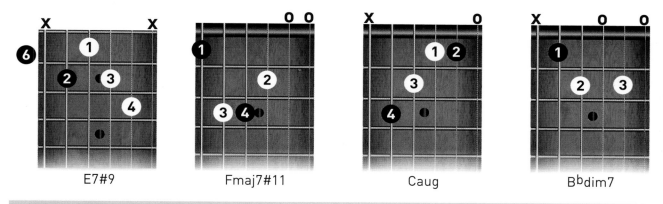

E7#9   Fmaj7#11   Caug   B♭dim7

UPLIFTING CHORDS

The major tonality and open sound of these chords creates an elating and inspiring atmosphere.

These chords are based on the bright, cheerful sound of major chords, with 9th and 11th intervals added to provide a lushness that works beautifully with a clean electric sound or an acoustic guitar. The Aadd9 and Badd11 chords use the same shape a tone apart; alternating between them sounds great.

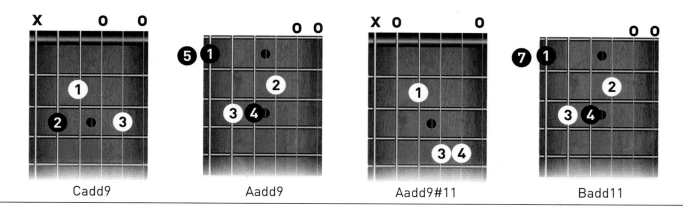

Cadd9   Aadd9   Aadd9#11   Badd11

LEAD GUITAR LESSONS

Don't fear the lead, learn it instead. Turn here to begin mastering the lead styles of some of rock's greatest guitarists and start your way on the path to soloing greatness. Sadly, we won't cover posturing or how to organise a legendary rider.

RHYTHMIC LEAD PLAYING

Just because you're playing lead doesn't mean you can forsake the rhythm. Take a tip from Alex Turner's Arctic Monkeys' style and get creative with phrasing.

Once you've learned a scale shape, your next step is to use it. That means turning the scale – a simple sequence of notes – into something more creative, namely some kind of melody or solo. Arctic Monkeys' Alex Turner and Blur's Graham Coxon give their solos a creative kick up the rear by making sure there's plenty of rhythmic phrasing on display and messing about with the rhythm of the notes they're playing.

Our short Arctic Monkeys-style solo below is made up entirely of eighth notes, which means that each bar is divided into eight equal notes, which are counted '1 & 2 & 3 & 4 &'.

Either play the numbered notes, which are 'downbeats', or the '&'s, which are 'upbeats'. To make interesting solos and melodies, blend together downbeats and upbeats – this is called 'syncopation'.

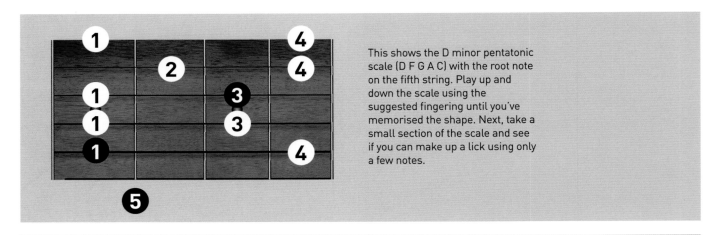

This shows the D minor pentatonic scale (D F G A C) with the root note on the fifth string. Play up and down the scale using the suggested fingering until you've memorised the shape. Next, take a small section of the scale and see if you can make up a lick using only a few notes.

MODERN INDIE LICK

Ensure consistent timing by counting the pulse of these bars as '1 & 2 & 3 & 4 &', while at the same time keeping your picking hand moving in a constant down-up-down-up motion to match. Play any notes that land on the downbeats with downstrokes and pick the offbeats with upstrokes.

BLUES STYLE VIBRATO

Your personal vibrato is a unique thing that will improve your tone and sustain, and give your playing new life. Take a leaf out of the King Of The Blues's book...

Vibrato is an expressive technique, performed by repeatedly bending and releasing the string to create a pulsing change of pitch.

A guitarist's vibrato makes a player unique and recognisable. Even though the basic technique is the same for everyone, if you compare how BB King sustains a note with the style of Brian May you'll hear a huge difference in the tone and feel.

There are two main factors that affect vibrato: pitch and speed. Blues players tend to use a more subtle change in pitch and a faster rate of bend and release, whereas rock players like Yngwie use a wider change of pitch, but a slower rate. It's up to you to experiment with these two factors and create your own personal vibrato.

VIBRATO EXPLAINED

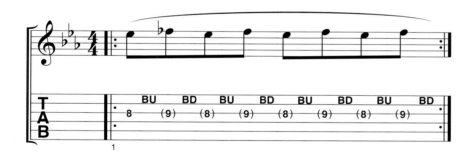

Vibrato is basically a series of upward and downward bends on a single note. Use your first finger for this exercise, turning your wrist so that the string is pulled down towards the floor. Aim to bend by about a semitone. Experiment by using each of your fingers and try bending upwards too.

CHICAGO BLUES LICK

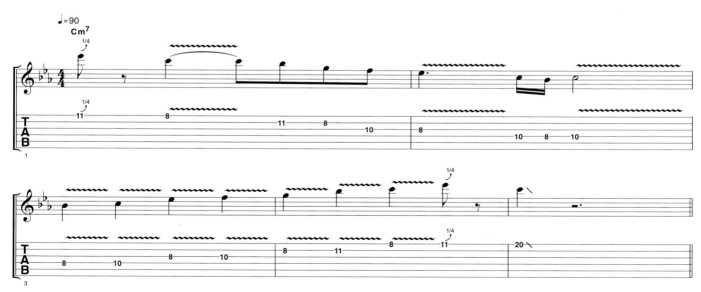

Use your first and third fingers throughout this C minor pentatonic lick. When adding vibrato on the third and fourth strings, it's better to pull the string down towards the floor, but on the first and second strings you must push the string upwards otherwise the string could slip off the fretboard.

ARPEGGIO LEAD

Test your note-separation skills with our Matt Bellamy-style lick and improve your fret/pick hand coordination by practising your arpeggio playing.

An arpeggio is made up of the notes of a chord, but the notes are played one at a time rather than all at once. Players, including Muse's Matt Bellamy, use arpeggios in two ways. The first approach is to hold a chord and pick the strings individually. Bellamy uses this in tracks, such as Muse's 2001 track Citizen Erased. This particular method can be applied to any chord and is largely better suited to a clean sound.

The second approach is to use arpeggios in a more lead-guitar fashion. The idea is to fret one note at a time, which can pose problems when moving from string to string while staying on the same fret. This happens quite a lot with chord shapes, such as the E minor shape shown below. In this case, roll your finger across the strings to mute the unwanted notes and keep the notes separated.

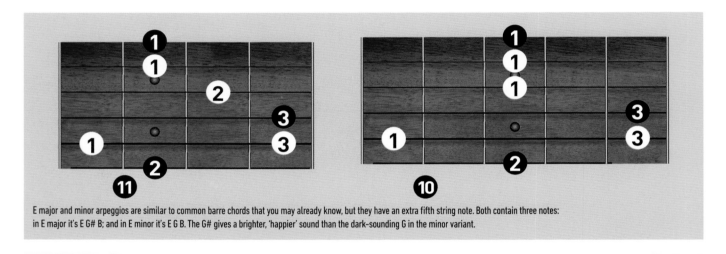

E major and minor arpeggios are similar to common barre chords that you may already know, but they have an extra fifth string note. Both contain three notes: in E major it's E G# B; and in E minor it's E G B. The G# gives a brighter, 'happier' sound than the dark-sounding G in the minor variant.

MODERN PROG ROCK LICK

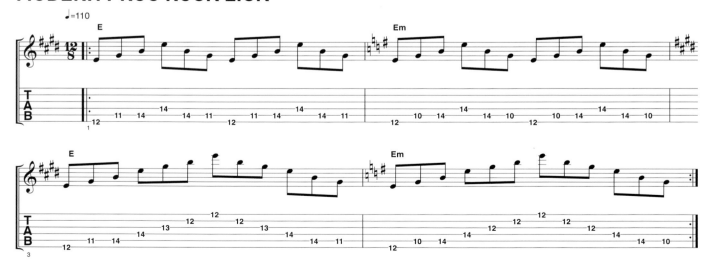

The first two bars show the E major and E minor arpeggios in one octave; the last two bars show the same arpeggios spread over two octaves. This is quite a formulaic lick, so you could easily try making up arpeggios of any other E and E minor chord shapes that you know.

OCTAVE SOLOING

Do you like to crank the volume? Then you'll need to fatten up your melodies. Help them cut through the mix by using octave shapes like Billie Joe Armstrong.

Jazz players have employed octaves in their leads for decades in order to be heard above a big band and you'll find octaves being used by contemporary players such as Green Day's Billie Joe Armstrong, too. Sometimes, a single-note melody just doesn't cut through the mix of a loud rock band. Of course, if you're the only guitarist in your band, you may not have problems cutting through the mix.

Adding an extra note either an octave above or an octave below the melody note is a good way of fattening up the tone, and making the volume of a melody closer to that of a rhythm part. The technical challenge of octaves is to mute out the idle strings, so you can strum freely without having to worry about open-string noise.

Place your first finger on the 7th fret of the fourth string to play the low A note. Next, place your fourth finger on the 10th fret of the second string. This is also an A note, but it sounds higher in pitch than the fourth-string A. The distance between these two notes is called an octave.

POP-PUNK OCTAVE SOLO

Fret the two notes of the octave shape with your first and fourth fret-hand fingers, staying relatively flat so you're gently resting against and muting the idle first and third strings.
If you're muting effectively, you should be able to strum the first to fifth strings and only hear the fretted octave notes.

PENTATONIC LICKS

Take the sound of 'five black keys' and you have the minor pentatonic scale,
a simple set of notes that unlocks a mountain's worth of lead licks.

L isten to Jack White and Dan Auerbach and you'll hear them use the minor pentatonic scale for simple melodies. In fact, Auerbach's band name, The Black Keys, is a reference to the minor pentatonic scale: the five black keys on a piano spell out the scale.

The E minor pentatonic scale is a relatively simple shape to play and an easy-to-remember sound and many classics are based on it, perhaps most famously the riff from Led Zep's Whole Lotta Love. Check out the scale shape and then try our lick below.

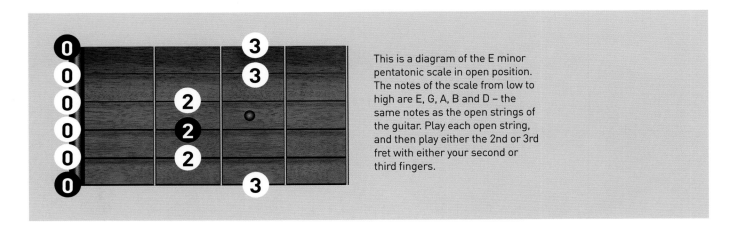

This is a diagram of the E minor pentatonic scale in open position. The notes of the scale from low to high are E, G, A, B and D – the same notes as the open strings of the guitar. Play each open string, and then play either the 2nd or 3rd fret with either your second or third fingers.

MODERN BLUES LICK

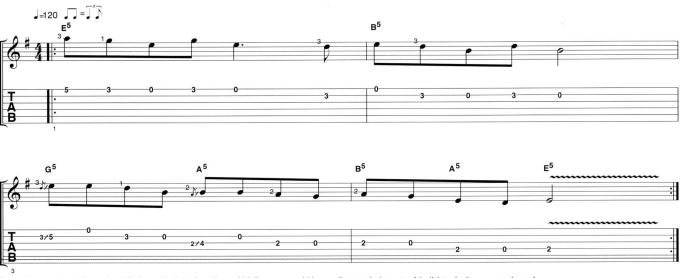

The numbers next to certain note heads in the standard notation tell you which fingers to use. Add some vibrato to the last note of the lick to give it a more vocal sound – this whole lick is played with a shuffle feel.

STRING BENDING

Use those arm muscles for the most fluid and expressive of all lead guitar techniques.
Learn the style of one of the greats and bend it like David Gilmour.

String bending is one of the most expressive aspects of playing. It's a simple concept: pick a note and then bend the string with your fretting finger to alter the pitch. Players such as David Gilmour have made bending into an art form; just check out his soulful solo in Pink Floyd's Comfortably Numb for proof. The wrist and forearm are the vital sources of strength for a proper bending technique. These muscles are bigger and better suited to the effort required. Sure, your fingers take fretting duties, but you bend the strings using forearm strength to push your fingers. You must use your ears, too. That means listening carefully as you bend the string to make sure you hit the note accurately.

Bending strings can put a strain on your fingers, so to avoid hurting yourself use the correct technique. When bending the third string, bunch up your first, second and third fingers in a line at the relevant fret. Next, turn your wrist to bend the string upwards. Your first finger's knuckle should stay in contact with the neck as a pivot.

BLUES-ROCK LICK

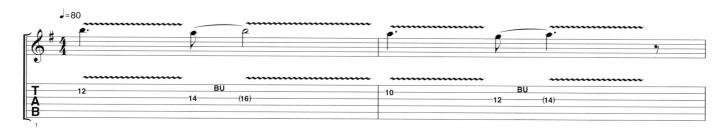

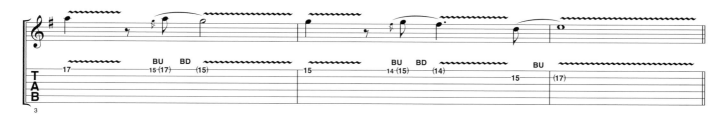

Play the opening 12th fret note with your first finger and as you listen to the note, try to remember what the pitch of the B note sounds like. Bend the following 14th fret A note with your third finger until it is the same pitch as the first B. Keep checking the notes like this throughout, to develop your ear as well as your technique.

ALTERNATE PICKING

Feeling the need for speed? Get your timing and accuracy on track with a little help from Gus G's formidable alternate-picking style.

Alternate picking is universally useful to practise on guitar because it applies to nearly all genres. It's found in its most extreme form in heavy metal with notable players including Paul Gilbert and Jeff Loomis using the technique to play intense riffs and high-speed solos.

The 'alternate' part of the title refers to the down-up pick motion, best used to create a constant stream of notes. Although this is a picking technique, a key element is synchronising fretting and picking. Keep both hands relaxed, move your pick hand from the wrist and start slowly.

ALTERNATE PICKING EXERCISE

There are three notes per click in this exercise, so use a metronome at a slow tempo to help you find the pulse. Start on the first click and pick the first three notes down-up-down. Start on the second click with an upstroke and pick up-down-up. Beat 3 starts with a downstroke; beat 4 with an upstroke, and so on.

MODERN METAL PICKING LICK

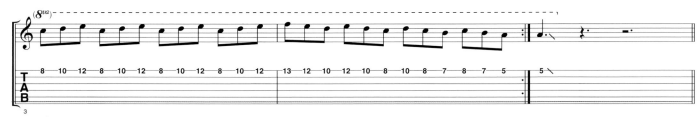

Move your picking hand from the wrist in even, alternate downstrokes and upstrokes. Start slowly and make sure that your fretting fingers and pick strokes are landing at precisely the same moment. First, ensure that you're comfortable with the first bar of music before shifting up the fretboard to the other positions.

CHORDAL SOLOING

Solos aren't all about single-note showboating. Bridge the gap between melodies and chords – just like Jimi Hendrix – to achieve an even fuller guitar sound.

Chords and scales are closely related. For example, the notes of an A major chord (A, C# and E) can be found in the A major scale (A B C# D E F# G#). Ornamenting chords with other scale notes is natural for a pianist, but it's not so obvious for a guitarist. However, it is a particularly useful skill to have especially if you're playing guitar unaccompanied, or if you're the sole guitarist in your band.

As opposed to the two hands of a piano player, we guitarists have to find ways of playing chords and melody notes with just our fretting hand. Jimi Hendrix's performance on tracks such as Little Wing and Hey Joe show how beautiful this approach can be on the guitar, and it's had an influence on more contemporary players, including John Frusciante who used this Hendrix style on Red Hot Chili Peppers' tracks such as the enduring Under The Bridge.

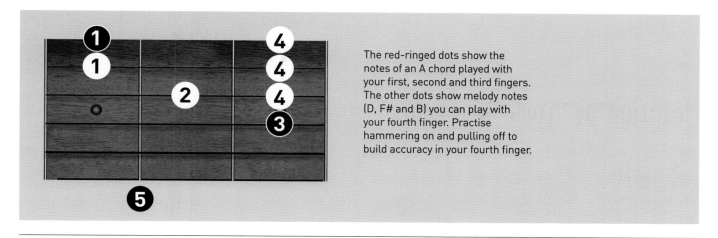

The red-ringed dots show the notes of an A chord played with your first, second and third fingers. The other dots show melody notes (D, F# and B) you can play with your fourth finger. Practise hammering on and pulling off to build accuracy in your fourth finger.

CHORDAL LEAD LICK

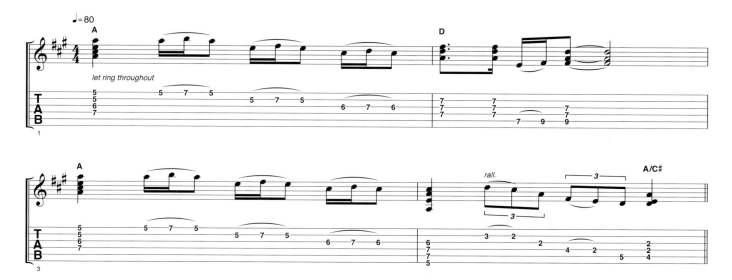

Each bar starts with either an A chord or a D chord. In each case, strum the chord and let it sustain for as long as possible while adding the melody notes with your remaining fingers. When hammering on and pulling off, do your best to avoid hitting the other sustaining strings.

GEAR

From tweaking your gear to using pedals, learning how to get the best out of your gear is a fun and vital part of sounding great when you play. In this section, we'll give you an insider's guide to getting to grips with your gear and provide tips on how to create the sounds you want to hear.

50 GUITAR HACKS

YOU NEED TO KNOW

We're always looking for shortcuts to help us make the most of our time. Over the following pages, you'll find 50 essential hacks to doing just that – easy, quick shortcuts to help you play better, sound better, gig better and get more from your precious gear...

Maintenance Hacks

Get your guitar in the finest fettle

1 REDUCE NUT FRICTION

If your string suffers erratic tuning, it might be because the string is catching in your guitar's nut. Sometimes this may entail the nut being filed, or replaced, but before you get extreme, try lubricating your nut slots. You can buy bespoke nut lubricants to do this, but an easier method is to use a pencil in the nut slot of the problem string.

2 Change Strings Faster

It's a myth that removing all the strings at once damages neck, but unless you're oiling the fretboard or cleaning frets, loosening and snipping off all the strings at once is not the best for speed. The more time the strings are off the guitar, the more chances there are for the neck to lose tension through movement, taking longer for it to stabilise again. Instead, restring one by one – it's quicker, and you'll need less time to retune.

3 Improve Tuning Stability

Having too much string on your tuners can cause tuning stability issues, and so can having too little? To reduce the risk of the string slipping when brought up to pitch, aim to have between two to four turns of string on each tuner post, with fewer on the wound strings.

4 Speed Up Floyd Rose Restringing

Restringing a Floyd Rose vibrato is a fiddly job but there is one annoying job you can spare yourself if you're in a rush. Instead of cutting the ball-ends off your strings to feed them into the vibrato, simply feed the strings backwards so that the ball-end is up at the tuners.

5 Intonate yourself

Having your intonation right is vital. Thankfully, it's a simple enough to do yourself, provided your electric has adjustable saddles. Get your guitar and a tuner, then play a harmonic at the 12th fret. Compare the harmonic's pitch to the note produced when you fret it normally – if it's sharper, move the saddle backwards slightly, if it's flatter, move it forwards (use the mnemonic FFF: fret, flat, forward). Repeat for the other strings and you'll be intonated perfectly!

6 Snip Strings Without Clippers

Okay, you've restrung your guitar but there are no clippers to be found. All is not lost – you can clip your strings with nothing more than your hand and some elbow grease. Firstly, take your loose bit of string and bend it against the machinehead so that it bends sharply against the string hole. Then bend it back and do the same the opposite way. Repeat this a few times until the string snaps, and repeat. This is much easier with the higher strings, wound ones can take some elbow grease, but it will work.

7 Make Strings Last Longer

Sweat from your hands corrodes strings into a dull, mess. So, whenever you finish playing, take a dry cloth and rub down your strings to get rid of any moisture, and notice how your strings now stay bright and zingy for longer. If you want to be extra conscientious, try washing your hands before you play, too!

8 Get New Strings In Tune Quicker

After restring a guitar strings need to stretch and settle. You can speed the process up yourself easily. Starting with the low E string, simply grip the string about half way along its length, and pull it up off the fretboard – not too much, just until you feel it get taut – release, and repeat! Do this on all your strings, and you'll find that your tuning is much more stable.

9 SET PICKUP HEIGHTS

To get the best out of your guitar, the pickups need to be set at the right height – the closer they are to the strings, the louder they'll be, but that's not what it's all about. Humbuckers are the simplest – fret the top and bottom E strings at the final fret and using a ruler, adjust the humbucker's side screws until treble and bass sides both sit evenly 2.5mm beneath the fretted strings. Single coils are more complicated – Strats should be adjusted to sit with the treble side higher than the bass for tonal balance. Fret the two outer strings at the final fret, then adjust the pickups so the polepiece tops sit 2.5mm and 3.5mm from the treble and bass E strings respectively. One thing to watch out for with single coils is wolf notes – these occur when the pickup's magnetic field is too close to the string's field of movement, preventing it from vibrating naturally. If you hear these, back off!

10 Trim Strings Perfectly

Knowing how many winds you need is all well and good, but how do you do it right? Well, if you have a Fender-style six-in-a-line headstock you trim your strings to the right length before you even start winding and still get the right number of turns. It simple really – as you fit each string on the headstock, simply measure your excess to the length of the next string's tuning post and then clip the rest off before winding it on. Of course, this trick won't work with three-a-side 'stocks...

Modding Hacks
Become the MacGyver of gear

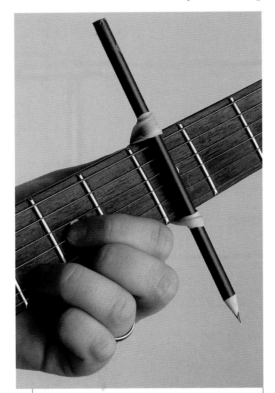

11 IMPROVISE A QUICK CAPO

There's nothing more frustrating than being caught short of a capo, but if you've forgotten yours, all you need to create an improvised substitute is a pencil and a rubber band! Simply lay the pencil over your strings in the allotted place, and then wrap the rubber band around each end a few times until it's tight and the strings sound cleanly. If you're without a pencil, you could try a pen, a fork... anything that's flat, straight and sturdy!

12 Make Your Les Paul More Resonant

Many LP users, thinks that they sound better with the tune-o-matic tailpiece screwed all the way down, improving the connection between wood and strings, and in theory making the guitar more resonant. However, doing this creates a steep break angle between the bridge and the tailpiece, making bending harder. The solution, as popularised by Joe Bonamassa, is to string

the tailpiece 'backwards' as if it's a wraparound bridge – this decreases the break angle, leading to easier bends and (allegedly) increased resonance with minimal hassle.

13 Cheap Home Made Strap Locks

Even if your strap isn't crying for help by repeatedly falling off your guitar's button, it could easily still happen in the heat of the moment onstage. You make a functional strap lock by fitting an old washer over the strap button to stop it popping off. The red rubber washers from big Grolsch bottles are an old favourite but you can use rubber plumbing washers as an alternative. If you want an even firmer option, unscrew the pins and using metal washers with the right sized holes.

14 Stop Your Controls Turning Easily

If your knobs are so easily turned that knocking them mid-song is a problem, there's an easy fix: remove your control knob and slot a rubber washer or O-ring (available from any DIY shop) over the post. Pop your knob back on and the washer will cause the friction between your guitar's body and the knob, making it much harder to turn. A word of caution – if your guitar has a nitrocellulose finish, the rubber washer could potentially mark or even damage the finish, so do this at your peril!

15 Make A DIY String Mute

String mutes are used by shredders to tame noise, overtones and sympathetic harmonies while they blaze up and down the neck. If you find yourself needing one in a jam, an old hair tie will do the job instead – fluffy 'scrunchies' are best, but any one will do in a pinch.

16 GIVE YOUR STRAT A BRIDGE TONE CONTROL

The Stratocaster bridge pickup is an immensely versatile beast, but one that's caged thanks to the lack of a tone control in Leo Fender's original configuration. Thankfully, changing this is a very simple fix that guitarists have been doing for decades. First, locate the wire connecting the Strat's second tone pot to the pickup selector switch (it'll be connected to the middle pickup at this point). Unsolder this, and move it one tag towards the middle of the switch and solder it back up. Done! Want to test it out? Crank up your gain and knock the tone down to about halfway, and you'll find that polite single coil sounds suspiciously like a humbucker!

17 Create An Emergency Plectrum

If you're a pick player, getting caught without one can be a nightmare, but don't fret - you already have the solution at hand. Look in your purse or wallet - we'll bet there's more than one loyalty or membership card in there you're never going to use again, so let's put it to good use. Simply take a pair of scissors, cut out a shape that suits your pick presence... and voila! One emergency pick.

Playing Hacks
Play better with less perspiration

Your volume and tone controls have huge expressive potential

18 Use Your Controls As An Instrument

There's potential to change your tone at your fingertips. Here are four ways to use your guitar's controls to get useful sounds without touching your amp or pedals:

1. Violining for expressive licks
For Jeff Beck-style volume swells, turn your guitar's volume down then gradually raise it as you play a note for a smooth, violin-like crescendo. It's easiest on long notes where there's time to coordinate all the movements. Generally, guitarists stretch out their fourth finger to reach the volume control as they pick. Alternatively, use a volume pedal if you have one.

2. Volume controlled gain boost
Turn your guitar up to maximum and then set your amp to the point where you're happy with its medium to high gain tone. Now dial back your volume and it will start to clean up as well as becoming quieter, leaving you a boost to call on mid-song when you turn up.

3. Two pickups. Two gain settings
If your guitar has a volume control for each pickup (such as on a Les Paul) you can set a medium drive tone on one pickup by lowering its volume to halfway, and a high gain sound on the other by keeping the volume maxed. Just flick your selector switch to change gain.

4. Woman tone
Get in the smooth ballpark of Clapton's fabled Cream tone by choosing the middle position on a two-humbucker guitar, turn the bridge pickup's tone to zero, add some overdrive and crank your amp's treble.

19 Tune Up More Accurately
Do you struggle to get your guitar as perfectly in tune as you'd like? Flip your guitar onto the neck pickup and roll the tone all the way down – this will reduce the overtones that can confuse electronic tuners, and give you a clearer signal with which to get yourself in perfect pitch.

20 Experiment With Different Picks
They say tone is in your hands but it's also in your plectrum, too, and a change in habits can have a real impact. Lighter gauges can be great for strumming feel, but they also encourage you to approach notes and vibrato in a more considered way. And if you're not cutting through rhythmically, a heaver pick can help. Try a few different textures and gauges of pick and you'll see what we mean.

22 Create Instant Dynamics With Your Picking Hand Placement

It's easy to fall into comfortable positions with our guitars, especially where we hit the strings. But where you pick in relation to the pickup can directly affect the sound and using it can give you new dynamics. Try playing over the pickup you're not using for a more acoustic-natured sound, now switch to the pickup you have selected – instant boost that cuts. The same dynamic principal applies to playing away from an acoustic's piezo or soundhole pickup, or indeed soundhole if you're unplugged.

21 QUICKLY FIND HARMONICS ABOVE THE LAST FRET

To master Van Halen and Dimebag Darrell style pinched harmonics (aka 'squealies'), you'll need to target your pick at a specific point on a string. Get started the easy way. If you're playing below the 12th fret, target your pick 24 frets higher than the fretted note. If you're playing above the 12th fret, aim 12 frets higher. Work out the exact spot in relation to your guitar – the harmonic might be in line with a pickup, a scratchplate screw, top horn, and so on.

Target your pick 24 frets above low notes...

...But 12 frets higher than notes past the 12th fret

10 Tuning hacks

Get your guitar in tune then get creative with a handful of alternative tunings using our handy hacks

23 Get in tune. Use a tuner!

E A D G B E

The electronic tuner is an essential bit of gear. Hardware tuners are affordable and there are loads of free tuner apps for smartphones as well. You just need to know the name of the strings (EADGBE from low to high); the gauge tells you when the string reaches the right note as you adjust your guitar's tuners. Tighten the string to go up in pitch or loosen it to go down.

28 Use Open D for one-finger major chords

D A D F# A D

Down two semitone   Down one semitone   Down two semitones   Down two semitones

Change your tuning from standard to open D (D A D F# A D) and your guitar's open strings produce the bright sound of a D major chord – that's because the notes of a D chord are D, F# and A. It also means you can play major chords simply by barring across all six strings with your first finger. Retune the first, second, third and sixth strings. The fourth and fifth strings are the same as standard.

D A D F# A D

D chord in open D tuning

24 No tuner? No worries!

E A D G B E

In the picture below you'll see that open strings are tuned to the 5th fret on the adjacent lower string. The only exception is the second string, which is tuned to the 4th fret of the third string. To tune up, simply choose the string you think is already most in tune, then adjust the strings on either side – and keep going till you've tuned every string. way.

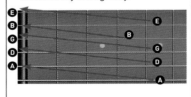

29 Slide into open G tuning

D G D G B D

Down two semitones   Down two semitones   Down two semitones

Just like open D, the idea here is to tune to the notes of a major chord, G this time, to give you a brighter sound and easy one-finger major barre chords. Open G (D G D G B D) was a favourite of slide player Duane Allman, and Keith Richards uses his own five-string version of the tuning, removing the lowest string from his guitar altogether – a vital part of the Rolling Stones' sound. Retune only your first, fifth and sixth strings.

25 Tuning trick for more accurate intonation

No guitar is ever 100 per cent in tune at every note on the fretboard – and when using the 5th fret tuning method mentioned in the last hack you may find the higher notes on your instrument sound less 'in tune'. If a song you play is based higher up the neck, try tuning with notes in that range of the fretboard for more accurate intonation.

30 Fix minor problems with open D minor tuning

D A D F A D

Down two semitones   Down two semitones   Down two semitones   Down two semitones

Open D tuning has one key drawback: if you're playing one-finger major chords it can be difficult to adapt the shape when a minor chord crops up. So tune to open D minor instead – this allows you to play one-finger minor chords that are much easier to adapt when you want to play a major chord. If you're in open D, simply lower the third string a further semitone to get to D minor.

D A D F A D   D A D F A D

Dm chord in open D minor tuning   **D chord in open D minor tuning**

26 Drop D: The one-finger powerchord trick

D A D G B E

Down two semitones

Make powerchords easier by tuning to drop D. Simply lower your sixth string by two semi-tones (same as two frets) from E to D. You'll be able to play one-finger powerchords by barring across the three bass strings at the same fret.

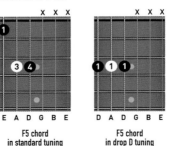

E A D G B E   D A D G B E

F5 chord in standard tuning   **F5 chord in drop D tuning**

31 Cut through a mix with Nashville tuning

E A D G B E

Up 12 semitones   Up 12 semitones   Up 12 semitones   Up 12 semitones

If you need a brighter sound to make strummed chords cut through a mix, Nashville tuning might do the trick. Simply replace the four bass strings on your guitar with their 'octave-up' counterparts from a 12-string set. This removes some of the muddy-sounding bass frequencies, helping your sound to cut through.

Gigging Hacks
Simple steps to better live playing

27 Drop C# and lower dropped tunings

C# G# C# F# A# D#

Down two semitones | Down two semitones | Down two semitones | Down two semitones | Down two semitones | Down two semitones

Drop C# is exactly the same tuning as our old friend drop D but in this case with all six strings tuned one semitone lower than drop D. Remember the drop C# pattern and you can also work out drop C (CGCFAD), drop B (B F# B E G# C#), drop Bb (Bb F Bb Eb G C) and drop A (A E A D F# B) by lowering all six strings by a further semitone each time. If your strings buzz try using heavier strings to counter the lower string tension.

32 Retune to make difficult chords easier

Andy Summers's 'add9' chord in Every Breath You Take is an infamous finger-twister. Simply raise the fourth string by two semitones (two frets) so the D note becomes an E and the riff is instantly playable with simpler 'E-shape' barre chords. Of course, this approach can throw up problems...

Aadd9 in standard tuning

Aadd9 with compensated tuning

33 Sort Out Your Strap Height
The low-slung guitar might be universal sign of a badass, but there's a sweet spot. We're not saying you have to have your top bout tickling your armpit but bashing it around your ankles isn't comfortable either. If you're struggling to play things live that you manage with ease at home just lift that strap a little– you'll be surprised how much easier it will feel.

Playing your guitar too high can look a bit rubbish...

But have it too low and you'll struggle to play cleanly...

But there's a sweet spot! Experiment until you find it

34 STOP PULLING YOUR LEAD OUT

Okay this might be obvious to many of you already but if you don't know it, you'll thank us! Keep pulling your cable out of your jack socket as you wander around the stage or practice space? Simply loop your cable through your guitar strap and then plug in – et voila! No more pulling your cable out with every innocuous tug or twist of the guitar!

35 Set Your Amp Tone Up For The Stage, Not The Bedroom
To make your amp sing in a gig or practice, you have to think about your place in the mix. So, for simplicity's sake let's say that the bass and drums take up most of the low frequency space, while the cymbals and vocalist occupy the highs – where does that leave you? The middle! SO, when you're setting your amp at a gig, give the mid control a twist to the right and notice how all of a sudden you can hear yourself cutting through!

36 Make Your Small Amp Sound Bigger
If you have a small valve amp but are struggling to cut through in a live environment, try kicking in a clean boost pedal into the front end of it. It'll never make your 1x10 sound like a stack, but a good boost will push the amp harder, bring out more rich harmonics, and increase the amp's natural compression, which can make small amps sound 'bigger'.

37 Keep Your Pedals Going In Emergencies
If you find yourself with a dead battery-powered pedal and no time to replace it mid-set, this one's for you. Keep a standard nine-volt battery in your gig bag, along with a nifty battery clip with the right sized power jack on the end. It's an instant power supply and not very expensive at that!

Recording Hacks
Shortcuts to better cuts

Gear Hacks
Make the most of your kit

38 USE YOUR PEDAL AS A RECORDING INTERFACE

You can spend a lot of money on an audio interface to record your guitar, but before you drop your hard-earned cash, check out your multi-effects pedal! Multi-effects have included USB audio outputs for many years now, and it's the simplest way of getting your guitar signal into your computer. The same goes for modeling amps – just hook it up to your computer, and you're recording for free!

39 Record A Dry Signal For Reamping

Get two tracks for the price of one by capturing a dry 'direct' version of your playing, as well as your mic'd amps sound when you record. That way, you have a backup if you want to reamp your sound later (if you're not happy with the recorded sound, for example), or double up your part with an alternate tone. How do you split your signal? Head to hack number 43...

40 Play The Same Parts In Different Tunings

Layering multiple takes of the same part and placing them within your mix can make you sound huge, but why not take it a step further? Play the same part using different inversions of the chords, either with different shapes, tunings or capo will increase the depth of your multi-tracked parts without just creating a wall of the same noise. For added variation, be sure to change your amp settings, too.

41 Create A Fake Acoustic Sound

Add texture to your electric guitar recordings capturing the acoustic sound of your strings. Place a condenser mic near the fingerboard or bridge, but be mindful not to breathe too heavily as you play!

42 GET CONSISTENT MIC PLACEMENT

Getting your mic in the right place to record a guitar amp can be a frustrating process, but once you've found that sweet spot, save yourself the hassle of having to go through it all again by marking the spot where you've found your slice of sonic perfection with a square or X of masking/gaffa tape. This also comes in very handy should some clumsy oaf knock the mic out of place on his way out of the room to get a coffee...

43 USE A STEREO PEDAL TO SPLIT YOUR SIGNAL

If you want to experiment with splitting your guitar's signal, or save real estate, scour your 'board for a tuner, modulation or delay pedal with dual outputs. Treat this as your splitter, and it's your low-cost gateway to the guitar signal dual carriageway!

44 Power Your Board From A Tuner

Many tuner pedals include a power output socket as well as an input. So, by powering up your tuner with one power supply, you can buy a 'daisy chain' of power cables for a few pounds to drive the rest. Add up the current draw of each of your pedals (the mA rating) and make sure it doesn't exceed your supply's maximum, check they use the correct polarity and you're all done!

45 Use Your Effects Loop

Those sockets on the back of your amp marked 'send' and 'return' actually do something. And it's good! Your effects loop allows you to divert your signal between the pre and power amp stages of your amp. Some effects (modulation, reverb, delay, etc) are designed to be placed after your gain has been applied. So, for example, by placing them at this point in the chain, you'll get a delayed distortion, rather than a distorted delay. You can also choose to place just a couple of pedals in the loop and use it as a way of bringing in multiple effects at once. There are no rules, so experiment!

46 Get More Out Of Your Amp & Multi-Effects Unit

Are you running your multi-effects unit straight into the front end of your amp? There's nothing wrong with that, but the mythical four-cable method could help make your effects sound better than ever. All you need is an amp with an effects loop, a multi-effects with send and return sockets, and four cables. Plug your guitar into your effects unit, then run a cable from your effects' output to the amp's effects in/return socket on the back. Then, you need to run a cable from the amp effects send into the pedal's effects return, and finally, from the pedal's effects send into the amp's main input. This not only will enable you to place effects in the amp's loop as you would with physical pedals (most modern multi-effects units allow you to choose where the loop occurs in the signal chain), but it can also totally change the character of your amp. If your pedal has built in amp simulations, and you're prepared to spend time learning how your multi-effects' signal chain works, you could bypass your amp's preamp (the bit that gives it much of its tonal character), and run your amp sim sounds (without cab modelling of course) straight into the power stage for added responsiveness.

47 Find The Sweet Spot On Any Amp

The sweet spot is the point where you feel your amp sounds best. It's subjective and how responsive you judge it can vary, but it's there. To find it, set your amp at the level you'd usually play at without any pedals or reverb engaged and turn all the EQ settings to 12 o'clock. Now dial down the treble and roll it up until you first notice a difference in tone. Do the same for middle and bass. If you have a master volume turn the normal volume setting down and gradually turn it up for the same test. Then use the master to control your level.

48 Change Your Valves And Make Em Last

Valve amps are great, but tubes don't last forever. Power valves (NOT preamp valves!) will start to wear out after about a year, depending on how much you use them, and will need to be changed. Want to extend your valve life? Turn your amp off straight after a gig and let it sit for a few minutes before moving it. Also when setting up, as soon as you've got a power cable to your amp turn it on and let it warm up as long as you can before you play.

49 Use Your Effects Loop As A DI

If you need to run a DI onstage for monitoring, or in the studio to capture a track fro reamping, you can hack your amp's effects loop! Simply use the 'send' half of it to run a signal out to another device and you're there. This will only work on some amps (our Blackstar HT Stage 60 does it), depending on how the effects loop is wired. Always make sure you have your speaker connected when trying this, too.

50 GET YOUR PEDALBOARD IN THE RIGHT ORDER

The order in which you place your pedals in your signal chain has a impact on your tone and while there are no right or wrong answers, there is a generally accepted order. The start point is generally wah, followed by any EQ or compression pedals. After that it's distortion/overdrive effects, then boosts, then modulation effects (chorus, flangers, phasers, etc). Delay and echo come next, and this is important. A delay pedal takes a snapshot of whatever sound is played into it, so if you want your echoes to reflect your full tone, it needs come at the back of the chain. Finally, we have reverb, which works well in conjunction with delay repeats, and indeed everything else, so stick it right at the back. Don't be afraid to experiment with the order though.

TIPS FOR BETTER TONE

MAKE YOUR GEAR SOUND BETTER TODAY!

Once you have the foundation, you can start to experiment with different gear to enhance your tone. Over the next few pages, we'll guide you through with tips and explanations of how to make your gear work for you!

CHANGE YOUR SPEAKERS

There are hundreds of different speakers on the market, from companies such as Jensen, Eminence, Celestion, Electro-Voice and more, and which one will work best for you largely comes down to taste. When considering swapping your speakers, it's worth bearing a few things in mind:

POWER RATING

This is measured in watts, and needs to at least match the output of your amplifie. If you're using multiple speakers, they should combine to match the output of your amp, so a 100-watt 2x12 combo would take two 50-watt speakers.

IMPEDANCE

You need to make sure that you don't go lower than your amp's rated impedance for the number of speakers you're using (marked on the back). If you do, you'll send the amp's output transformer into meltdown and fry your amp.

EFFICIENCY

Most speakers will have an efficiency rating in dB. It's typical to find speakers rated at around 90 to 100dB: the higher the rating, the more efficient it is, meaning it will sound comparatively louder to those with a lower figure.

MAGNET

Classic amps from the 1950s and early 60s, made use of alnico-equipped speakers. As these got expensive to produce, ceramic magnets became the standard. The Celestion G12M 'Greenback', G12H and Vintage 30 have become classic ceramic designs.

WHAT THEY SOUND LIKE

It's impossible to say how a speaker will sound in any given cab, but as a guide, we've compiled a chart of some of the most iconic speakers by their power rating, magnet type, and the players that used them.

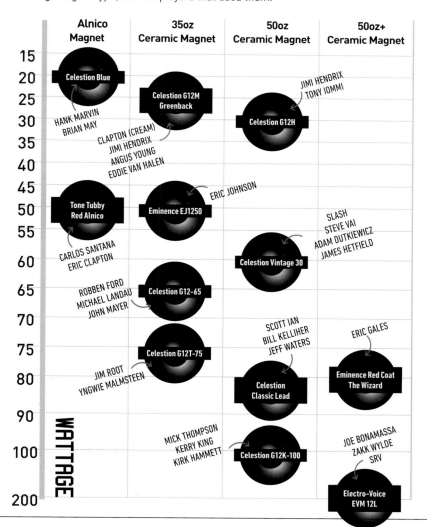

WATTAGE

	Alnico Magnet	35oz Ceramic Magnet	50oz Ceramic Magnet	50oz+ Ceramic Magnet
15				
20	Celestion Blue			JIMI HENDRIX / TONY IOMMI
25		Celestion G12M Greenback		
30	HANK MARVIN / BRIAN MAY		Celestion G12H	
35		CLAPTON (CREAM) / JIMI HENDRIX		
40		ANGUS YOUNG / EDDIE VAN HALEN		
45		ERIC JOHNSON		
50	Tone Tubby Red Alnico	Eminence EJ1250		SLASH / STEVE VAI
55				ADAM DUTKIEWICZ / JAMES HETFIELD
60	CARLOS SANTANA / ERIC CLAPTON		Celestion Vintage 30	
65	ROBBEN FORD / MICHAEL LANDAU / JOHN MAYER	Celestion G12-65		
70			SCOTT IAN / BILL KELLIHER / JEFF WATERS	ERIC GALES
75		Celestion G12T-75		
80	JIM ROOT / YNGWIE MALMSTEEN		Celestion Classic Lead	Eminence Red Coat The Wizard
90				
100		MICK THOMPSON / KERRY KING / KIRK HAMMETT	Celestion G12K-100	JOE BONAMASSA / ZAKK WYLDE / SRV
200				Electro-Voice EVM 12L

EL34   6L6   6V6   EL84

KNOW YOUR VALVES

The sound of your valve amp isn't entirely governed by the glowing glass bulbs, but they do play a big part in shaping your tone.

EL34

The EL34 is the driving force behind the sound of a classic Marshall stack being pushed into overdrive. Referred to as the 'British' sound, it's smooth, mid-rich, crunchy overdrive. See Marshall 1959 Super Lead (after 1969), JCM800, Blackstar Series One

6L6

The 6L6 is the classic 'US' sound. Typically, a 6L6-powered amp will have increased low and high end, plus a greater headroom before breaking up. When a 6L6 does break up, you'll get aggressive thick distortion. Used in: Fender Bassman, Mesa/Boogie Dual Rectifier

6V6

Often used in lower-watt heads. It has a smoothed-out frequency range, lower output than a 6L6, and adds compression to your sound at achievable volumes. Used in: Fender Champ (various models), Princeton Reverb, Deluxe Reverb & Tweed Tremolux

EL84

The sound of the EL84 is often typified by the timeless bell-like tone of the Vox AC30. The valve produces a smooth, chiming breakup and is ideal for use in smaller, low-wattage amps. Used in: Vox AC30, AC15; Fender Blues Junior; Orange Tiny Terror

GIVE YOUR STRAT A BRIDGE TONE POT!

This one's massive, and won't cost you a bean (assuming you own a soldering iron). Vintage-style Strats use the second tone pot for the middle pickup, but it's the bridge pickup that's often a bit shrill. It's easy to swap the tone control from middle to bridge by locating the wire connecting the second tone pot to the middle pickup on the selector switch. Move it one tag towards the middle of the switch, changing it from the middle to the bridge pickup.

DOUBLE UP YOUR AMPS

Do you love one channel on your amp, but feel it's lacking elsewhere? Maybe you're the only guitarist in your band, and you need to fill out the sound. Using two amps is actually pretty simple – with the help of an AB-Y box, you can switch between the two like massive distortion pedals, or use them both at the same time for ultimate power!

USE THE RIGHT-SIZE AMP

Valve amps need to be working at their 'sweet spot' to sound best. For most Marshalls and Fenders, that's just between four to eight on the master! If you find a valve amp sounds somehow 'cold', 'brittle' or harsh, it might be that it's just not turned up enough to be working properly. Joe Perry of Aerosmith, for example, uses small amps, suitably mic'd up, even for stadium gigs. We've seen Jeff Beck doing the same.

LOSE SOME BASS!

What sounds like the ultimate guitar tone when you're practising alone at home won't sound so good when you're playing as part of a band. You'll want to dial in some more bass when playing quietly than you will when you're playing loud. Too much bass – especially with lots of drive, and when using neck pickups – can mean a muddy, indistinct bottom end that clashes with the bass guitar and the kick drum when all three go for it.

PICK YOUR PICKS CAREFULLY

They're the cheapest part of the tone equation after the hands you got for free, but picks have a profound effect on tone. Thin picks made of softer materials such as celluloid produce a flatter tone than stiff nylon picks, which can enhance snap and clarity. Thick picks are good for single-note speed and articulation, but can be awkward to strum with.

DON'T FORGET THE VOLUME CONTROL!

Standard guitar volume controls cause a loss in treble when you turn them down. That's because, as a side effect of altering volume, they act as a low-pass filter. To get round this, you can do a treble-bleed modification. This is either a capacitor, or a resistor and a cap, wired, usually in parallel, to the pot. Popular combinations are a 150k resistor with a 0.001uf cap, or 100k/0.002uf. See www.guitarelectronics.com for in-depth examples.

EL CAPACITOR!

Key to your guitar's tone control is the capacitor. This controls the 'roll off' of tone when you turn it down. The lower the cap's value, measured in microfarads (uf), the less high end it will remove. So, if you reckon your guitar sounds too muddy and it is fitted with a 0.047uf cap, try fitting, for example, a 0.022uf or smaller cap instead. A lower value cap will also make more of the pot's turning range useful.

ACTIVE PICKUPS? UP THE VOLTAGE!

Many more dynamic guitarists claim that active pickups lack headroom and therefore compress the signal and their playing too much. One common mod is to double the voltage by using two nine-volt batteries (instead of one) to power the pickups and double your headroom! EMG shows you how on its site, or you could try the EMG ES-18 external power supply. Tidy!

TUNE UP!

Do we really have to remind you that the first step to sounding great is to be in tune? You'd be surprised at the number of guitarists that still try to tune by ear and get it wrong. Tuning has come a long way, with products such as the all-six-strings-displaying TC Electronic PolyTune making it (almost) cool!

OR TUNE DOWN...

If you thought drop-tunings were just for metal, think again. Certain tunings just sound better. Try taking everything down half a step from standard to Eb (Eb Ab Db Gb Bb Eb) for an instant tone boost a la Hendrix. Likewise, QOTSA, Mastodon and even Biffy Clyro have taken things low (C#) for a great modern-rock sound. Apply some fuzzy distortion, and you'll be like a stoner pied piper!

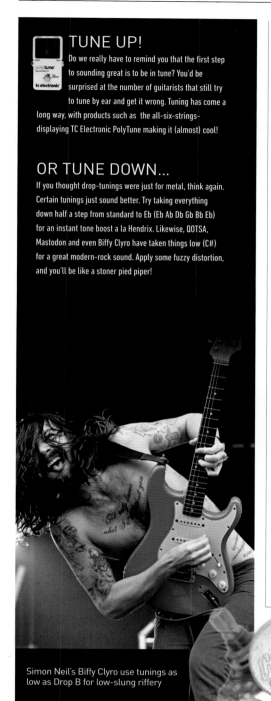

Simon Neil's Biffy Clyro use tunings as low as Drop B for low-slung riffery

DIAL IN YOUR SETTINGS

CHRIS GEORGE, MARSHALL AMPLIFICATION
"If you're using an amp for the first time, set all the dials straight up in the 12 o'clock position so you're getting equal values of everything. From there, fine-tune the settings. Or try Zakk Wylde's method – max everything out, then take away the parts you don't want!"

MATT SCHOFIELD

"You'll find that every pot has an obvious cusp point in its rotation – every single one – where it goes from not doing much, to where it really kicks in. So I sweep through the pots one by one and find those spots. All amps will do this – bass is especially easy to hear. Nothing, nothing, then bang – there it is!

"If you do that, the amp is set as evenly as it can be; not too trebly, not too dark, but just right. With everything set right on the cusp, you can then go ahead and push it over by digging in, or pull it back by playing softer. It makes everything really responsive and sensitive to what you do. The rest is up to you!"

PICKUP TYPES

 Single coil
Single coils have one coil, which gives the sharp, spanky tone that defines guitars like the Strat and Tele. If you're looking to upgrade yours, consider whether you want traditional low-output tones or more modern, high-output sounds. Since single coils are more susceptible to noise than humbuckers, a variety of noiseless options exist, too, most notably from EMG and DiMarzio.

Try these:
- Fender Texas Special Strat Pickups
- Seymour Duncan Vintage Staggered SSL-1

Humbucker
To combat interference, the humbucker is equipped with two coils that create a reverse polarity, which 'bucks' the hum. The first patented humbuckers were Gretsch's Filter'Tron, designed by Ray Butts, and Gibson's 'PAF', designed by Seth Lover, both of which were patented in 1959. The humbucker has evolved since it was introduced, with huge output from both passive and active 'buckers. Again vintage or modern voicing variants to choose.

Try these:
- Seymour Duncan JB
- EMG 81

P-90
Designed by Gibson in 1946, the P-90 is commonly known as a soapbar because of its rectangular shape. Although it's technically a single coil, it has a larger output thanks to a wide coil that accentuates the mids. If your tone is getting lost in your band's mix, the P-90 is a great middle ground between a single coil and a humbucker, and is used by the likes of Billie Joe Armstrong, Pete Townshend, Neil Young and Tony Iommi among many others.

Try these:
- Gibson P-90 'Super Vintage'
- DiMarzio Soapbar

STEEL YOURSELF

This one's for those who have Fender (or similar) Strats with a zinc, or leaded-steel vibrato block (ie, most of them). Swap the standard vibrato block that's factory-fitted for a non-leaded steel replacement. If you play loud and live, you'll hear a noticeable improvement in the sustain, depth and focus of your tone. Make sure you get the right size for your guitar, though.

PLAY WITH YOUR POTS

You can improve a low- or mid-price guitar by replacing the standard potentiometers. Of key interest is the pots' resistance value: the cheaper they are, the more they tend to vary. A Strat can sound very different with 300k or 200k pots (the 'correct' value is 250k). Likewise, 300k and 500k pots sound quite different in a Les Paul or SG.

TURN DOWN THE GAIN

Heavy distortion is a warm, comfortable place to be, and you might think it makes your tone massive. In fact, too much gain often equals too much compression, and that means nobody can hear you properly. It's why clean sounds often seem louder than dirty ones. Back off the gain, and you'll find your tone will sing out more clearly in the mix.

FX PEDALS

From overdrive to octavers and beyond, the world of effects is an exciting one – but to get the most out of them, you need to understand how they work. Over the next few pages we list out the major pedal groups and how to use them. Be warned though: any guitarist will tell you that pedal addiction is very real and can greatly affect your wallet.

OVERDRIVE

Overdrive, distortion and fuzz all increase the gain of your signal in different ways. Generally, overdrive is the mildest of the trio and has two primary roles: to boost the gain to drive your valve amp into distortion; and to simulate the sound of a valve amp distorting. Most overdrives use gentle 'soft clipping', unlike distortions, which use harsher 'hard clipping'. Clipping describes the way in the guitar signal is compressed when it becomes distorted. The harder it is driven, the more the peak of the waveform is flattened (clipped) to resemble a square waveform with increased harmonics and a lower dynamic range.

Overdrive tends to produce a smoother, warmer sound, allowing your amp's tonal characteristics and your guitar's tone to shine through. This makes overdrive stompboxes ideal for an organic boost that's used to push the front end of a valve amp, maintaining note clarity with driven open chords or when you're breaking into solos.

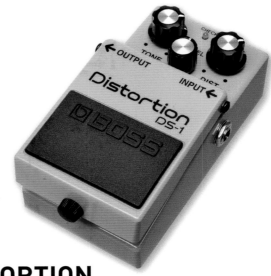

DISTORTION

From rock to metal distortion is the subject of most guitarists' first foray into pedals. The harder clipping of distortion can give tones a serious kick. Think of as an amp stack in a box, rather than something to complement an already overdriven valve amp. Here, the sound wave peaks tend to be squarer than the smoother peaks created by overdrive. Some pedals enable you to alter your EQ compared to an overdrive, too. This is especially true of heavy metal-type distortions that can offer super scooping of midrange, to accentuate 'chunk'.

High-gain pedals can be useful for distortion at any volume – simulating the break-up sound of a valve amp when you're unable to use it at the volume needed to get those valves cooking. They can also push a breaking-up valve amp to greater extremes of gain. Hard clipping saturation usually compresses your tone, accentuating sustain and harmonics making an ideal sound for leads compared to most traditional overdrives.

GET THE SOUND

DRIVEN RHYTHM

LEVEL TONE DRIVE

Add a touch of reverb and set the gain at about 9 o'clock for a big open boosted sound

PIERCING LEAD TONE

LEVEL TONE DRIVE

Add delay with the drive's gain and tone controls at 3 o'clock for a piercing lead tone

MARK KNOPFLER-STYLE DRIVE

LEVEL TONE DRIVE

Neck humbucker + medium drive + wah at a fixed setting = Money For Nothing tone!

TRY THESE OVERDRIVES

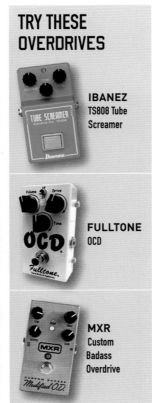

IBANEZ
TS808 Tube Screamer

FULLTONE
OCD

MXR
Custom Badass Overdrive

GET THE SOUND

DROP-TUNED METAL

LEVEL TONE DRIVE

Drop your tuning and experience the full-on chunk that liquid distortion can provide!

SCOOPED RHYTHM

LEVEL TONE DRIVE

Scoop the mids out for a Dimebag-style razor-sharp distortion sound

SLOW METAL LEAD

LEVEL TONE DRIVE

Boost your gain and tone, then add some delay for a sustained lead sound

TRY THESE DISTORTIONS

BOSS
DS-1 Distortion

PRO CO
Classic RAT

BLACKSTAR
LT Distortion

FUZZ

Fuzz wins in this trio of gain – it was first to the pedalboard, dating back to the early 60s. It polarises the opinion of some players, but fuzz can be a gain effect full of attitude that has enhanced everything from The Rolling Stones' (I Can't Get No) Satisfaction to The Smashing Pumpkins' Siamese Dream.

A vintage fuzz tone is warm, woolly and fat and increases sustain. These classic units tended to use germanium transistors to clip the signal, but back in the 60s their tolerances were not consistent, hence old Arbiter Fuzz Faces often vary wildly in gain. Modern examples often use silicon diodes for harsher clipping.

So what makes the fuzz fuzzy? The clipping threshold is lower than a distortion pedal – and the resulting wave is almost totally square. With that comes a series of strange and abrasive harmonics, and in extreme pedals an almost synth-like square wave sound. There are different ways to achieve this kind of clipping depending on the model of fuzz, and that makes them popular with DIY builders and modders.

GET THE SOUND

STONER ROCK LEVEL TONE DRIVE
Punch the gain (but don't go too mad), then lower your tuning for woolly stoner grind

MODERN FUZZ LEVEL TONE DRIVE
Pushing your fuzz through a flanger adds a wild spacey sheen, so just plug in, baby

RETRO FUZZ LEVEL TONE DRIVE
Retro 60s-style fuzz is as popular now as it was then. Here's a garage fuzz tone

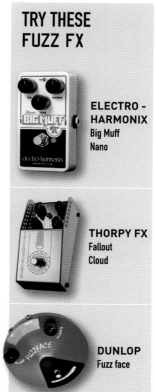

TRY THESE FUZZ FX

ELECTRO-HARMONIX Big Muff Nano

THORPY FX Fallout Cloud

DUNLOP Fuzz face

PITCH SHIFTERS HARMONISERS

DigiTech's Whammy transposes between notes using a foot pedal

Pitch effects weren't always authentic but it has evolved into effects incorporating pitch shifting, harmonisers, octavers and DigiTech's pitch-bending classic, the Whammy pedal. But what are the differences?

A pitch shifter transposes the pitch of your guitar up or down, while a harmoniser blends your original signal with a pitch-shifted interval to create dual guitar lines. An octave pedal is basically a harmoniser fixed to produce notes an octave or two octaves below, while DigiTech's Whammy uses a wah-style rocker pedal to bend your note.

However, it's not quite as black and white as that, because many of today's pitch-based pedals, such as the DigiTech Whammy (5th Gen), offer a combination of all of these effects. Until a few years ago, pitch-shifting more than one note at a time (polyphonic) didn't really work, but the latest breed of pitch-altering effects enable you to shift all six strings at once for electronic drop/capo tunings.

Regardless of which pedal you own, most pitch pedals operate in a similar way. For harmony effects, you select the key you're playing in, set the interval you want the pedal to create, and blend the signals together. For pitch-shifting effects, you simply choose the interval (usually in semitones), and for whammy effects, you set the maximum bend range you'd like the pedal to achieve, then use the pedal to bend your notes up or down as you solo. It sounds amazing.

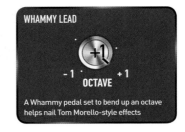

WHAMMY LEAD

A Whammy pedal set to bend up an octave helps nail Tom Morello-style effects

HARMONISED LEAD

| LEVEL | KEY | HARMONY |

Set a harmoniser to diatonic 3rd intervals to create Iron Maiden-like lines

OCTAVE RIFF

| DIRECT | OCTAVE 1 | OCTAVE 2 |

Blend in an octave below your guitar signal and use a fuzz for a cool garage-blues sound

OCTAVE

Pioneering players from Jimi Hendrix to Jack White have experienced the highs and lows of octave effects

PITCH SHIFTER

From Gilmour-mellow to drop-tuned metal, the pitch shifter can elevate your lead playing to the stratosphere and beyond

HARMONISER

Select a key, and clever little demons inside the box will play along at specified intervals to create harmony parts and unique effects

WHAMMY

Step on it for expressive pitch-shifting fun

TRY THESE PITCH FX

DIGITECH Whammy

BOSS PS-6 Harmonist

ELECTRO - HARMONIX POG2

FILTER PEDALS

You can use filter pedals to either accent or quite literally filter out particular frequencies of a sound. Think of a filter as a door that only lets certain frequency ranges through. Low- and high-pass filters allow the low and high-end frequencies to 'pass' respectively, while a band-pass filter works within a predetermined frequency range and filters out the low and high-end frequencies either side.

The EQ on your amp is essentially a series of fixed filters, sculpting the shape of your tone by removing different frequencies at the amount you set. However, it's when you start shifting those frequencies in which the filter is operating that things get interesting...

FILTER TYPES

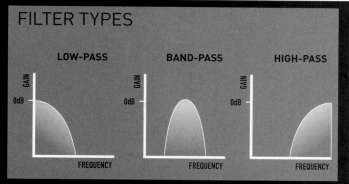

LOW-PASS   BAND-PASS   HIGH-PASS

This diagram shows the three most common filter types (low-pass, band-pass and high-pass) and how they affect your signal at different frequencies

AUTO-WAH

Auto-wahs (or envelope filters) work differently from a traditional wah pedal in that they don't use a rocker pedal to control the sound. Instead, they are controlled by your playing dynamics: how hard or softly you hit the strings. Essentially, you set a sensitivity level for the effect and once your picking reaches that level, the wah effect is triggered. Most auto-wahs let you decide the sweep's direction (low to high, or high to low) and sweep speed (how quickly it rises and how quickly it falls).

These controls let you create extremely fast movements, so it's possible to create sounds with an auto-wah that you'd find difficult with a regular pedal. Some auto-wahs (such as the Boss pictured) use a low-frequency oscillator (LFO, controlled by the rate knob) as you'd find in a modulation pedal to control the sweep of the wah – this gives you consistent rhythmic sounds without tiring your foot!

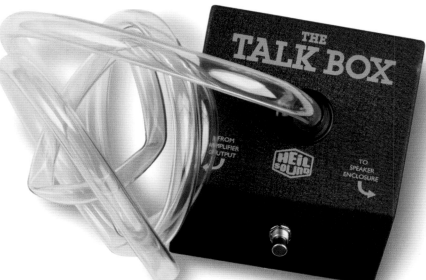

TALK BOX

As well as providing the vocalised effect on Bon Jovi's Livin' On A Prayer, the talk box (not to be confused with a vocoder) was made famous by Peter Frampton, Foo Fighters, Aerosmith and many others.

The talk box itself doesn't actually create the filtered effect: this is done by your mouth. It works by amplifying your guitar signal into a plastic tube, which is placed inside your mouth. When you change your mouth's shape, the tone is filtered in the same way as your voice. The whole lot is then picked up by a microphone, and pumped out to your audience through a PA system.

You can grasp the idea behind it without your guitar or a talk box: try singing a continuous note, then shaping your mouth to create different vowel sounds. Notice how the sound you sing never changes, but the tone can go from 'ahh' to 'ee' to 'ooh', and so on. Heil Sound's Talkbox is the most common unit for creating this sound, while the Danelectro Free Speech Talk Box lets you create the effect 'in-line' to your guitar amp, without the need for a PA.

WAH

The wah pedal can add percussive effects, bring rhythm parts to life, or add vocal expression to solos. They usually create a band-pass filter and the 'centre frequency' of the wah sound is changed using the rocker pedal. In classic wah examples such as the Dunlop Cry Baby, the rocker pedal is attached to a control pot, similar to those on your guitar.

When the pedal is swept from the heel-down to toe-down setting, the pot turns and the wah-wah sound corresponds to the movement. Mechanical pots can often wear out, introducing a scratchy sound to your pedal, or they can even stop working entirely. To combat this, companies such as Morley make wah pedals that use a sensor inside, rather than a moving pot.

Wah pedals don't usually have any controls apart from the rocker pedal and an on/off switch, but some come with additional circuits to increase the vocal quality of the pedal or add overdrive.

CHORUS

Known for the watery shimmer they add to electric guitar tone, chorus effects are designed to imitate the shimmer sound of a chorus of singers trying to pitch the same note. Chorus effects split the signal from your guitar into a 'dry' half and a duplicate 'wet' signal that has a series of short delays and pitch variations applied to it. This wobbled-up signal is then blended back in with the dry signal. Discrepancies in pitch and timing between the wet and dry signals generate a 'comb filter' effect: a series of harmonically ordered notches in the frequency spectrum of your guitar tone that resembles the teeth of a comb. This filtering effect alters with the varying pitch and delay times of the wet signal, controlled by the rate and depth knobs.

Chorus pedals are available in both analogue and digital varieties with analogue usually sounding warmer and digital versions tending to be both crisper and cleaner.

GET THE SOUND

HENDRIX LEAD
Use your wah in front of a valve-style overdrive for a vintage Jimi-style lead tone

TALK BOX
The 'talking guitar' effect Peter Frampton popularised with his Heil Talkbox

AUTO WAH
SENSITIVITY   RANGE   RESONANCE

An auto wah works off pick dynamics, so is best placed before distortion/compression

TRY THESE WAHS

DUNLOP
Cry Baby

BUDDA
Budwah

VOX
V847 Wah

GET THE SOUND

80S CLEAN RHYTHM
LEVEL   RATE   DEPTH

Use compression and some reverb with your chorus for a pristine 80s clean sound

PARADISE CLEAN
LEVEL   RATE   DEPTH

Which way to Paradise City? Ramp up rate and depth with your amp just past clean

JAZZ CHORUS
LEVEL   RATE   DEPTH

Try a stereo chorus pedal with moderate rate and depth through two clean amps

TRY THESE CHORUS FX

ELECTRO-HARMONIX
Neo clone

BOSS
CE-2w
WAZA Craft
Chorus

TC ELECTRONIC
Corona
Chorus

PHASER

Phaser became a classic effect in 70s rock, used by everyone from the Eagles to Van Halen to add a psychedelic edge to electric guitars. To understand how phasers work, let's turn to basic physics. In their simplest form, sound waves have regular peaks and troughs. Now imagine two identical sound waves aligned so that when the one peaks, the other is in a trough. These sound waves are 'out of phase'.

Phaser pedals split your guitar's signal into a dry half and a wet half that passes through filters, knocking the two signals out of alignment. When the filtered (wet) signal is mixed with the dry signal again, phase interference occurs that creates cancelled-out gaps in your signal's frequency range. These gaps are moved across the spectrum by a low-frequency oscillator which morphs your guitar's tone between bassy and warm, to toppy and brittle in regular cycles.

FLANGER

Flangers have a sinister metallic quality that makes them popular with metal bands such as, well, Metallica. As with chorus and phaser, the flanger generates its trademark sound by splitting the signal from your guitar into a dry unaffected half, and a wet signal that has a smidgen of delay on it. The delay times involved are shorter than in a chorus effect, with a typical duration of just a few milliseconds.

When the dry and delayed signals are blended together again, phase interference between them causes harmonically ordered 'notches' to appear in the frequency spectrum. The position of these notches is then swept up and down by a low-frequency oscillator controlled by the rate knob that alters the delay time of the wet signal – just like a phaser. This produces the swirling sound. Flangers differ from phasers as the notches in the flanger signal are equally spaced across the frequency range.

GET THE SOUND

VAN PHASIN'
RES · RATE · DEPTH
Set your phaser with the rate and depth set just below halfway for Van Halen swirl

FUNKY PHASER RHYTHM
RES · RATE · DEPTH
Slow rate settings and medium/high depth settings create a cool funk rhythm sound

JIMI PHASE
RES · RATE · DEPTH
Faster rate settings and a low/medium depth add gentle fluttering phase to cleans

TRY THESE PHASERS

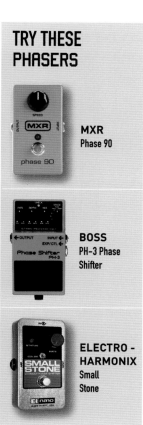

MXR
Phase 90

BOSS
PH-3 Phase Shifter

ELECTRO - HARMONIX
Small Stone

GET THE SOUND

CLEAN METAL FLANGER RHYTHM
FEEDBACK · RATE · DEPTH
Run a scooped clean tone through a flanger with slow rate and moderate depth settings

JET FLANGER
FEEDBACK · RATE · DEPTH
Set rate to a medium sweep. Turn up the feedback for the classic 'jet plane' flange

ALIEN FLANGER
FEEDBACK · RATE · DEPTH
Go nuts! Low depth and high rate settings will give metallic laser-gun flanger effects

TRY THESE FLANGERS

MXR
Micro Flanger

ELECTRO - HARMONIX
Electric Mistress

TC ELECTRONIC
Vortex Flanger

ROTATING SPEAKER

The Leslie speaker is an icon. It started out life designed for the organ market, but it wasn't long before guitarists wanted in on the swirly action. It's a common misconception that the speakers in a Leslie spin around, but that's not the case. The classic Leslie 122 model consists of two speakers: one treble and one woofer. In front of the treble speaker sits a 'horn' and in front of the woofer sits the 'drum'. It's these bits that do the spinning, and the 122 model offered two speeds: fast or slow (controlled by a brake circuit). As the drum and horn rotate, the direction of the sound relative to your ears changes, seemingly causing fluctuations in pitch.

However Leslie's are heavy, they're mechanical items that can break down, and to work, most require a special non-guitar-friendly preamp. Leslie simulators take the backache and connectivity problems out of employing that swirly sound.

TREMOLO & VIBRATO

That metal stick that you waggle to bend the pitch of your guitar strings? It's not a tremolo. It's a vibrato unit. But vibrato is also the name of a popular guitar effect and both a picking-hand and fretting-hand playing technique. Confused? So was Fender when in 1954 it christened the Stratocaster's vibrato system the 'Synchronized Tremolo'.

Tremolo is a periodic variation in the volume or amplitude of your guitar's signal. At its most dramatic, it creates a choppy stutter, but more subtle flavours give your sound a retro cool.

Vibrato is a periodic variation in pitch. You can get it by waggling your whammy bar or moving your fingertip as you fret a note. Vibrato stompboxes operate with a rate control setting the speed that your volume/pitch throbs at, and depth adjusting how much of your signal is being affected.

GET THE SOUND

FAST LESLIE

SLOW — FAST

A fast Leslie effect is exactly what you need for Soundgarden's Black Hole Sun intro

SLOW LESLIE

SLOW — FAST

Slowing things down can give guitar parts a huge sense of space in a stereo field

SLOW/FAST LESLIE

SLOW — FAST

Organists love the transition of switching between a Leslie's slow and fast settings

TRY THESE LESLIE STYLE FX

STRYMON
Lex Rotary

ELECTRO-HARMONIX
Lester G

BOSS
RT-20
Rotary
Ensemble

GET THE SOUND

SURF TWANG

RATE — DEPTH — MIX

Set the rate and depth/intensity controls to a medium level, add reverb and twang away!

TREMOLO BOULEVARD

RATE — DEPTH — MIX

Turn depth high and speed to a 16th-note pattern for Green Day's Boulevard... sound

GATED TREMOLO

RATE — DEPTH — MIX

Place your trem after a wah, tap single notes and add delay for a synthy sound

TRY THESE TREMOLO VIBRATO

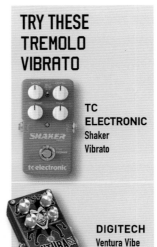

TC ELECTRONIC
Shaker
Vibrato

DIGITECH
Ventura Vibe

BOSS
TR-2

VOLUME-BASED EFFECTS

These swells and great levellers are key to certain guitar styles

Spare a thought for the unsung heroes of the pedalboard. If a Whammy pedal is a brash show off then volume, EQ and compression are the three dependable dullards – they keep themselves busy and quietly get the job done.

GET THE SOUND

PRINCE-STYLE FUNK RHYTHM

COMPRESSION   ATTACK   SUSTAIN

Compress single coils and play 16th-note grooves for good clean Prince-style funk

ANDY SUMMERS COMPRESSION

COMPRESSION   ATTACK   SUSTAIN

The Police man used modulation with compression to make single-note riffs ring

GILMOUR-STYLE LEAD

COMPRESSION   ATTACK   SUSTAIN

Turn up the sustain, add some reverb and practise those mighty Gilmour-ish bends

TRY THESE COMPRESSORS

BOSS CS-3 Compressor Sustainer

MXR Custom Comp

TC ELECTRONIC Hyper Gravity

COMPRESSION

Compression is used on almost every piece of recorded music we listen to. The idea of compression in recorded music is to level out the dynamic range of a sound by removing loud jumps in level. For guitar players, it can be used to boost your signal, increase sustain for soloing, create the snappy attack that you hear on country and funk guitar parts, or even bring out a fingerpicked part.

Imagine someone manually controlling your volume for you, so every time you hit a note above a set volume level (threshold), they turn it back down by a percentage.

That's essentially how a compressor works. Studio compressors usually feature more controls than their stompbox counterparts, which often only have a few knobs. Attack usually governs how quickly the signal is attenuated (the reduction of amplitude) after the volume reaches the threshold level, and sustain controls how much the signal is turned down by.

Once you've compressed your signal, you'll need to turn the whole lot back up again, and that's what your level/output control is for. The result is a much smoother, less variable signal with noticeably less dynamic range and a greater consistency in volume.

EQ PEDALS

A graphic equaliser or EQ pedal is a simple effect. Just like the bass, middle and treble controls on your amp, it offers control over the shape of your sound. Rather than giving you one control for each frequency range of your tone, though, a graphic EQ splits your sound into finer 'bands' for more specific fine tuning. Six or 10-band EQs are common in guitar pedals.

It may look daunting, but a graphic EQ works exactly the same as the one on your hi-fi. The bands to the left cover bass/low mid, and the bands to the right cover the treble frequencies. Each of the sliders either boosts or cuts its respective frequency, and in most cases the middle of each slider's range is 'flat' or unaffected.

A solid EQ pedal can be used for a number of tricks: you can scoop your mids for a thrash sound; create a 'telephone' effect by cutting the bass and treble and boosting the midrange, or even use it as a flat volume boost by pushing all of the frequency bands equally. It's also handy for either killing or introducing feedback onstage or levelling out any unwanted tonal variations when you're switching guitars.

GET THE SOUND

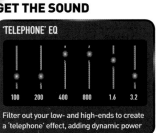

'TELEPHONE' EQ

100   200   400   800   1.6   3.2

Filter out your low- and high-ends to create a 'telephone' effect, adding dynamic power

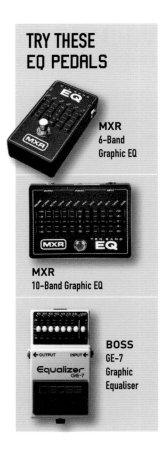

TRY THESE EQ PEDALS

MXR
6-Band Graphic EQ

MXR
10-Band Graphic EQ

BOSS
GE-7 Graphic Equaliser

VOLUME

You've already got one volume control on your guitar and one on your amp, so why do you want another pedal to turn your guitar up and down?

Well, firstly your hands should be busy playing the guitar. This leaves your feet to control impromptu volume boosts/cuts. You can also use your volume pedal to 'swell' your notes, for manual tremolo, or gradually fade in the effects in your effects loop. Granted, it's not essential, nor is it for everyone, but try it on your 'board and you'll be surprised at how creative a tool a volume control can be.

GET THE SOUND

AMBIENT VOLUME SWELLS

Set the pedal to silence your sound. Fade up volume and add delay and reverb. Cosmic

TRY THESE VOLUME PEDALS

ERNIE BALL
VP JR

MORLEY
MMV Mini Volume

BOSS
FV-500l

DELAY

You already know what delay sounds like, but probably refer to it as echo. Defined as the distinct repetition of sound, dedicated delay effects were first seen in recording studios in the 1950s in the shape of cumbersome tape-echo units that used actual reels of magnetic tape to record and play back sound. Solid-state technology brought delay to a more practical stompbox format in the 1970s. Although the most common delays these days are digital, many replicate the natural warmth and grain of much-loved early tape echoes and analogue delay pedals.

Common delay sounds in rock and pop music range from short 'slapback' echo effects to multiple repeats with a long decay. Slapback sounds are synonymous with 1950s rock 'n' roll, while examples of delay with multiple repeats range from the signature chime of The Edge's dotted eighth-notes in U2 to the epic widescreen guitars of post-rock bands such as Sigur Rós, Mogwai and Explosions In The Sky.

REVERB

Unlike delay, reverb is a blend of the reflections that occur when sound bounces off the surfaces around you, decaying gradually as soundwaves are absorbed by your surroundings. We only notice reverberation when it's at its most dramatic – in a cathedral or a tunnel, for example – but everywhere has its own unique reverb sound.

The first reverb effects used in recording studios were the result of microphone placement in a space with chamber reverb, plate reverb (a large 'plate' of sheet metal with a pickup attached to it to capture vibrations), and spring reverb (similar to plate reverb but cheaper and more compact because of the coiled nature of the spring).

Most of the reverb you hear in recorded music today is digital in origin, the arresting splash of the spring reverb tanks in 1960s Fender 'blackface' amps is still the most desirable reverb sound as far as most guitarists are concerned.

GET THE SOUND

ROCKABILLY SLAPBACK

FEEDBACK — TIME — MIX

Set time to 60ms, feedback at two-three repeats and blend at 50 per cent, daddio

EDGY EIGHTH-NOTE DELAYS

FEEDBACK — TIME — MIX

Set dotted eighth-notes with three-four repeats. Play straight eighth-notes over it

CASCADING DELAYS

FEEDBACK — TIME — MIX

Set your pedal to repeat in crotchets, with three or four repeats. Play straight 16ths

TRY THESE DELAYS

TC ELECTRONIC
Flashback Delay

LINE 6
DL4 Delay Modeller

ELECTRO-HARMONIX
Memory Boy

GET THE SOUND

REVERB SWELLS (SEE VOLUME P62)

LEVEL — TIME — TONE

Try using reverb, delay and a volume pedal (or your guitar's volume control) for swells

SOUL/BLUES SPRING REVERB

LEVEL — TIME — TONE

A generous lashing of amp (or pedal) spring reverb will give you a great Black Keys tone

DOUBLE REVERB

TIME: 0.3 SECS — TIME: 3 SECS — LEVEL

Use two reverbs – one short, one long – to create a thickened lead sound

TRY THESE REVERBS

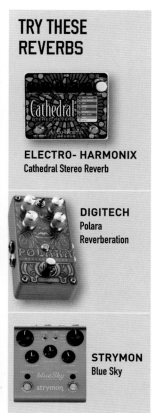

ELECTRO- HARMONIX
Cathedral Stereo Reverb

DIGITECH
Polara Reverberation

STRYMON
Blue Sky

Marshall
HIWATT 100
Marshall
Marshall
Marshall
Marshall
1960

Words: Amit Sharma Photography: George Fairbairn

J MASCIS

Legendary Dinosaur Jr fuzz king J Mascis invites us for a walk through his guitars, amps and *that* pedalboard...

How many fuzz pedals is enough? For a guitarist such as J Mascis, there will never be enough free space on the 'board. Each of his stompboxes brings its own chemistry and colour, unlocking new worlds of tone. And then, of course, there are the ones that didn't fit but simply had to come along for the ride anyway. TG tracked down one of the original pioneers of alt-rock and true legends of fuzz to look at the equipment responsible for his unfathomably overdriven wall of sound...

GUITARS

FENDER JAZZMASTER

1 "I once had all my guitars stolen on tour and needed to buy new ones. This happened to be at the local guitar shop, which I'd never really been interested in going inside before. It came from a local guy who bought it new in 1963 or whatever. I spotted it, tried it and thought it worked out pretty good. I like playing Jazzmasters, my whole style is almost built around it. Originally I wanted a Strat but didn't have enough to get one, so had to settle for the Jazzmaster. The neck felt right and it's what I learned to play on... so I've just stuck with them ever since."

FENDER JAZZMASTER

2 "This is my main backup. I don't use it much... it does sound different to my main guitar. The pickups are from 1964 or '65, so they sound a little stronger than the other '63s I use... A friend of mine worked at a guitar shop quite close to where I live and told me it was going pretty cheap. I bought it without even seeing it and was happy with what I got."

RICKENBACKER 620-12 12-STRING

3 "I got this guitar very recently because there's some 12-string guitar parts on the new album. The one I had at home didn't seem to work, I tried a Vox Phantom but it wouldn't stay in tune. Then I tried a Rickenbacker hollow body but the pickups were just too loud and it fed back a lot. So a friend lent me one of his guitars, and it just seemed to work really well. I found the exact same model online and bought it right there and then. It worked out."

DANELECTRO ELECTRIC SITAR

4 "I first used an original one in the studio and really liked the sound of it. Then a few years later Jerry Jones started making copies of them, so I started using those. We use it on the first song on the new album, Goin Down, and it's also played on The Wagon. This one is really cheap, I bought in the States specifically to tour with."

FENDER THINLINE TELECASTER

5 "I got this from Fender... it was a Squier thinline but they had some pre-made necks with jumbo frets, because I didn't like the original neck. Then I put some Custom Shop Seymour Duncans in there and somehow it all came together. They're somewhere in between a P-90 and a Filter'Tron. I use this guitar on Goin Down, Start Choppin and I Walk For Miles. It definitely sounds heavier than the Jazzmaster because of the pickups. It does feedback but I can control it. To be honest, everything is going to feedback once that Big Muff is on! It's like it sounds different night after night. Sometimes I can't sustain any notes over all the feedback."

EFFECTS

ZVEX LO-FI LOOP JUNKY

6 "I got this before an acoustic show in New York. I thought it would be good to get a loop to jam with myself a little bit. I thought this was cool because it was all-analogue and very easy to use. It seems to cut off a lot of the high frequencies; it just can't reproduce them because of the chip in there. They make you sound a lot darker, so it's like having two separate tones. You can even make your guitar warble as it plays back. Then I started using it for the electric shows for those noisy jamming parts or even in between songs so no one has to hear silence!"

MOOG MF DELAY & IBANEZ ANALOG

DELAY MINI

7 "I started using the Moog for recording, I just liked the sound of it. They brought out the smaller version that fits on my pedalboard. It has an expression pedal which I've been using to turn the speed up and down to get the wacky sounds I like. I use it on Gargoyle – which we usually play last – Watch The Corners, sometimes on Get Me... whenever I feel inspired to switch it on. I really like the short echo on the Ibanez. I've been using it for the solo on Heaven, it's a bit of a different sound to the Moog, but they're both analogue. Plus it's pink..."

BOSS RV-5 REVERB

8 "I've had this for a while. I always try to check out different reverb pedals, but this is the one I keep coming back to. Usually, I prefer not to use a Boss pedal if I can, but this one works better than anything else I've tried."

CUSTOM AUDIO JAPAN TWIN TREMOLO

9 "I really like the square wave sound of this pedal... you can get it going really choppy and super fast. I used to have the rack-mounted version, but Custom Audio told me about this Japanese pedal version and I had to get one!"

TUBE WORKS REAL TUBE OVERDRIVE

10 "This is responsible for my main clean sound... it only has a little bit of drive dialled into it. I can turn down the volume and it still sounds really good. I like doing that so when I turn on the Big Muff it gets louder... though with four amps, it's always loud!"

KR MUSICAL MEGA VIBE

11 "At first I used to use a Roger Mayer Supervibe, which was a rack-mounted vibe unit. The Mega Vibe is closest I've heard to that thing in a pedal version. I'll use it on Knocked Around, Gargoyle, Freak Scene with the flanger added for colour and volume."

ELECTRO-HARMONIX ELECTRIC MISTRESS FLANGER/BOSS TU3-S

12 "This was the first flanger I ever bought and I guess I love it because it sounds more extreme than most of the others I've heard. We use it on Freak Scene, Forget The Swan, Does It Float... There was no room for the tuner so we put it on the Electric Mistress. The tuner is a new smaller version that I saw in

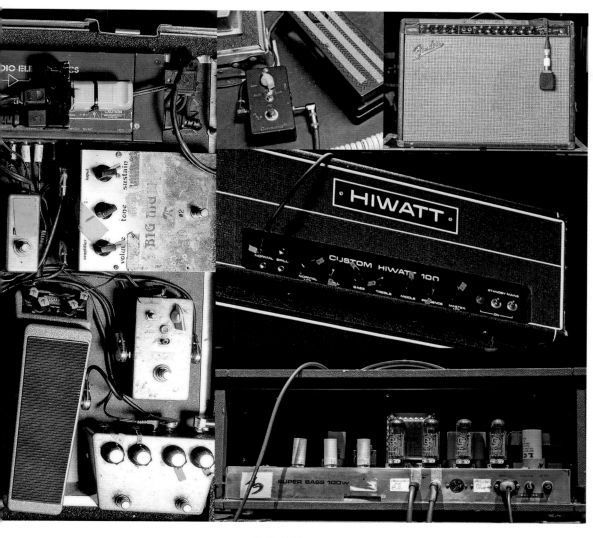

AMPS

FENDER TWIN REVERB REISSUE

18 "At home I use a 1966 Twin Reverb, I wish I had one over in England. But for this tour I'm using the reissue... it gives a little more top-end to my sound, so I'll try to use more of it for my solos. It's another ingredient in the soup. A pinch of Fender, some Marshall, a bit of Hiwatt..."

HIWATT DR-103 CUSTOM 100-WATT HEAD

19 "I think I got this about six years ago or something like that. I'd never used Hiwatts before that, but I found the combination with Marshall made for a cleaner, more treble-y sound. It's equally as loud, probably louder actually. It's always on, all my amps are always on and dialled in fairly clean. They sound pretty lame without any pedals, they're just super clean."

MARSHALL 1968 SUPER BASS & MARSHALL PLEXI REISSUE

20 "The purple Superbass Plexi came from a friend of mine, who bought me it when I was last over in England and it's from the early 90s. I'm a big fan of purple! It has that classic heavy Marshall sound. The black one I've borrowed from Marshall, it's a new Plexi reissue. It sounds good to me. At home I have a Plexi Super PA from 1968, but I can't bring everything with me when I come over and Marshall are kind enough to lend me what I need. The cabs are borrowed, too, new ones that they're just bringing out. At home I use older cabs, I figure if it worked well back then, why shouldn't it work well right now? Believe it or not, I actually use full stacks at home, too."

a shop and thought it was perfect for my needs. You don't have to turn it on and off, it's just always on and I like that."

ELECTRO-HARMONIX BIG MUFF

13 "This one was made in 1976. I don't know how much it's worth, they've probably come down since the internet... maybe up to $1,000. It's probably the most important pedal on my board because it's where my distorted sound starts. I might add stuff on top of it but the Big Muff is always in there. I got this on our first American tour in 1987, from a pawn shop in Arizona. Before that, I was using a Deluxe Big Muff, and for a while I used both – but as it turns out I liked this one better so stuck with it alone. I've had it fixed a few times but it's still going..."

MC-FX SUPER-FUZZ COPY

14 "These were made in Australia, I'm not sure if they're in production anymore. I have original Super-Fuzzes, but I love the sound of this one and, again, it fits on my 'board. I kick it in for solos and extra fuzz when things get super crazy."

RANGEMASTER/TONE BENDER MK1 COPY

15 "One side is a Rangemaster copy and the other is a Tone Bender Mk1 copy. This was made by Jim Roth from [American indie-rockers] Built To Spill, he gave me a Tone Bender copy a while ago. I really liked it but had it remade with a Rangemaster to save space."

ZVEX DOUBLE ROCK

16 "I actually asked them to build two overdrives into one pedal. They made it for me and now they've started producing them commercially. I'm usually pretty set on which distortion I'll use from song to song, but sometimes during solos I'll switch on different ones when I feel like it."

HOMEBREW ELECTRONICS GERMANIA 44 TREBLE BOOSTER

17 "...I found this one on tour somewhere in Belgium and I didn't miss a show without that Rangemaster sound I use for a lot of my solos. I'll use this for I Want You To Know to give my sound a bit of a treble boost and an extra kick. It's probably the one I use most randomly, whenever I feel like it."

MAKING MUSIC

Collaborating with other musicians, playing live and recording your own music is one of the primary reasons that most guitarists pick up their instrument in the first instance. It may sound like a huge undertaking, but by breaking it down into manageable goals and working with others, forming a band and capturing your tracks – either for fun or with big ambitions – can be hugely rewarding. Here, we show you how to do it, with plenty of advice on how to make it easy and sound great fast.

COLLABORATING

Thanks to the constant advances in technology that connects there are no longer any boundaries to making music with other people – try it!

Writing and recording music alone is immensely satisfying, but bringing other people's creative ideas into the mix can often enhance both the experience and the end results. But sometimes, life gets in the way of intentions; our day jobs, the distances between us and the challenge of finding the right environment to write with others can all be obstacles in our way.

But they can be overcome with our good old friend – technology. Things have moved a long, long way since John and Paul first sat down together with their acoustics. With ever-faster internet speeds available to more of us and new apps and great software being released every day, it's now not a case of if you collaborate, but how. And even if you're not into the idea of collaborative songwriting, working with other players is a great way to exchange ideas and get tuition advice.

THINGS HAVE MOVED ALONG SINCE JOHN AND PAUL FIRST SAT DOWN TOGETHER

FIND A FRIEND

Before you go online with your intentions to collaborate with other musicians, think about what you're looking for and what you're offering. Have a look at websites such as Join My Band, Musolist, MusoFinder, BandMix, Gumtree and Forming Bands, where musicians will often be located by the closest city to where they're based. Search or consider posting your own profile or advert to get started.

THE FIVE RS OF CO WRITING

1 REFLECT Give the other musician or musicians a recording of your song idea, and let them go away with it to reflect and try out different ideas; the time will pay dividends.

2 RELAX Have you hit a wall at a writing session? Sometimes it really helps to just play something you know together, have fun performing, and then go back to the writing again with a fresh creative attack.

3 RECORD Never, ever presume the other person you're writing with will remember what you were working on last time. Record everything you do that is worth further development.

4 RIDE Your car is also your vocal booth. Are you a vocalist struggling to find the time to sing over instrumental ideas you've recorded or have been given? Play it in the car on a loop, and try singing ideas over it.

5 RATION Throwing loads of different song ideas at someone to work on can allow them to pick, but it can also be overwhelming and defocusing for some people.

The greatest musical resource available in the digital age is still other musicians

There are plenty of online directories packed with musos

TRY THESE

MEET & JAM

Looking for other musicians to play with in your area can be a daunting task. But this website allows you to sign up and not just find other musicians nearby who are looking for collaborators but also to book rehearsal studios to play in, and keep a profile page to organise your plans once you do have a musical partnership or band.

EVERNOTE

A great app for iOS and Android that allows you to store song ideas and share them with others. Record audio ideas on your phone, tablet or desktop with the app; write lyrics and share notes on the song with collaborators. Simply hitting the share button will email your idea, or you can also share notes via Twitter and Facebook.

WHOLEWORLDBAND

This iOS app is all about getting musicians to create together in 'a global recording studio'. Upload your music idea (eg, a chord progression) as video with a note requesting what you need, then other musicians contribute and you can combine the results. There's even a system in place for potential earnings from your creations.

You can record sessions with a remote producer

Remote collaboration

WRITING

It might initially seem awkward using the likes of FaceTime, Google Hangouts and Skype for real-time voice and video communication, but for musicians, they're the next best thing to jamming in the room when songwriting. Alter Bridge's Mark Tremonti and Myles Kennedy have used Skype to continue working on songs for a new album while in different parts of the country. A decent webcam and high bandwidth are essential to prevent muffled and stuttery sessions while you try to pen your first hit.

RECORDING IN REAL-TIME

It's possible (and relatively simple) to track remotely in real-time using a plugin such as Steinberg VST Connect Pro software that works with Cubase 7 and Nuendo 6 DAWs (Digital Audio Workstation software) on PC or Mac.

Everyone involved in the sessions will need Connect Pro. Then, via an access key, you'll be able to work with a remote artist who you can see tracking their instrument via a video connection. Cubase also offers monitoring for the performer, and you can send and receive MIDI. You'll need a minimum 256kbps upload speed on your connection.

Alternatively, Source-Connect Source Elements is a high-quality audio streaming solution that isn't so limited by the DAW you use. It enables real-time, broadcast-quality connections between audio systems anywhere in the world. The downside is the price starts at US$650 for the Standard version. Still, there's a free 15-day trial...

Gobbler integrates with certain DAWs to transfer files

WEB-BASED COLLABORATION

How about everyone involved in a project uploading their parts, ideas and comments to a central 'hub' for demos in their own time? AudioCommon is an ambitious venture founded by musicians Philip Cohen and Chris Dorsey. Users of the site create a project, then build teams and upload audio content they've recorded to cloud storage. They're even offering real-time collaboration, too, but if you have a situation where musicians are in different time zones, the ability to work on projects whenever you want to and add notes for others is a great benefit.

FILE-SHARING

If you want to take charge and get your collaborators to send you their recordings, the quickest way is via cloud-based services such as Dropbox, Google Drive and Gobbler. The latter is aimed at musicians and you can integrate Gobbler into Pro Tools, Logic and Sonar, and it will also scan your hard drive to back up chosen projects to the cloud storage.

Japandroids have had huge success as a two-piece

PLAYING IN A TWO-PIECE BAND

A duo isn't a disadvantage: find out how to harness the power of two to your musical advantage

Duos are taking over the guitar world: just look at the phenomenal success of The White Stripes, not to mention rising acts such as Japandroids, Blood Red Shoes and DZ Deathrays. What these bands have in common is their refusal to compromise – they don't treat their line-up as some kind of hindrance.

Instead, they use their setup to their advantage, stripping songs back to their core elements and rocking the hell out. Don't get us wrong, there are downsides to only sharing the stage with a drummer – for one, the banter will be less sophisticated – but

BEFORE YOU PLUG IN, DECIDE WHAT YOU WANT FROM YOUR BAND

there's no reason your sound should suffer. Through creative use of gear, playing style and songwriting, your duo could be as big as any four-piece rock band, and without adding two members along the way. Read on as we explain how to grab a two-piece of the action...

THINK ABOUT YOUR SOUND

Before you plug in, decide what you want from your band. Are you into trashy bass-less garage-rock like The White Stripes or early Black Keys, or do you crave something heavier and more layered? Your overall vibe plays an important role in shaping your gear choices; if you want to sound like a three-piece, you need enough pedals and amps to trick the audience's ears into thinking you are. Either way, prepare yourself for some serious work: as the only melodic instrument in the band, it's going to be up to you to provide both rhythm and lead – no pressure!

FOUR THINGS TO THINK ABOUT

1 STAGE PRESENCE With only two of you on stage, it could look a little lonely up there, so plan how you're going to perform: try spreading out à la early Black Keys gigs, or feed off each other's energy and rock out.

2 LOOPING Can't replicate the overdubs from your recordings? It might be time for a looper. Whatever model you choose, make sure your drummer can hear your loops – go out of time, and the whole song could fall apart.

3 BACKING TRACKS Don't be afraid to use recorded tracks for bass and extra instruments. Your drummer will need to work to a click track, which could limit your ability to improvise, but you're guaranteed a full sound.

4 DIRT Fuzz is the natural ally of the two-piece, thanks to its suitability for both guitar and bass. Use it wisely, though: a relentless onslaught of full-on dirt can be fatiguing, so experiment with different drives for your guitar and 'bass' sounds.

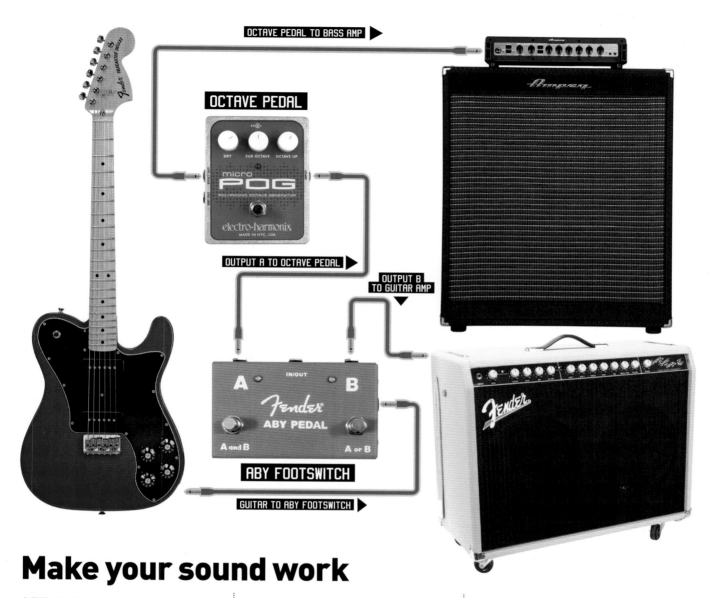

OCTAVE PEDAL TO BASS AMP ▶

OCTAVE PEDAL

micro POG
POLYPHONIC OCTAVE GENERATOR
electro-harmonix
MADE IN NYC, USA

DRY · SUB OCTAVE · OCTAVE UP

OUTPUT A TO OCTAVE PEDAL ▶

OUTPUT B TO GUITAR AMP ▼

A · IN/OUT · B
Fender
ABY PEDAL
A and B · A or B

ABY FOOTSWITCH

GUITAR TO ABY FOOTSWITCH ▶

Make your sound work

GET AMP'D
Fewer band members can mean only one thing: more amps. Dan Auerbach forces his roadie to cart three huge rigs around, while Japandroids frontman Brian King employs no fewer than five on stage. Careful setting of each amp's EQ enables it to fill out the frequencies you lose from an absent bass player, but you'll need a serious signal splitter to run more than two at once. Don't ignore bass amps, either; employing even a small bass combo can help you to round out your low-end, especially if you're running a parallel effects rig – let us explain...

FAKE THE BASS
A few choice stompboxes replace a bassist: first split your signal using an ABY footswitch, or any stompbox with a stereo output. Next, grab an octave pedal or pitch-shifter – ideally one with polyphonic tracking – and crank up the one-octave-down mix, then run one output of the ABY switcher into the octave pedal. Now, send the other ABY output to a guitar amp and hook the pitch-shifter up to a bass amp (or bass DI to the PA), and there you have it: instant bass. Everything you play will be tracked down an octave and outputted through your bass rig, while your guitar playing will remain unaffected through your guitar rig – look at the diagram above to learn more.

PLAY TO YOUR STRENGTHS
The danger with playing guitar and bass at once is that octave-down chords can sound a little... strange. Fortunately, with so much power behind you, single-note riffs take on a new lease of life, and are likely to form the bulk of your playing. Meaty powerchords also work a treat, and don't be afraid to venture above the 12th fret, either: the lower-octave output will fill out anything you play at the dusty end, and makes it easy to weave melodies around riffs.

BE DYNAMIC
With only one other member in your band, it's crucial to work with your drummer. Respond to each other's playing dynamics and be sure to switch it up: take the 'bass' in and out, add or remove distortion, and play riffs in different octaves. If you're struggling to fill out your sound or replicate overdubs in recordings, it could also be worth investing in a looper for further layers.

GIGGING

Preparation prevents poor performance, but if things go wrong these key items will save the day!

YOUR GUITAR
Make sure your guitar is set up how you like, in tune and well protected for the journey to the gig

GUITAR TOOLS
Pack string cutters, pliers for tightening, and Allen keys to tweak your action and vibrato system

GAFFER TAPE
Fix your mic stand, setlist, cable, van exhaust, leaky shoes.

SPARE STRINGS
Strings aren't immune to breaking in soundcheck – spares are essential

SPARE GUITAR AND STRAP
Tune it up before you go on. Your fans will escape to the bar if you hold things up changing a broken string mid-song

TORCH
It gets dark onstage: get an app for your smartphone and you won't have to worry about forgetting your torch

ESSENTIALS

PEN AND PAPER
You need to have these on hand to jot down your setlist

TUNER PEDAL
Never forget this. Get the best you can afford: there is no excuse for starting out of tune

AMP BACKUP
If you can't take a spare amp, try a modeller with cab simulator that can be DI'd straight into the PA. It's not ideal but it's an option if another band on the bill can't help you out

BLU-TACK
If your pick tends to fly out of your hand mid-song, stick spares to your mic stand or guitar so replacements are always at hand

BATTERIES
You'll need some spares if your power supply goes down

FIRST AID
You don't want to bleed on your fans or let a headache ruin your big night – pack some plasters and painkillers. And the singer's secret weapon: throat pastilles

SPARE PEDAL
Get a budget spare for your essential pedal. For the super-prepared, a multi-effects unit could save you from serious pedalboard problems

EARPLUGS
It might get loud so earplugs can increase the clarity of onstage levels

ELECTRONIC CLEANING SPRAY
A quick fix for crackling connections. Make sure it's in your gigbag

CABLES
Pack instrument, patch, speaker, XLR and daisy chain cables. Don't buy the cheapest: quality lasts and you always need more cables than you think

PICKS
Minimise the chances of losing one from sweaty mitts by packing picks with grippy surfaces

MAINS ADAPTOR
Never assume that the venue has enough power points or extensions. It's well worth investing in your own multi-socket extension adaptor that's RCD-equipped, with surge and overload protection

THE SOUNDCHECK

Take the time to get your band's sound right and then you can focus on the fun part

Don't be this guy! Get your party pants on after the show

DO...

- Learn the names of the sound engineers: treat them with respect and thank them at the end of the night.

- Set your amplifiers to sensible volume levels onstage. Moderate levels allow the engineer to have more control over the overall front-of-house balance meaning that monitors don't need to be pushed to levels where they begin to feedback in order for singers to hear themselves.

- Turn your amp on at least a few minutes before you start – it lets your valve amp warm up a bit.

- Tune all your guitars again as close to the start of your set as possible and make sure they're on hand and on stands. Things have a tendency to get knocked over in the heat of the moment.

- Choose a song for soundcheck that will test the sound mix in the best way for all the instruments in your band.

- Listen carefully to the mix of instruments coming through the monitor speaker wedge – can you hear yourself and the rhythm section clearly to keep time?

- Check as many of your sounds as you can: clean/crunch/distortion channels all need to be checked so they're at the right level. Ditto effects.

- Talk to the other bands you're playing with and find out what backline will be shared. While it's common for a headline band to let support acts share drum shells and stands, it's not for breakables like amps.

DON'T...

- Drink alcohol excessively before. It won't make you play any better!

- Assume you'll be able to share gear and turn up with minimal kit. It's common courtesy to ask first.

- Crank your volume if your amp is being mic'd through the PA – you don't need a very loud onstage volume. Let the sound engineer get the levels. And you may not need your cab or combo front-on to the audience if it's being mic'd – angle it in a position best for you.

- See soundcheck as a rehearsal or jam. One or two short songs should provide more than enough opportunity for the sound engineer to set up a decent mix. Taking liberties won't do you any favours with the other bands on the bill.

- Leave your pedals running with the input plugged in for long periods of time, if you're using nine-volt batteries with your effects pedals – it drains the power.

- Get bogged down with your onstage sound if you're playing outside. Put trust in the sound engineer's front of house mix – the nature of the external environment means your concern is playing in time, and the sound engineer's is making sure the audience get a good mix.

- Play blazing lead lines when the sound engineer is tweaking the bass drum sound – they won't appreciate it.

- Lose sight of the bigger picture – it's about attitude as well as the rig you're setting up. And remember that you get back what you put out. If you're professional and polite, that's what you'll get from the engineer and the other bands.

DON'T PLAY BLISTERING SOLOS WHILE THE ENGINEER IS TWEAKING THE BASS DRUM...

Keep that smile on the sound guy's face and you're in for a good show

Broken a string? Let your singer pick up the flak with some crowd-friendly banter

THE GIG

There's more to impressing the crowd than your blazing chops

Get your gig prep right and all that's left is to show the crowd what you're made of!

DO...

- Write a setlist for the show. Unless you're playing a wild free jazz set, you'll need a list of the songs you're playing and the order in which you're playing them.

- Demand the audience's attention. Open up with a song that will make an impact.

- Take a drink onstage with you – especially if you're a singer. You may be surprised to find your throat can get as dry as the Mojave desert onstage.

- Realise that things can go wrong – it's just part of gigging. Have contingency plans in your head in case the worst happens, including an instrumental piece the rest of you can play to fill time if one of the musicians has a problem.

- Look people in the eye while you're performing – engaging with your audience is more than just about sound.

- Signal to the engineer if you need to communicate with the desk mid-gig: for example, if you can't hear your guitar through the monitors or you're too loud.

- Relax, listen to the sound engineer and remember that, ultimately, it's about the audience, not the band. Nobody cares that much about your tone except you, so stop stressing about it.

DON'T...

- Amplify your guitar when you're tuning up. You should tune quickly and silently between songs. Buy an electronic tuner with an easily visible display.

- Forget to say the name of your band between songs. If you're a support act and don't have a banner, you can't assume anyone knows who the hell you are.

- Allow long silences between songs. While the guitarist or bassist tunes up, it gives the singer an ideal opportunity to crack a joke or fill the silence by plugging the band's website or merchandise.

- Mess with your amp settings during the gig based on the monitor speaker mix – it isn't a reflection of what the audience and engineer can hear out front.

- Take forever to pack up your gear. Unless you're the headline act, the next band want to get onstage before the audience drifts away and loses interest. There will be plenty of time for excessive alcohol consumption and chatting up groupies once your equipment is off stage.

- Be sheepish with the audience. Forget apologetic amateurism and smack them right between the eyes with your set!

Hydrate: keep a bottle of water onstage to lubricate those vocal cords

STONEHENGE
STAIRWAY
[DRUM SOLO]
FREE BIRD
JAZZ ODYSSEY

Kicking into Free Bird during your drummer's solo is just embarrassing... sort a setlist!

Don't assume you can use the headliner's sweet selection of gear. Always check first!

RECORD YOUR BAND

Essentials for tracking a band playing live together

There are many ways to record your music, and you don't have to be in a traditional studio environment to get good results. Capturing musicians playing together can reap rewards in terms of dynamics and practicality, and showcase your band's chemistry together. Here's out 10-step guide to getting started with it...

1 GET THE RIGHT GEAR FIRST

As well as your instruments and amps, you'll need a laptop capable of running DAW software such as Cubase and Logic, or if you're old-school, a multi-track portastudio. You'll also need an interface that can take multiple XLR inputs; eight would be ideal to cover amps, drums and room mics, too. With that in mind, you'll also need plenty of XLR cables, and it's worth labelling them with each source (eg Guitar Amp 1) so the signal paths don't get confusing. Dynamic mics for amps are a must, as is a set of condenser and dynamic mics for the drums. If possible, an extra condenser or two to use as ambient mics are useful for capturing more of the overall sound of the band in the room. You might decide to DI some sources too; bass and acoustic amps are prime candidates as they often feature XLR outputs.

2 PREPARE

Before setting up to track your band, make sure you choose a song, or songs, to record that you can play consistently well live. You're going to be capturing the instruments live and while you may leave solos and vocals (see point 8, Overdub Session) for a separate session, you need to nail your live parts and make sure the band dynamic and tone is as good as can be. Having a friend who can engineer is so useful, as it allows you to focus on your performance and speeds up the process of checking levels, and starting/stopping recording. Next, you need to choose your location. It could be your usual practice room or even a village hall, but you'll need enough space to position your band and not have excessive unwanted reverb...

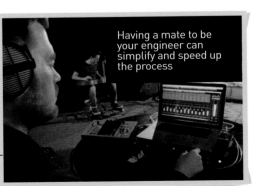

Having a mate to be your engineer can simplify and speed up the process

3 POSITIONING THE BAND

During recording 'spill' or 'bleed' is inevitable between them. This is when the instrument on one mic is picking up the sound of another. It tends to happen less with the close mics you'll have on amps, but the drums are a loud instrument so spill from them is highly likely. Because of this, it's advisable to record your vocals in a separate session rather than have a sensitive condenser mic picking up the other instruments as well. You can minimise bleed between the other instruments by positioning the musicians in a semi-circle or horseshoe shape so they're spaced out from each other but still close enough to communicate but amps aren't facing each other where they could cause feedback.

4 DRUM MIC'ING BASICS

Using a four-mic setup for the drums to capture clean sound, start with the overhead mics first. These capture the sound of the kit being played in the room and help produce a clearer cymbal sound. Start by positioning them six feet above ground level and aimed down at the kit. It's vital that they are equal distances from the kit to avoid mic phasing (which happens when the sound is hitting each mic at different times). For the kick drum, the closer you position the mic to the batter head (the side that is hit) the more attack you'll get from the sound. You may also choose to place a pillow inside the kick drum as a muffler to reduce unwanted overtones and help give a punchier, less boomy sound. For the snare, position the dynamic mic a couple of inches above and an inch from the edge of it. The further you move it away, the more room ambience you'll get. And to reduce the amount of hi-hat cymbal sound hitting the snare mic, make sure it's facing directly away from the hi-hat.

5 RECORDING GUITARS

Dynamic mics are rugged enough to cope with the high-frequency sound pressure levels coming from amplifier speakers. A single-mic setup with the mic directed at the speaker cone and almost touching the grille cloth can get you a good sound, especially if you tweak the positioning and it's important to monitor the effects on tone when you change the positioning; dead centre will be punchier, positioning to the edge adds a darker tonality. When you've found your sweet spot, mark it with a cross of tape on your grille. If you have enough XLR inputs on your interface, you may want to add a condenser several inches away for more of an ambient element but make sure

you engage the -10-decibel pad setting (if it has one) to help you prevent clipping.

6 RECORDING ACOUSTICS

If you're an acoustic player you can track live with the band by mic'ing an acoustic combo amp or using its DI. Your choice of pickup and preamp comes into play here. If you want to give magnetic soundhole or piezo pickups more of the 'acoustic' sound of a mic'd guitar, carefully dialling in your tone with an onboard EQ or preamp pedal can reap rewards. An acoustic in the mix with a band needs mids to stand out though, and less of the bass you might dial in when playing solo. Inevitably, there's compromise involved.

7 TROUBLESHOOTING

When the live session is underway make sure all guitarists and bassist have a tuner pedal and constantly re-tune between takes. Why risk sabotaging your song before you've even played a note? And once you start, if someone makes a significant mistake, be prepared to stop. You've got to give your best chance at a performance you can live with. This is where the extra pair of ears of the laptop engineer are especially useful; particularly via headphones, they might hear a problem with the performance or signals that you don't.

8 OVERDUB SESSION

You'll get the instrumental core of your song tracked in the live stage but you may want to save solos for an overdub stage, using amp and effects modelling plugins to nail a take and tone that you're comfortable with. You may also choose to overdub parts to really add impact to your song's parts, such as adding ringing overdriven chords in the chorus. Think about how you can enhance it without losing that live energy you've captured.

Remember to re-tune between takes – even being a little out can ruin a take

Make sure your overhead drum mics are equidistant to avoid mic phasing

9 VOCALS

When recording the live instrumental, remember to keep vocals in mind with your playing dynamics so when you add them, the musicians are already reacting to the parts where vocals will be, such as taking things down a notch with their playing when the first verse comes in. For the singer, it's important that they try to keep that live dynamic in mind for their own recording takes, again using the interface and laptop setup. Get comfortable with the band recording and try some run-throughs before even touching that record button; this will serve as a warm up for vocal chords that should make tracking easier in the long run. It's important that the vocalist is comfortable in the recording space so make sure they're singing up to the condenser mic to open their vocal chords and ensure they have a monitor mix of both their vocal level and the song that they're happy to sing with. Add the kind of effects that you would use post-recording for this monitor headphone mix; reverb can really help a singer's performance as opposed to a dry uninspiring signal, in the same way as it does for a guitarist.

10 GOOD FOUNDATIONS

Listen back and evaluate all the takes you have as a band before moving forward to the mixing stage. If you get good takes at the live and overdub stages that reflect the dynamics of your song well, it makes mixing your song a much more straightforward process as you'll be reflecting what's already there. And that's one of the great things about tracking the bulk of a recording live; it helps capture the energy of musicians playing a song in a more organic way that can be harder to replicate by simply tracking all of the instruments individually.

RECORD YOUR GUITAR

Forget what you've heard about red light fever, recording your own music can be one of the most fun and rewarding experiences you'll have with your guitar, and guess what? It doesn't have to be difficult or expensive! Here we show you exactly what gear you need, how to get it working and how to get a great sound from a simple set-up with both your electric and acoustic.

MULTI-TRACK RECORDER

Hardware recorders have a limited track count, offering four, six, eight, 12 or 16 tracks per-song, but they have their benefits, too. They're simple to use, they're self-contained portable units so you can take them to a practice room or gig easily, plus they often have effects, CD burners and USB connectivity!

AUDIO INTERFACE

This little box is simply the bit that allows you to get decent quality audio running in and out of your computer. Computers have rudimentary onboard audio interfaces, but this box will override the on-board hardware in your computer and give you better quality audio. Your choice of interface will be governed by how many channels you want to record at once, and the types of inputs you need (mic/instrument)

GUITAR

Before you record, it's worth checking out all of your guitar for buzzes, noises and intonation. A quick setup doesn't cost much – or if you're handy you can do it yourself – but the benefits of having your gear in order now will pay off later. Get a set of fresh strings on your guitar, give them plenty of time to stabilise, and you'll be sure that you're capturing the best sound possible from your instrument

MICROPHONES

You don't need a cupboard full of expensive microphones to get a great sound, but if you're recording electric and acoustic, we'd suggest getting your hands on at least one dynamic microphone, and one condenser microphone (see Mic Check p43). If you don't want to buy them, you can always look into borrowing (ask around) or hiring some mics (check with your local music shops or practice spaces). With some careful preparation and placement, these will have you covered for most situations

DAW RECORDING SOFTWARE

A DAW (or digital audio workstation) is the software you'll be using to actually record with. There are many different options out there (Cubase, Logic, GarageBand etc), but most essentially offer the same thing. Many interfaces come with a stripped-back free version to get you started out of the box

COMPUTER

Don't get hung up on whether you're using a PC, Mac, desktop or laptop; it doesn't matter. If you're going to be doing lots of recording, you might want to invest in some extra storage, however, as full-fat audio files can mount up after a while

WHAT YOU NEED TO RECORD

Before you really get stuck into recording at home, here's the gear you'll need to get the job done...

GET CONNECTED

When the time comes to put all the gear together that last thing you want to hear is nothing at all – here's how to hook it all up properly...

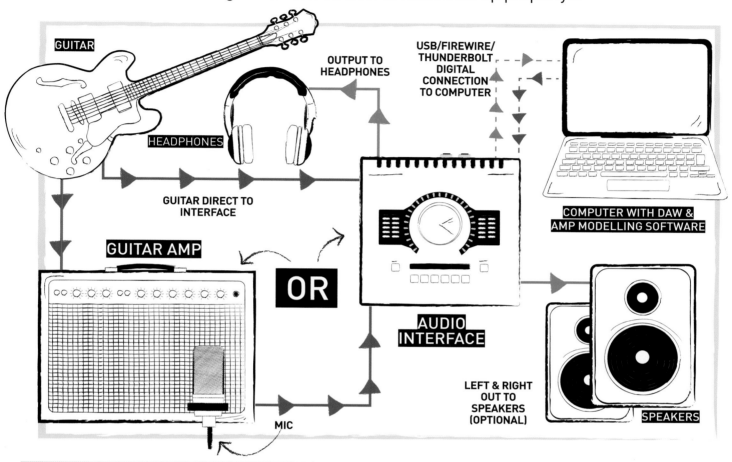

THE SOUND OF SILENCE

There's nothing more frustrating than getting all of your connections together, then hearing nothing. If you've done it as per the manual and you're still stuck, here's how to find and solve problems before your inspiration dies...

Check your connections
A loose jack here, or a forgotten USB cable there can bring everything to its knees. While you're doing a complete check make sure your guitar's volume control is turned up!

Got power?
When using a condenser mic, make sure you've turned on your interface's phantom power switch, otherwise you'll hear nothing.

Check your settings
We can't walk you through the settings for every piece of recording software, but here's roughly how they all work. First, make sure your computer is talking to the interface as the main audio input and output device. On a Mac, you'll find this in the 'Sound' menu. For PC check your device manager.

Check your DAW software
Think of the DAW as another signal in the chain; the audio goes from your instrument to the interface, into the computer and into the software. So check your software is set to use the interface as its input and output device. You can often find this in a menu at the top of the screen: it will be called something like 'Audio Setup', or 'Audio Preferences'.

Assign the correct input
This is common when using an interface with different inputs, and recording multiple tracks. Sometimes, you'll find that if you are recording on 'Track 4' your software will look to input four of your interface for the signal. Fine. But if your guitar is plugged into a different input you record nothing. You can usually change which input you want to use on each track's 'inspector'.

Turn on monitoring
Many DAWs replicate the signal routing of old tape machines, so you'll need to press the 'monitor' button to hear yourself. This is also found in the track inspector, and often resembles a speaker or headphone icon. Remember the fader in your recording software controls the monitoring volume, so you can turn it up or down – it won't affect the recorded level of your signal.

Don't forget the hardware
Some interfaces have mute buttons or monitor volume controls, or switchable dual master volumes that control your speaker or monitors. Ensure you are adjusting the correct control for the output you're trying to listen to.

UNDERSTAND YOUR AUDIO INTERFACE

Get to grips with the gadget that makes computer recording happen...

INPUTS

The first decision you have to make when you're looking for an interface to record with is how many inputs – and what type of input (instrument or microphone) – you'll need. This will govern how many tracks you can simultaneously record to their own tracks in your recording software. For example, if you're a singer-songwriter recording guitars and vocals and using software instruments, a simple two-input interface that includes at least one microphone preamp will most likely be fine.

I f you're recording on a computer, the interface is an essential ingredient in your set-up. The interface is the part that connects your guitar, microphones, headphones and speakers to your computer. Think of it as a central hub for all of your different audio inputs and outputs.

Like so much music kit, audio interfaces range from ultra-simple and affordable to complex and expensive, but the market is awash with reasonably-priced, feature-packed boxes.

You can record two audio sources at a time on different tracks, then overdub extra parts such as solos or backing vocals later.

If you're working in a band set-up with drums, and want to record the entire rhythm section playing together while keeping all of the instruments on their own tracks for mixing later, then, of course, you're going to need a lot more inputs. There are plenty of interfaces available with eight or more microphone inputs, and they have really come down in price over the last few years.

Make sure your audio interface has all the inputs and outputs you need!

Some practice amps can be used as audio interfaces, such as this Yamaha THR

THE INTERFACE IS ONE THE MOST ESSENTIAL INGREDIENTS IN YOUR SET-UP

CONNECTIVITY

The next thing you need to think about is how the interface will connect to your computer. It used to be that interfaces were circuit boards that you had to mount within the computer, but these days they're pretty much exclusively external boxes that run off a USB, Firewire or Thunderbolt (for Apple people). Check the connections on your computer to make sure it's compatible, and also think about power. If you're likely to be recording in an environment where electrical sockets are sparse (acoustic guitar in a church, vocals in a bathroom, etc) having an interface that can power itself from your laptop's battery will be a handy feature.

Finally, it's worth noting that some interfaces can connect to portable devices such as a phone or tablet as well as your computer, giving you the ultimate in portability.

Having an interface that can power itself over USB or the like is handy

RECOMMENDED

Take the stress out of shopping for an interface with our top picks!

THE MOBILE RIG
Recording on a phone or tablet gives you a set-up you can take anywhere

IK Multimedia iRig Pro
For just over £100, you get a simple box for plugging in your guitar or a microphone (although not at the same time) to an iPhone or iPad, plus it also works a treat on Apple Mac computers. Pair it with IK's bundled amp modelling and recording apps and you have a straightforward setup to take anywhere.

Shure Motiv MVi
There aren't many Android compatible interfaces on the market that do it all, but this little box from Shure does. It looks a bit like an alarm clock but gives you a combi socket for a mic or guitar, it will also work with PC or Mac.

Presonus AudioBox iTwo
Just because you're going mobile, doesn't mean you have to be limited to one input at a time. The AudioBox iTwo is compatible with either iPad or Mac and offers two inputs — one for mic and one for your instrument, as well as MIDI, balanced 1/4-inch outputs, and an internal analogue mixer for under a £100. The Studio version bundles a condenser mic and 'phones for just £50 more.

THE SINGER-SONGWRITER SETUP
Recording your songs alone in your bedroom? Here's the gear for you

M-Audio M-Track Mk II
£69. That's all it'll take for you to bag one of these rock-solid, easy-to-use interfaces. It's got everything you need on it and comes bundled with some great plugins from studio effects legends, Waves.

Focusrite Scarlett Studio
This is a complete out-of-the-box solution to get you recording immediately. For around £179 you'll get a decent interface, a condenser microphone and a pair of studio monitoring headphones. If you want to take the fuss out of getting geared-up, start here.

UAD Apollo Twin
Okay, so it's not the most affordable (expect to pay around £625), but as well as being loaded with two premium inputs, the Apollo Twin runs UAD plugins. This gives you access to world-class software recreations of classic studio gear, effects and amp modelling. It's an investment, but well worth it.

THE FULL-BAND STUDIO
Need enough inputs to record your whole band? These interfaces won't let you down

Tascam US-4X4
If you want to record a small band, this affordable (under £200) interface from Tascam will give you four simultaneous inputs; that's more than enough to try all of the techniques we'll cover in our tutorials, plus you could record your drummer with a simple four-mic set-up.

M-Audio M-Track Eight
The M-Track Eight offers value for money for around £300, you'll get eight mic inputs, metering for each channel and two headphone outputs. It also comes bundled with Cubase 7 LE and some Waves plugins to help with your mixing. Bargain.

UNDERSTANDING MICROPHONES

The chances are you'll want to record an amp, acoustic or even vocals – that means you'll need something to capture that sound...

You don't need to spend a fortune to get a microphone that'll have you covered for recording your guitar. The most important thing is to choose the right kind of mic for the job. For this tutorial, we'll be sticking with the two main types of microphone used for recording guitars, these fall into 'dynamic' or 'condenser' categories.

DYNAMIC MICS

Dynamic mics are the type of mic you'll see most commonly, and are great all-rounders for recording guitar cabinets, drums and even vocals. Their passive design means that they don't require any power to work, and they're also less sensitive than condenser microphones. This lower sensitivity means that a dynamic microphone can usually handle very high Sound Pressure Levels (SPLs) without getting damaged, making them a great choice if you need to close-mic a loud source like your guitar amp. They're affordable, rugged and will work on any interface with a mic preamp.

RECOMMENDED DYNAMIC MICS
SHURE SM57
The SM57 is the Swiss Army knife of any studio, from bedroom set-ups to multi-million pound facilities. Stick it in front of your amp, on a snare drum, or use it to record vocals. It's about the best £100 you can spend on recording gear.

JZ MICROPHONES GTR-1
You may not know the name, but the GTR-1 from JZ Microphones is a serious contender. It's designed specifically for mic'ing guitar cabs, and its flat design means it'll sit as close as you want to the grille on your speaker. Plus you'll pick one up for a similar price to an SM57.

AUDIX I5
No prizes for guessing that Audix has positioned the i5 as an alternative to the 57. It's got a rugged build quality, can handle SPLs of up to 140dB (that's louder than a jet taking off), and will cost under £100.

CONDENSER MICS

A condenser microphone is a classic studio choice. Its applications range from acoustic guitar, to vocals, to the ambient mic'ing of a guitar cab. Condenser mics have a few extended features when compared to their dynamic brothers. First off, most condensers will require power from an external source, which is sent down the XLR cable, so you'll need to make sure your interface has phantom power. If not, you can buy external preamps or phantom power units to take care of this for you.

Because of this circuitry, condenser mics can pick up a wider range of frequencies and greater sonic detail than a dynamic mic. This isn't always an advantage, though, as with increased sensitivity comes a lower resistance to very high SPLs. If you place them too close to a sound source, you could risk damaging the mic. On top of this, the condenser will 'hear' a lot more background noise – fridges, computers, traffic etc – so you need to make sure you choose your mic and environment extra carefully.

RECOMMENDED CONDENSER MICS

RODE NT-1A

The Rode NT-1A has been a household name since it launched, with about 1.5 zillion of them sold to-date. A street price between £150 and £190 will get you this low-noise condenser, a proper elastic cradle mount and a pop shield to tame those Bs and Ps on your vocals.

SE X1

SE Electronics have a habit of packing a lot of bang for not much buck, and the X1 continues this with features such as a -10dB pad (for use on louder sources) and a bass roll-off (to cut down on low-end rumble). Bag it on its own for about £100, or push the budget to £150 to get it bundled with a cradle, pop shield and Reflection Filter for recording your vocals!

AKG C1000S

This small-diaphragm condenser has got you covered for multiple applications, with a -10dB pad switch, bass roll-off, and switchable cardioid or hyper-cardioid patterns. It can also be powered with a battery, so you can plug it in even if you don't have phantom power! All in all, super-handy.

DYNAMIC MICS ARE GREAT ALL-ROUNDERS

> "CONDENSER MICS PICK UP A WIDER RANGE OF FREQUENCIES AND GREATER SONIC DETAIL"

MIC CHECK

Use a dynamic mic if...
- You're placing the mic very close to a loud source

- You don't need as much high-frequency detail

- You want to minimise spill from other sources

Use a condenser mic if...
- You want to capture a wide frequency response (acoustic guitar, vocals etc)

- You are recording an instrument with a lot of dynamic range

- You want to record from a greater distance (ie ambient room mics)

PICK UP PATTERNS

Every microphone has what's known as a polar pick-up pattern, which determines the shape of space around the mic's capsule that it can 'hear'. It can sound technical, but it's actually quite simple. Here are some of the most common.

Omni-directional
An omni-directional mic picks up sound from all directions. They work well at capturing 'group' sounds, for example, more than one acoustic guitar or vocal chants, but are a big no-no if you want to eliminate spill between instruments.

Cardioid
If your mic doesn't have switchable patterns, chances are it'll be a cardioid design. The name comes from the fact that it picks up sound in a heart-shaped pattern around the front of the mic's capsule, so it's great at picking up the sound in front and to the sides of the mic, while rejecting sound from behind.

Super cardioid
These types of mic give an even tighter pick-up pattern to the front of the mic than a standard cardioid, but the trade-off is that they don't reject sound from behind as well. This is great if you want to increase isolation between instruments in a live recording, you'll just need to consider the placement of the sources so that they aren't bleeding into each other.

OMNI-DIRECTIONAL

CARDIOID

SUPER CARDIOID

MAKE THE MOST OF AMP MODELLING

No room to record? Neighbours on your back about noise?
Amp modelling is your silent partner...

D on't let space or noise restrictions stop you from recording your guitar at home. There are loads of great software amp modellers available such as Native Instruments' Guitar Rig and IK Multimedia's AmpliTube. In fact, many DAWs come loaded with great amp modelling on board for free. Here's how to get the most out of amp modelling.

First, make sure you're connected up as illustrated in the diagram on page 97. Once you've loaded your DAW, create a new audio track. Amp modelling is then applied as a 'plugin'. Think of a plugin as a program within a program, your DAW acts as a 'host' to the amp modelling software, and all of your settings and signal chains are saved into the song, so it'll remain exactly as you leave it when you next open your song.

You'll need to use it as an 'insert' effect, rather than a send, otherwise you'll hear a blend of your guitar's dry, clean signal along with the effected sound when playing.

TWEAK PRACTICE

One benefit of amp modelling is that it is inserted into the output of your DAW's signal chain. This means that what is actually being recorded is your dry guitar sound, so if you decide to change the EQ, gain settings or even the type of amp after you've recorded, you're free to do so!

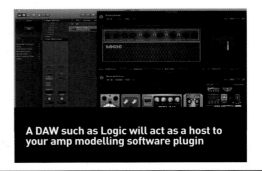

A DAW such as Logic will act as a host to your amp modelling software plugin

FLICK THROUGH SOME DIFFERENT AMP AND SPEAKER TYPES, YOU MIGHT FIND THE PERFECT MATCH WHERE YOU LEAST EXPECT IT

Amp modellers give you the freedom to swap and tweak 'til you're happy

MAKE DECISIONS

The last point is indeed one of the greatest virtues of amp modelling software, but at some point you will have to make a decision on your tone in order to finish your song. Learn how to recognise when you're finished, then move on to the next part.

TRY EVERYTHING

It's easy to fall into preconceptions when using an amp modeller – big rock tune? Use a stack! But it's also a great idea to try out some unexpected models, too. Flick through some different amp and speaker types and see how they fit in your mix and you might just find the perfect match where you least expect it.

BUILD COOL SOUNDS

In the real world, every time we want to add a pedal, amp or speaker to our rig, we're plagued by switching boxes, cables, and noise. As well as this, you'll need the space, and resources to get your hands on such gear. But this is virtual, baby! Rigging up two amps at once is easy, and you

won't find a ground hum in earshot. The modern laptop is more than powerful enough to handle it. This is also true of creating crazy effects patches. Want three fuzzes, a wah, and four delays? The only limitation is your imagination and processing power, so get stuck in!

MIC MECHANICS

Many amp modellers give you control over the type of virtual microphone that's used on your virtual cab, and you can usually change its position, too. Play around with blending different virtual mic types and placements together, and you can often scratch the tonal itch that EQ and gain settings can't reach.

GET HARD

Okay, we know this bit is predominantly about software amp modellers, but many multi-effects units and amps can act as an audio interface, with on-screen control over your amp. This will take some of the strain off your computer, and allow you to silently record the settings you know and love without any noise from microphones.

ROCKING IN THE FREE WORLD

Three software amp modellers that won't cost you a penny!

IK Multimedia AmpliTube Custom Shop
www.ikmultimedia.com
This expandable version of IK Multimedia's AmpliTube is totally free, and comes with four amps, five cabs, nine stompboxes and more! If you like it, you can download more models, but you have to pay for them…

Native Instruments Guitar Rig Player
www.native-instruments.com
Guitar Rig Player gives you one amp (based on a Marshall Plexi), plus a host of effects including delay, modulation and filters.

Kuassa Amplifikation Lite
www.kuassa.com
Kuassa's Amplifikation Lite is 100 percent free, and provides you with a three-channel amp equipped with EQ and cabinet modelling. It's not the flashiest, but it is solid, and won't cost you a bean.

Modern modelling will let you tweak every bit of an amp's recorded sound

RECORDING YOUR ACOUSTIC GUITAR

Recording your acoustic needn't be difficult. All you need is a good mic and the right surroundings

The sound an acoustic guitar produces is self-contained, and relies on you as the player to influence it. This can be done with different string types, picks, but most of all, the room. There are tricks for getting different acoustic guitar sounds on your recording, and in this tutorial we'll show you just a few of them. You can achieve brilliant-sounding acoustic tracks with just one microphone, some careful room selection and mic placement. Here's how...

ONE MIC

Acoustic guitars are capable of outputting a range of levels and frequency responses. So the most common way of capturing an acoustic guitar with a single mic is to use a condenser. But before you position the mic, listen to the guitar in the room. Your environment effects the sound; empty spaces with hard reflective surfaces (a bathroom, for instance) will give a bright, lively sound, a room with a carpet, sofas and curtains will soak up a lot of the reflections, giving you a dryer, punchier acoustic tone. Experiment with different rooms to see which gets you the sound you prefer.

Position the mic 30cm in front of your acoustic, aimed at the join between the body and neck. This will keep it out of the way of your picking hand and avoid muddy low-end from the soundhole.

DIFFICULTY Easy!   **YOU WILL NEED:** ✓ CONDENSER MICROPHONE   ✓ ONE MICROPHONE INPUT   ✓ ONE TRACK

STEREO SET-UP 1 X/Y CONFIGURATION'

Capturing your guitar in stereo can give you a wide-sounding acoustic part for your tune. When you record in stereo, it's best if you can use a pair of identical microphones, so that the signal picked up by each will be equal. For this method, we're going to use an X/Y placement. This is where the capsules are crossed over, so that they're an equal distance from the source. Position them around the 14th fret of your acoustic. Pan them left and right and bask in the super-wide stereo!

DIFFICULTY EASY! **YOU WILL NEED:** ✓ TWO CONDENSER MICROPHONES ✓ TWO MICROPHONE INPUTS ✓ TWO TRACKS

STEREO SET-UP 2 SPACED PAIR

The second way of recording in stereo is using a spaced pair. It's similar to the X/Y idea, except for this time we'll physically move the microphones apart to achieve an even wider sound than before. Place one microphone between the bridge and the soundhole, and aim the other at the fretboard. Pan the tracks left and right respectively when mixing to achieve a spacey, stereo effect.

DIFFICULTY MODERATE **YOU WILL NEED:** ✓ TWO CONDENSER MICROPHONES ✓ TWO MICROPHONE INPUTS ✓ TWO TRACKS

STEREO SET-UP 3 OVERHEADS

The acoustic guitar has an organic sound, and there's an argument that it should be captured more ambiently. A good method for achieving a very natural acoustic sound is to try positioning a pair of microphones at the player's head height as shown. This way, you'll be recording 'what they hear' rather than an artificially close sound.

DIFFICULTY MODERATE **YOU WILL NEED:** ✓ TWO CONDENSER MICROPHONES ✓ TWO MICROPHONE INPUTS ✓ TWO TRACKS

THE DOS DONT'S OF RECORDING ACOUSTIC

Do Experiment with different rooms. this can make a huge difference to the sound of an acoustic guitar

Don't Tap your foot too loudly. If you need to use it as a count then take your shoe off and place a cushion underneath your foot

Do Try different picks and strings. These are some of the biggest tone-shaping devices at your disposal, so it's definitely worth it!

Don't Move too much while recording. You should be aiming to keep the guitar a consistent distance from the microphone

Do Remember to switch off phones, boilers/air conditioning and anything else that could make noise during your take. If you're a heavy breather, try and keep it quiet!

Don't Stress too much about string noise? Coated strings can help minimise string noise and consider using some string lubricant such as Fast Fret or similar

YOU CAN ACHIEVE BRILLIANT-SOUNDING ACOUSTIC TRACKS WITH JUST ONE MIC

PICKUP/MIC BLEND

If your acoustic has a pickup, you can get two contrasting tones from one take by blending the sound of your pickup with the ambience of a microphone. Simply plug your guitar into your interface's instrument input (keeping your preamp's EQ 'flat' so you can tweak the tonality later), then record the mic signal on a separate track using the one mic method – you might want to play with the distance of the microphone. Once you're done, try panning the tracks, or running the pickup track through amp/speaker modelling to create some extra texture.

DIFFICULTY EASY! **YOU WILL NEED:** ✓ ELECTRO-ACOUSTIC ✓ CONDENSER MICROPHONE ✓ MIC/INSTRUMENT INPUTS ✓ TWO TRACKS

RECORDING YOUR GUITAR AMP

Recording your amp isn't rocket science, and once you understand a few
basic principles, you'll be getting a great sound in no time

While many of us will record our electric guitars straight into a DAW and use amp and effects modelling to create the sounds we want, there's just something about recording a proper guitar amp in a live room, particularly a full-fat valve amp. As with recording an acoustic, however, mic'ing up an amp is a process that requires a bit of knowledge, and a fair bit of trail and error to get the ideal sound.

START WITH YOUR GUITAR

A great guitar sound starts at the business end of your signal path. With your guitar set-up with fresh strings that are played in, you've got the first link in the guitar chain sorted.

GET YOUR SOUND

Fine-tune your pedal and amp settings to get them the best they can be to your ears in the room. Try moving your amp to different positions in the room – or even a different room if possible– and see where it sounds best. Set your drive, EQ and overall level to a place where you feel comfortable, then move on to the mic.

SPEAKER EASY

If you're getting a great sound in the room, the only job the mic has to do is capture it. But the position of your mic in relation to your speaker can radically change the sound. Put simply, depending on where you position the mic, you can change the sound it's capturing from bright to dark. The brightest tone is found dead centre of the speaker – right on the dust cap. As you move the microphone to the edge of the speaker, you'll find the sound gets progressively darker. Distance will also play a key role in your resulting tone – placing the mic very close to the speaker will capture the amp's sound in detail, with a lot of attack and definition. With this type of set up you're recording the sound of the speaker, with hardly any room sound.

The further you move the microphone away from the speaker, the more you'll capture the room sound and its reflections, adding ambience and depth to your sound.
The examples on the facing page also illustrate how multiple mics can affect tone.

THREE WAYS TO MIC YOUR SPEAKER

1 CLOSE-MIC'ING

A dynamic mic will handle the high SPL of your cab, so you can place it as close as you can physically get it. Start in the centre of the speaker cone, and move it towards the edge of the speaker. It's worth enlisting the help of a bandmate at this point to monitor the sound the mic is picking up through headphones against the sound in the room. If you're recording alone, do this yourself.

Once you've found the right position for tonality, try moving the mic back/towards the speaker and listen to how it changes the timbre of the sound.

DIFFICULTY EASY!	YOU WILL NEED: ✓ GUITAR AMP ✓ DYNAMIC MICROPHONE ✓ ONE MICROPHONE INPUT ✓ ONE TRACK

2 AMBIENT MIC'ING

Ambient mic'ing will capture more of the sound reflections in the room, as well as the amp, and can help your guitar to sit in the mix well later. Because you'll be placing the mic further from the source, we recommend using a condenser mic; the extra sensitivity and frequency response will keep your sound full, even at distance. Start with your microphone about a foot (30cm) away from the grille. As with close mic'ing, the tonality of your captured sound will change, depending on which part of the speaker you aim the mic at – bear in mind that this effect will be lessened the further you get from the speaker.

DIFFICULTY EASY!	YOU WILL NEED: ✓ GUITAR AMP ✓ CONDENSER MICROPHONE ✓ ONE MICROPHONE INPUT ✓ ONE TRACK

3 CLOSE/AMBIENT BLEND

Using a blend of close and ambient mic positions gives you the best of both worlds in terms of maximum attack, and spatial effect from each position, plus the ability to balance these sounds in your final mix. Replicate both set-ups above. With two mics in fixed positions, the phase will be at a set frequency. It can be used to make your sound fuller or thinner, depending on which frequencies are affected. Phase is pretty much unavoidable, but it can be minimised using the 3:1 rule. The idea is that your second mic should be positioned three times the distance from the source (your amp) as the close mic. Ultimately though, you shouldn't let this worry you too much. You're not going to break anything. Use your ears, listen to the two mics together, and if it sounds good, it is good!

DIFFICULTY MODERATE	YOU WILL NEED: ✓ DYNAMIC MICROPHONE ✓ CONDENSER MICROPHONE ✓ TWO MICROPHONE INPUTS ON YOUR INTERFACE ✓ TWO SEPARATE TRACKS TO RECORD

TRACK TRICKS

Our unmissable tips to make recording amps easier

Mark your spot
Once you've found your ideal mic placement, mark the amp with tape or chalk so you can find it again.

Cone home
To see where the speaker starts and finishes take a look around the back if it's is open-back or shine a torch through the grille to see its outline.

Use small amps
Getting a great amp sound from a valve amp means cranking it up. Do this with a 100-watt stack and you'll end up with sirens on your recording! Instead, try a low-wattage amp to minimise the volume, and give a more usable result.

Gain killer
When you're recording, it's easy to go overboard with the drive, but when you stack up layers of distorted guitars, it gets messy. Get the gain to your usual level, then back it off a notch.

Double up!
A classic guitar recording trick is to double your track with an identical part. Play as tightly as you can, pan them left and right, and bang... instant huge tone. For an added twist, try changing your gain, EQ, pickup settings or even the guitar on one of the parts.

The voicing
One of the best ways of adding thickness to double-tracked guitar parts is to use different voicings of the same chord. Try playing one part as open chords, and then switch to barres for the next track.

Dare to DI
Recording a DI'd clean version of your part straight from your guitar is the ultimate safety net. You'll be able to re-amp your part later either live or with a modeller, or simply have a backup if anything goes wrong with your amp track.

Play guitar, MAKE MONEY!

Words: Stuart Williams, Rob Laing, Chris Bird   Photography: Simon Lees

Your guitar is a valuable cash-generating tool. Follow these tips from TG's band of professional experts and you, too, could make a living out of doing something you love

BECOME A TECH

Teching is a viable career that requires skill and know-how. Alex 'Vman' Venturella has tech'd for Fightstar, Coheed And Cambria, Mastodon and many others. Here, he reveals what the job is really about

**Alex Venturella
Guitar tech**

How did you get into the world of guitar maintenance?
"I remember getting my first electric guitar and I was always tinkering with it. I must have been about 16 and I put a huge ding in it, and there wasn't much on the internet then on how to fix it. So it was books, and then I got into basic repairs. It all kind of flourished from there, really."

What was your first job as a tech?
"I was a guitar teacher and I would fix students' gear. There was a local shop in Edgware, and every now and then the guy there would send me stuff that he couldn't fix himself. It was a word of mouth thing, and I've never set up a website or a shop, which is the way I like it. My first paid gig was when Charlie [Simpson] left Busted. I remember just fixing some of his gear and he asked if I wanted to come and work for Fightstar. I was with them for about five years."

What kind of work would you generally find yourself doing when you're on the road?
"Whereas most guitar techs or people I see on the road don't touch fretwork or adjust the necks, and if a nut wears down they'll just put a bit of paper in there, I would do heavy modifications, fixing fretwork. And electronics as well; I've always taken pedals apart and fixed them. I've always tried to do that instead of ringing up a company and getting a new pedal in."

Was there much learning on the job?
"The technical side I was great at, but I didn't have the roadie etiquette. I looked at it more as a kind of holiday camp in the beginning. For the first couple of years, I didn't take it seriously, whereas now it's a professional thing – you can't be messing around on the job."

Do you think it helps that you've been a gigging guitarist as well?
"It's like a pride thing. I want the guitar to play as good as someone who pays for a guitar setup. So on the road, I want the guitarists to have a guitar that I'm chuffed about too. That's the way I've always looked at it."

How have you earned money between tours?
"I repair gear – that's always been an income. It can range, though. One day, you've got 20 guitars through the door, the next you've got just one in a week. That's why teching has been my main money-earner. When I come home, it's more relaxed, more of a holiday."

What are the typical repairs that you'll get?
"Amp repairs, like trying to get a dead amp working again, all the way to refretting, some finish work. I've never done major overhaul work, but with a refret I try to give my experience to customers so they don't keep having to come back. It varies because you never know what you're going to get."

Can you recall any particularly challenging jobs?
"I get that with different amp companies sometimes. Some companies like to use printer ports [for the footswitch]; you're trying to fix a switching system and you have to go online and try and find where all the pins run out. When it's basic MIDI, it's in and out of there."

What are the most common things that tend to go wrong?
"It'll usually be if we've got hired-in gear. Onstage, the guitar rigs should stay constant. I always check measurements every day to make sure the necks haven't moved. But the more that you get into it, the less problems you might have. Six or seven years ago, I'd be running around a lot more onstage, whereas nowadays I'm sitting more on a chair looking at an iPad. That's a good sign – it means you're doing your job."

Is getting a tech job all based around reputation?
"The Coheed one was a good example. Their tech had to fly to Australia for another gig, so [the promoter] rings me up and asks if I can do the show. So I turn up and meet the guys, and they have these big MIDI switching systems. Claudio [Lopez] had a lot of gear and he was like, 'Don't touch anything – leave it alone.' But there was ground hum in his rig that was horrendous. He said it had been there for years and to leave it alone. I went and fixed it anyway. Then after the show he came up to me and said, 'Man, that's the clearest my rig has ever been.' It was just a few ground loops here and there. Three weeks later, I got a call asking if I wanted to come and work for the band. Some techs are not repairmen, but I'd jump in."

So repair knowledge is really the secret of your success?
"Exactly. At Mayhem festival there were a bunch of bands who couldn't afford to take a tech on the road. It's them in a van going across the States, which sucks. And they break their gear a lot because it's cheaper gear. So I would go over to the smaller stages and see friends I knew over there and set up as a kind of guitar fixer. Not for money or anything,

but you just get bored and you want to help people out. Like Job For A Cowboy, they just had problems every night, so I was fixing their basses, guitars, and putting new pickups in. I was more like a handyman!"

What's an average day like for a guitar tech on a UK tour?
"A medium-sized band at a 2,000-capped venue, you're looking at getting up at 9 or 10am, checking the venue out and having a walk around. Check that load-in is going to be on time. Get the gear in, and then depending on how big the production is, you have to make sure lighting is in first, and front of house is all set up and you're not crossing wires. That's another problem you run into. Even some bigger bands now can't afford proficient expensive techs, so people cross paths with each other. Whereas with a more experienced crew it's like clockwork. You knock a soundcheck out later in the day, fix all the problems from the last night's show. You hit show time, and then it's packdown again."

What's the most challenging task you've encountered?
"Challenging in terms of it being a time restraint, I've had to rewire a pedalboard a couple of times when the artist is unhappy with it and they want to change it around. You've got an hour until you're onstage. That's always a pain in the ass."

Being a tech means a lot of travel and being away from home is that underestimated by newcomers?
"It is, yes, I always see on Facebook with friends [who are techs, too] that have kids and them having to say goodbye to their kids, and then they're gone for three of four months. That's really tough, and it's a pretty shitty job if you want to keep up a steady relationship. I think that's something that gets overlooked when people see being on tour as a kind of party zone and just having fun. The reality is it's a bit of a solo mission."

Do you modify gear a lot?
"Opeth actually used one of my amps on their new record. It was a Soldano clone that I built, and one of my overdrive pedals. I build pedals, too – I took four of my favourite overdrive pedals and went through each one asking, 'why does it sound that way?' Then I made my own version of it. With the amps, I'm a big Soldano fan, so I took a bit of a Diezel preamp and stuck it with a Soldano power amp stage. It's fun."

You're a big fan of Mastodon, and became part of the band's family in a sense as a tech...
"It's pretty amazing. About seven years ago, I sent a message to them on MySpace, saying, 'Hey I'm a guitar tech, I'd love to come and work for you – you're my favourite band.' I didn't hear back or anything, but lo and behold years later I was on the tour bus one day and went through my old messages and found it. It made them chuckle. So if you put your mind to it, you can eventually work for your favourite band."

START TECHING!

World tours with your favourite bands are the ultimate dream, but if you want to make it as a tech, you need to learn your craft. Here are some ways that you can get going...

GET FIXING
Learn about basic repairs. Practise on your gear, buy cheap broken guitars and fix them, then when you're confident, offer your services.

DON'T FORGET ELECTRONICS
Okay, so fiddling under the bonnet of an amp can be dangerous, and shouldn't be attempted if you're unsure of what you're doing. However, learning to change valves and replace/fix dodgy controls and sockets is a valuable skill. Having a go at making your own pedals can also be a great way to learn about the inner workings of your gear.

APPROACH LOCAL STORES
Guitar shops will often have an in-house technician, but it's worth checking around. Be honest about your abilities, get ready to change a lot of strings, and learn how a kettle works.

PUT YOUR NAME OUT THERE
Find local musicians in need of a setup and offer a reduced rate to help get your name around. A regular setup (action, intonation, string change and check-up) will cost between £35 and £50.

LEARN ABOUT SIGNAL PATHS
Amps the source of many mid-set panics for guitarists. Get to know how signal flows around a guitar rig, and how you can improve it. From here, you'll be the ultimate onstage wingman.

GET TO KNOW YOUR SCENE
Go to gigs, meet the best bands in your area, get to know local sound engineers, and help them out. Word of mouth is your main reputation builder, so become the go-to guitar tech by being reliable, professional and knowledgeable.

Good luck getting that in tune for the soundcheck...

RECORD REMOTE SESSIONS

Turn your home office into a money-making recording studio

When not on tour, Ollie Hannifan is recording guitar parts remotely. Here, he explains how it works, and how you can do it too

**Ollie Hannifan
Session
guitarist
theguitarparty.com**

How did you get started playing these remote sessions?
"It was just friends who were doing similar things; trying to get their own projects going or doing things for other people, and they'd need stuff doing, so they'd ask. They'd either send it over and get me to do it, or they'd come to mine."

Did you have to do some unpaid work to begin with?
"Yeah, to begin with there was quite a lot of unpaid work, to be honest. It was bands that needed some stuff doing, I ended up working with them for about six months and in the end I got paid with a guitar, which was nice! I remember I actually had to ask in the end; after a certain point I had to say 'I can't do it anymore if there's no money', and they agreed to pay me a daily rate. But I did have to decide that for myself."

Did this period help to produce paid work?
"Yeah, definitely. Definitely people that I've worked with before, or in bands or live situations have offered me work. I've had a few offers specifically for online work from people that I haven't met, through other online session players."

So who are your main clients?
"It's mainly singer-songwriters, but also corporate stuff. I do a lot of stuff for a dance company, reproducing songs, which I really enjoy. Anything from Michael Bublé to Avril Lavigne and everything in-between, a lot of pop. Understanding the original is key, and then going a little bit off-piste."

Do you charge per track?
"Yeah, unless you're doing a whole album, then you could work out a day rate if there's a whole bunch of stuff to record; but I usually charge by the song, so an acoustic and an electric guitar part."

Were there things you struggled with at first?
"Yeah, I think getting used to the software takes a little while. For a start, I couldn't find the on switch for my Mac, so that was a good start! I hadn't used Logic for quite a few years. I'd been using Windows for years and I just couldn't figure it out. But in the end I discovered loads of YouTube tutorials, which were great! In terms of getting stuff done, I always

used to find it quite stressful because I didn't take enough breaks. When you're recording by yourself, and you're hitting start and hitting stop, and trying to play it, I used to get in a rush and end up spending more time on it than it needed. Whereas now I spend much more time practising in advance until I can nail it, and then I'll record it, instead of trying to learn it as I record it."

What gear do you need?
"Getting that first setup can be quite intimidating, because it is quite an investment. The amount you'd have to make to make back what you're spending is quite a lot. I use an iMac at home, and I have a DigiDesign Eleven rack and a decent

"IT'S WAY MORE ABOUT UNDERSTANDING TONE, PLAYING IN TIME AND BEING TASTEFUL"

mic for acoustic stuff, and that works great. I've actually done quite a lot of fully professional stuff using just that. Recording yourself is good for your playing anyway, and it allows you to be creative."

What about recording acoustic?
"I've forgotten which model I use, it's an SE Electronics one that costs about £300. It just sounds clear, and I spent quite a bit of time trying out different mic placements around the guitar; that really helps. I think that if you have a nice,

reasonable mic, it will pick up what it's hearing. So, with acoustic stuff it's much more to do with things like different picks and mic placements to get the sound, and eventually you will get what you want."

Do clients get hung up on valve tone?
"I've never had that. I've got all that stuff, but living in London I just can't play through a loud valve amp. To be honest, I've never been asked to use a real valve amp in that situation."

What level of ability is needed for playing online sessions?
"It's way more about understanding tone, playing in time and being tasteful. That's way more important than technique. When it comes to recording, it's probably going to be a singer-songwriter's song, so it's all about making it sound good, and like a part rather than a guitar solo. If you can provide something in time and creative, then that's the most important thing. Imagine you were playing it live in a pub, that's how it needs to sound – the right chords at the right time, and have a good feel."

Do you need to read music?
"In this environment, nobody has ever put a piece of sheet music in front of me. But, certainly, for a lot of the live stuff I do, I have had that. Learning to read, I would say it's essential, but if you want to do this as a hobby or make a bit of money, I don't think it's anything to get too upset about."

How do you work out the parts?
"Quite often, it's just by ear, which is something I enjoy doing. Having learnt to play the guitar by playing along to loads of songs, and learning how songs are structured and how chords work together is probably the best thing."

Do you restrict how much time you spend on a track?
"Now I do, yeah. It's a good idea to give yourself deadlines; as soon as you have a timeframe it'll help you get it done. I usually charge per track, and some tracks can be really quick, other tracks take longer."

Do you encounter odd timings?
"It's pretty much straight 4/4 stuff. Anyone writing songs in 11/8 is likely to have their own band members to play it. I'm in a prog band myself, and you don't get many prog players needing session guys."

What do you do if the client isn't happy with your tracks?
"I have had that, but it's never been a problem. It's easy to get offended, when actually it's not really worth it. They hear it differently, and you just need to accept that. If they're employing you then that's the deal."

Do limit to how many times you re-submit a track?
"To begin with, it can be difficult to please the client first-time around. There are going to be things they're not happy with, and there are going to be things that they want to be redone."

How to... RECORD SESSIONS

OLLIE'S TIPS FOR SUCCESSFUL REMOTE SESSIONS

Experiment with mic placement to get a good acoustic sound

GET SET UP

You'll need an audio interface (or way of recording your guitar), a microphone for acoustic guitars and some good-quality amp models (hardware or software) as a minimum. You'll also need a computer and internet access, but as Ollie says, don't get too hung up on gear.

"I did a whole solo album on my old PC – a £300 PC World laptop. So it can totally be done, you don't have to buy the top-grade stuff. And the other thing is, half the tracks I've laid down, they don't need the most amazing tone you can ever imagine. Half the time clients want something that sounds a bit nasty or rough, because that's the vibe they're after."

UNDERSTAND YOUR GEAR

You might not need the best guitar or flashiest outboard gear, but you will want to spend some time learning how to get the best from what you've got. "I think tone is really important – I don't mean a pure valve tone – I just mean a good sound. Whatever it is, if you understand your gear you can get a good sound. I think as soon as they hear your sound, they're pretty much sold."

PLAY FOR THE SONG

When it comes to recording other people's tunes, leave your ego at the door and forget the noodling. "That's what people want to hear – an acoustic part strumming through their song or an electric rhythm part. They don't usually want a blistering solo these days, you don't hear blistering solos on the radio. People just want to hear their track with guitars on."

AND PLAY IT PROPERLY

Time correction? Digital editing? It's no replacement for a well-played part, Ollie reckons. "I was always a bit guilty of not playing the part right and then fixing it. Whereas now I'd much rather learn to play it well, and only edit it if I really have to. It's the best way, but it's tempting to get used to the whole studio thing and overuse it. Even if you have to play the same riff or groove for three minutes, it's always better to play it rather than loop it or copy and paste."

A guitar, a laptop, a mic, an interface and a copy of TG – what more do you need?

GET YOUR ONLINE PROFILE SORTED...

Having a website and social media profiles will be key to getting work. It's your shop-front for potential clients and will give you a chance to showcase your talents. You can also point people to your services through ads on sites such as Gumtree, Meet & Jam and airgigs.com. However, keeping it simple is the easiest way to get started. "I made a mistake when I first made my website. I asked a designer to do me a design and then a web builder to make it. It ended up costing me much more than it should have done, whereas if you just use a WordPress template, it's so easy. I did mine in a few hours just by watching some tutorials online and I had a website that I was able to control. People don't ask you to work for them based on your website, they ask because of your sound. So having a showreel, and getting your personality across – maybe with a video – is important as well."

...BUT DON'T GET DISTRACTED BY IT

Use your social media reach to attract clients, and keep people up-to-date about your latest musical adventures, but don't let it steal your focus. "It's easy to get YouTube, Facebook, Twitter, etc, set up, but it's also easy to spend too much time on it and get distracted, worrying about what other people are doing. Getting your own thing out there, being confident about it and saying 'This is me, this is what I can do', I think that's better. It's more important to practise!"

GET AS MUCH INFO AS POSSIBLE

A happy customer is a repeat customer. So get a very clear brief about what the client is expecting from you, and it'll make for a smooth session. "Getting a clear idea of what they want, and having a conversation rather than just emails, about what they want is a good idea. The more information you get in advance, the better it's going to be and the quicker you'll be able to do it."

DON'T GET CAUGHT OUT

Once you've finished, you'll need to deliver the tracks. Avoid getting stitched up by only sending short sections of the song to show the part you've recorded, then send the full, isolated tracks once you get the fee. "You can send an MP3 of the track with your guitars in it, but not send the stems until you've been paid."

START A FUNCTION BAND

Ollie Thomas is one quarter of successful wedding band, The Zu Zu Men, playing a range of popular music in a unique style. Here he explains just what it takes...

**Ollie Thomas
Guitarist
vocalist**

thezuzumen.com

How long have you been playing in function bands?
"I've been playing in function bands for around seven years. This particular band has been going for around three years, but I was playing in another for four years. With this one, we were just playing small gigs in bars; it was a lot of fun, so we decided to do it properly and see if there was a way of making a living out of what we enjoyed doing."

How many gigs do you play in an average month?
"We do two wedding gigs a week during the summer, so usually
seven or eight in a month. On top of that, we do public gigs, too – festivals and regular pub gigs, which are great adverts. If someone's having a wedding and they want to come and see if you're what they want, they can."

Do you pick up a lot of new gigs from the public ones?
"Yes, because unless people are at a wedding then they're less likely to see you. Often, people at our regular gigs will approach us for their wedding, or their friend's wedding. So it's a good idea to have cards you can give to them with your contact details on it, and not just say 'Well, here's my number'. You need to be ready for that eventuality. If you're prepared and you're representing yourself well, then it's more likely people will come back. If you're writing your

name on someone's hand or something like that it could wash off, and it's not a good look!"

What do you do outside of the 'wedding season'?
"It does drop off – some people do like to get married in winter, but not as many – so if you're trying to make a living from this, then you'll want to book in lots of bar gigs during winter. But the business never stops, because that's when people start to get their weddings together."

Do you find more and more people are having weddings during weekdays?
"Yeah, that's definitely true. It's opening up a lot more than I expected. So you have to be ready for the weekday ones, especially if you or any of your band members have other jobs. You normally have to take the next day off because you won't finish until 2am or something."

Do you specialise in any kind of music?
"No, we make a point of not specialising in any kind of music. If you limit the styles you play then you're potentially limiting the number of gigs you're going to get. If you're a function band then you have to accommodate everyone of all ages, because you never know what kind of audience you're gonna get. So the more styles and songs you can play, the

more likely it is people are going to latch on to you. You can't be too precious about that sort of thing and get too 'muso' about it. A lot of bands and musicians take themselves very seriously, and although what you do should and has to be taken seriously, that side of things should be left behind closed doors. If you go to play at a wedding thinking you're Radiohead, then you're gonna find yourself some stumbling blocks. The idea is that you want to make people smile and dance, so you can't take yourself that seriously. It won't work."

How many songs do you have in rotation?
"Hundreds! We tend to learn songs along the way. We've got maybe 200 to 300 songs that we have on rotation to fall back on. We never stick to a setlist, instead we tend to read the audience – what they're reacting to and what they like. We're always adding to the set, too."

Is there a song that comes up as a request at every gig?
"Yeah, there's always three or four songs that we get asked for. Mr Brightside has got to be number one, it comes up over and over again. We get asked for Stereophonics quite a lot, and Arctic Monkeys and The Jam too."

How do you go about selecting the songs you learn?
"In the beginning, we put a set together from songs that we'd all learnt in previous bands. For the ongoing stuff, it's the ones that people request the most, plus you hear stuff on the radio, or remember an old tune you like. Sometimes, we'll all put 10 songs forward, then from those 40 we choose the ones that work the best. We might learn 40 songs and then only really carry on with 10 or 15 of them."

Do you have to learn a new 'first-dance' request for every wedding you perform at?
"Yeah usually, probably about 70 percent of the time. We actually offer that as part of our fee. Within reason, I mean if there's an orchestral piece or something then we might have to say 'Umm, could you maybe just do Is This Love or something?' But it's beneficial to do that, because it's nice for people to have something played especially for them, because it's their day."

Your band has quite a strong look, is this important?
"Yeah, I think it's important to have a look or a style that sets you apart, as with any business. I think you need to make it an event for the people that are booking you. It should stand out, and you're entertaining people so it's important to be entertaining. And it gives some sort of uniformity to what you're doing. You can't very well turn up to a wedding in a pair of shorts and a baseball cap."

Do you need to cover a lot of bases sonically?
"Not too much. I keep it quite simple, I have a few pedals; a reverb and delay, an overdrive and a wah – which I hardly ever use. My amp is a Fender Twin, so I use a boost to drive it a bit harder. We bring spare guitars with us, but only really in case a string goes."

Do you worry about making sure you use the right gear for each different song?
"It doesn't matter too much about the absolute specifics of a sound. I think it depends on the player. I've got a Strat and an

© Jesse Wild

SG, we just try to play the song right and get the tones right on whatever you're using. It saves time with swapping around guitars, but you don't need to be too precious. People aren't really going to be listening out for that, apart from other musicians and the band. We do songs in our own style as well, so it's less about the sound; as long as the people are enjoying it and we're playing it right then that's what's important."

"WE'VE GOT MAYBE 200 TO 300 SONGS THAT WE HAVE ON ROTATION"

So people are looking out for the parts that they recognise, rather than the specific sounds?
"Exactly. For example, we play Take On Me sometimes, and I learned the main riff on guitar and play it distorted. It's the riff that they notice, not that it was originally played on a keyboard!"

Do you give a breakdown of what you'll provide?
"Yeah, absolutely. It's important for people to know what they're paying for. Even if they just want a general quote, I tend to send through a list of every eventuality. For example, we're a four-piece, but we can also play as a three-piece – of course, this costs less. And underneath, we'll say 'For this amount, you'll be getting:', with bullet points, and include the insurance, lighting and length of time, etc. It's just better that way because then everyone is clear about what they're getting and it saves problems down the road."

Talk us through the average wedding gig...
"Usually, people want us to start playing at about eight-ish. What that means for us is that we have to pick up our gear at about 3pm, load up and drive to the venue. If it's relatively

Make sure you get your look right and you'll stand out from the competition

"YOU NEED TO MAKE IT AN EVENT FOR THE PEOPLE THAT ARE BOOKING YOU. IT SHOULD STAND OUT"

local, it's normally about an hour's drive. We'll try to get there for around 6pm. Once they've finished their meal and speeches we'll get in and start setting up. It usually takes about an hour-and-a-half to set up all of our gear and do a quick soundcheck.

"Then we'll play the first dance, and straight into the first set. Usually, we do an hour then have a break, then another hour to 90 minutes. Then we pack down, which takes about an hour. We'll normally be heading out by about 12:30, then once we've driven back to where we store our gear, we pack it all back in. So we're not usually finished until about 2/2.30am."

Do you have insurance for your gear, and liability?
"Most venues will want to see at least public liability insurance (PLI). Some will want PLI and PAT testing certificates for your gear. You kind of have to get that, because even if they don't always ask for it, maybe half of them will. That's a definite need. Usually, it's not too expensive, and you're covered for millions of pounds' worth of accidents!"

What about shared costs for the band?
"With all of the gigs that we do, we split up the fee into our percentages for each member, then a percentage goes back into the band. So we'll use that money to pay for band equipment and insurance. It's up to us individually to insure for our own gear."

Writing your number on a beer mat won't cut it – get some cards made up

How to... GET BOOKED!

Guitarist and vocalist Ollie Thomas on the dos and don'ts of playing in a function band

SET YOUR GOALS
"Make sure that everyone in the band is on the same page from the start. Not only that everyone has the time to do it, but that they have a similar vision for what you're doing. How often you'll be gigging – if you're successful, you can forget about weekends – where you want to take it. Otherwise, it can get pretty messy. You've got to make sure that you're with people that you get along with, and that if there are any problems then you can discuss them properly without ruining your friendship, thus ruining the band."

BUILD YOUR WEB
For most people, booking a wedding band is a huge deal. Make it easy for them by building a website with shots, sound clips and videos of your band. "Having a good online presence is important, too, with a website, Facebook, etc. It's worth investing a little bit on that with photos, too. Put demos on your site from Soundcloud or YouTube – potential clients can see that you can actually do it."

PLAY THE PART, NOT THE TONE
Chances are, the type of music you will be playing may have hooks and riffs that weren't written for guitar. If you can't replicate the sound exactly, fear not! "If it's recognisable and it sounds good, it's fine. It's the song that you're learning, if there's a hook that people are going to automatically latch on to then it's important that you get that right."

GET EQUIPPED
PA systems, lights, microphones for speeches, these are all things that are commonly requested at functions. "It's really good to be self-sufficient if you can be. If somebody books you, you want to be able to give them as easy a ride as possible. You learn a lot along the way. You'll find that people ask the same sort of things, and those are the things that you have to listen to because those are the things that will get you booked or not booked. If it's a reasonable request and you can do it, then do!"

OFFER ADDITIONAL ENTERTAINMENT
"We bring an iPod that has a mix of general wedding/background music. Just fun, inoffensive party music that's not already in our set. If they have a set on an iPod that they want, then we can just plug it in. Sometimes, they'll want to have music after we've played, too, so we'll leave the PA set up while we pack everything else down, and agree that once we're finished with everything else then we'll pack the PA down."

TOOLS FOR TRADING
Work eBay's features

Search
You can sort your search in many different ways (time, distance, listing type). For late bargains, check out auction-style listings that are about to end. To get an early bargain, filter your search by newly listed items that have a 'Buy It Now' option.

Use categories
Searching by product name is great if you know what you're looking for, but viewing a category and filtering as above can produce some cool surprises.

Make offers
If there's a 'Best Offer' option, use it and push your luck. Don't worry about offending the seller – they don't have to accept it...

Set alerts
eBay's mobile app can notify you when items you're watching/bidding on are ending, or have been listed. Set up alerts and 'saved searches' for newly listed items and eBay will notify you when they are added..

Time your bid
There's often a flurry of bidding activity in the last 60 seconds of an auction. By bidding on a seemingly cheap auction three days before it ends, you're effectively only pushing the final price up. Decide a maximum price you're willing to pay for the item (don't forget postage costs) and stick to it. Try to wait as long as you can to place your bid (the last 30 seconds is advisable). If you don't win, don't worry, another one will be along shortly!

BUY AND SELL GEAR

How to turn old gear into new money

Buying and selling used gear is a great way to make extra money. If you know a decent amount about guitar gear and are savvy, it's actually very achievable!

Choose your level
Buying/selling gear requires a minimum level of capital – you don't have to start out trading vintage Les Pauls. Effects are abundant on eBay, and you can pick up some bargains if you're clever. Choose an area you know about, and do your research.

Buy from the right places
To seek out bargains, you need to be looking where other people are not. eBay, local papers, Gumtree and even supermarket noticeboards can be great places to keep an eye on. There's a lot of other junk to wade through, but persist and it'll pay off.

And sell in the right ones, too
When it comes to selling your gear, you need to do the opposite; expose your advert to the biggest and most relevant audience possible. This is often eBay, but guitar forums, Facebook groups and dedicated reader ads pages such as the ones found in our sister mag, Guitarist, will put your gear in front of the right people.

Use eBay's tools
Take advantage of eBay's search tools (see above) to find the best deals. You can also exploit sloppy typing by using Fatfingers; a site that searches eBay for spelling mistakes, meaning you might spot a badly-listed bargain.

Make it presentable
Once you've snagged a bargain that you can make some money on, it's time to get selling. Tidy up the gear – a sad-looking guitar with broken strings, missing controls and covered in grime can be transformed with some cheap replacements and a clean. Make sure your gear works and looks good before you sell.

Sell, sell, sell!
Be clear about what you're selling, what's included and what isn't. Write a description detailing the product, what it does, how it sounds, the features included, and point out any defects, too (cosmetic or otherwise). If you're selling on eBay, good photos are a must. Shoot in good light at the highest resolution possible, and upload three or four photos from different angles, including any damage.

Don't forget the fees
eBay and PayPal charge a commission for listing, selling and receiving payments. This will eat into your profits, so don't forget to factor this, plus the cost of postage into your buying and selling rates.

Then deliver
Communication and honesty are key. Package the item properly, stick to the delivery times you state, and stay in touch with the buyer until it's delivered. Your reputation as a seller hinges on the feedback of happy buyers.

Stay safe!
Online buying/selling is built on trust, but things can go wrong. Get as much contact info from the person you're dealing with as you can. PayPal offers an extra level of payment protection, and if you're using eBay, always do transactions through the proper channels.

START TEACHING

Earn some cash by passing on your skills to others

If you can play to a decent standard you have a wealth of knowledge you can exchange for cold, hard cash. Two years ago, BIMM graduate Richard Hillyer gave up his day job and started Mobile Guitar Tuition. Here's his advice on getting started...

**Richard Hillyer
Guitar Tutor
richardhillyer
music.co.uk**

How did you get started teaching?
It's only recently, in the last two years, that I've turned professional. I did have a job before. I used to work at Sainsbury's. It just wasn't for me. I did it for a very long time. I did it about six years.

I went to BIMM in Bristol and I did a course on professional musicianship. As part of my course, I had to look at maybe setting up a business and that sort of thing. I branched out from there. I started thinking about setting up the business properly, taking on more than one client, properly advertising, getting a website together, and all of the online stuff.

As part of BIMM, I had to do a market analysis and see who was out there, what they were charging, and competition in my area as well to see who I would be up against. So that's what I did. That's how it came about. I took on one student. Then they told a few friends and all that sort of thing. It was word of mouth. Then I got another couple of students. It just built up over time, really.

Did you have to invest in any equipment?
The massive thing I had to buy was a car to get around. That was the main thing I had to invest in, a decent, reliable, car that was going to get me around from A to B, without any problems.

I had most of the equipment I needed, but I did buy a Taylor GS Mini just because I wanted something I could travel around with. I also bought an iPad for my teaching materials, so I could have Spotify on my iPad. I use Spotify for all the songs that we're learning, which means we can refer to it quite quickly.

How about teaching grades, do you do that?
Yes, I do. I teach grades. I teach the Rockschool and the RGT Grades. I teach Electric and Acoustic Grades. it's pretty popular. It's especially popular with children, because they like to have an achievement. They love getting certificates. They love all that sort of stuff because they can put it up in their room. It's really nice for them to get a sense of achievement.

Where do most of your lessons take place?

It's mobile guitar lessons, so I travel to most of my students. I think it's quite a popular service because parents don't have to stress about getting to you, and travelling across town and things like that. I charge a small little fee for covering petrol and other things.

Then I'd say that probably about 10 to 15 per cent of my business is Skype lessons. Skype is obviously more convenient for me. I can do it from anywhere where I've got my computer.

How have you gone about building up the Skype tuition side of the business?

I've got a website. So it's advertising and pushing that. That's what I'm doing now as well, offering both services just to give people options. I teach somebody who's got a disability, so he can't get out and about. He doesn't like people coming to his house because he gets very nervous, so he prefers to use Skype. He's more relaxed and it works for him.

How do the Skype guitar lessons work from a technical point of view?

I use a very simple set-up. I think that's the best way to go instead of having a really complicated set-up. I've got my MacBook Pro and it has a decent HD web camera built into it. I literally just use that for the video. The same on the other end, the other person has a webcam and they do exactly the same thing.

What about audio, do you just play live in your room or is there a DI'ing sort of scenario?

No, I play live in the room [using the onboard microphone] and it usually works out pretty well.

Do you run into any technical problems when you're teaching this way?

You can't play at the same time [as each other]. You have to play and show them and then stop and let them play back. When I first did it, it was quite strange and you're playing over each other, but I've got used to it now. I know that you've got to stop and let them do it. I also send them backing tracks for them to practise with.

How useful is word of mouth for finding students?

It's very important to have a good rapport with your students, and with their parents – if they put in a good word for you to anyone else they know. They're always in with all the schools and things like that so it's always really good, but I think word of mouth is pretty important.

How important is your online presence?

You have to have a good website. Obviously, a recognisable website so people can see if you're a brand. Facebook is pretty important as well, everyone's on Facebook aren't they? I've used Facebook Ads a few times.

What about flyers?

I've done flyers. I had professional flyers printed and I went round music shops and put them out in there. I've also got them up in shops in the local area.

Is there a lot of 'business' stuff to take care of, too?

I knew it was a big part of it. I knew you had to have a business head and be switched on and do your tax returns and things like that, but I didn't realise how on it you have to be with all your accounts. It changed my mindset completely. I had to keep all my receipts. Before, I used to probably just put them somewhere or bin them. Obviously, I keep all my petrol receipts, to claim back; any purchases I buy for equipment or anything like that to claim back at the end of the year. I have to keep all that all up together, so it was a bit of a learning curve to be honest, but I've got used to it now. I keep a spreadsheet myself on my computer. So every day I'll sit down on an evening and I'll update it. As long as I do it every evening I know I'm on top of it!

"I'D SAY 10 TO 15 PER CENT OF MY BUSINESS IS SKYPE LESSONS. I CAN DO IT FROM ANYWHERE"

Remote lessons via Skype can be a really convenient way of teaching students

How to...
START TEACHING

Even if you're not thinking of getting into teaching as a full-time profession, it's important to go about it in the right way. Here are some key points to consider when getting set up

DON'T LIMIT YOURSELF

If you can competently play and understand more than one style of music, then don't stick to teaching one style. "I teach all sorts of styles to be honest, blues, rock, pop, funk. I can see the benefits of being a specialist and teaching one sort of niche, but it opens you up to more business if you can teach more styles."

LISTEN TO WHAT THE STUDENT WANTS TO LEARN

Don't push your students to learn things they don't want to. "Some students are not interested in doing grades at all, and want to learn for fun, but I think it's a good option to have and suggest to them if they're not sure where they want to go."

NO STUDIO? WORK AROUND IT!

Not everyone has a dedicated studio space to teach in, but as Rich has proved, there are other ways. "I still live at [my parents' house]. That's one of the reasons why I went mobile from the beginning, because it was a bit like a train station. There'd be someone coming in, someone coming out. With it being my parents' house, it didn't really work too well. Luckily, I do my Skype lessons in the day, so my parents are at work. It works quite well."

THINK ABOUT PRESENTATION

Ditch the dog-eared pad and scratchy handwriting! Your students will thank you for it and you can build up a library of lessons to re-use. "I use something called Neck Diagrams. It's great for drawing out chord diagrams or scale diagrams. Then I can copy the diagrams into Word and make a really nice document to give to students. Also, Guitar Pro, I use that for printing out tablature."

SOCIAL MEDIA IS YOUR FRIEND

When it comes to teaching, word of mouth has become word of Facebook. Keeping a decent profile page can give potential students a place to find out about your services. "I've been trying to get on there every day and post something, even if it's just a video of one of my students playing, just to keep everyone interacting and keep your name on the scene. If you set up a Facebook page and don't update it, people start switching off, start leaving your page and not being interested in it."

IT'S NOT JUST ABOUT TECHNIQUE

There's more to learning guitar than the technical side of playing. Being able to advise on instruments, effects and even tuning is important, too. "I think it's good if you can teach a student how to tune a guitar, or how to use certain effects to help get the sound they want to get. I think it is good to be able to set up the instrument as well, if you can teach them how to do that. They're all valuable skills that you need to learn.

"It's all stuff that I didn't learn with my teacher, unfortunately. I had to learn along the way."

THE 'T-WORD'

It's important to know where you stand with tax. "You need to do that, otherwise you can get yourself in a lot of trouble if you don't keep an eye on your accounts. I have an accountant as well. She just submits [my tax return] for me.

"I sit down with her and she reads it all over, checks everything's okay and all in order, then we submit it together."

Don't give your students hand-drawn chord diagrams, use a program such as Notion

BECOME A DEMO GUY

Show those Saturday afternoon shop shredders how it's done

YouTube views can earn you money over a period of time, but offering your services to a local store could pay even more. Here's how to become a video demonstrator in your spare time

Video
You'll need a way of recording and editing your videos, but this doesn't need to cost a fortune. Your smartphone will most likely shoot video to a decent standard, and if you have only one camera, you can shoot close-ups and other gear shots afterwards.

Audio
People want to know how a piece of gear really sounds; this means you need to capture your audio as transparently as possible. Electric guitars can be captured directly using an amp modeler, but don't rely on the mic from your phone. Get a decent mic for capturing amps and acoustics and record into a mutitrack, field recorder or DAW. If your amp has an emulated output, consider this. You can use the audio from your phone to help with syncing later...

Keep the chat brief...
People want to hear the gear, not you, so open with some playing, keep the talking to a minimum and get to the good bit, quickly.

Keep it simple
You know who's better at being Guthrie Govan than you? Guthrie Govan, and there are loads of videos of him online already. Play realistic parts well, and remember, this is about the gear, not your technical chops. Try to steer clear of playing over other

people's songs, too – YouTube can block videos containing copyright material, and it could affect your ability to earn money from your video.

Editing
Simple editing software is all you need to put your videos together. Programs such as iMovie are cheap (free if you buy a new Mac), plus GoPro Studio is available from GoPro's website for free, and works on PC or Mac. You don't even need a GoPro camera to use it! Keep your edit snappy, and use the alternative angles/close-ups where applicable.

Build your following
If you're planning on becoming a demo guy for a shop or gear company, you need to show that what you can do actually works. Use a relevant and professional name, build up a following, title and tag your videos so they're easy to find, and encourage people to subscribe to your channel.

The pitch
When you've built your online video empire, it's time to start approaching potential clients. Do your research before making contact with them; what brands/price-points does the shop stock? Is it suited to your style? Does the shop already have an online presence? What benefits will your demos be

to the store (driving sales, raising awareness)? Get this info straight and you'll have the workings of a punchy, targeted pitch.

Seize your moment
Music shops are busy places – particularly independent stores – so you need to time it right. Find out who you need to talk to (the manager, not the work experience kid) and call ahead to arrange an appointment with them. Visit stores in person, preferably armed with a laptop/tablet loaded with your videos. Be professional, polite and realistic about what you can do and what they will get out of this arrangement. Avoid Saturdays, and don't turn up 10 minutes before they shut.

Make it work
Any guitar store that is producing its own video demos has one main objective: to sell the gear it's demoing. Branding, watermarks, repetitive mentions of the store's name and price of the gear are common features of these kinds of videos, so you'll need to include these. Also, don't forget to include a link to 'buy it now' in your video's description.

SONGWRITING

Starting – that is the biggest hurdle to songwriting. No matter what you say there is a song inside you that wants to come out. And the sooner it does the better: because once you've written one song more will follow. Over the next few pages we will arm you with confidence and inspiration, supply you with hints and tips, and even point out helpful gear to get you writing songs right now.

START WRITING SONGS TODAY

You want to write a song – so where do you start?

You've been staring at that blank sheet of paper for half an hour. Any minute now your musical opus will appear in all its glory, forever to be referenced in the great annals of rock history. Hmm, if only it were that easy...

What's more likely is that you'll hit a blank after kicking off with G, Em and C, and then procrastinate by putting all the bins out and wasting hours achieving Major General II rank on Call Of Duty. Now what?

Getting started with the songwriting process is a common hurdle. Strumming a few chords seems to provide the opening of a song – but what have you actually written? Chord patterns are sometimes false friends, because by keeping you brain occupied they can steer you away from more difficult creative decisions, such as the chorus melody or the central meaning of the lyric.

It's a delicate art, certainly, but we're going to help jump start your creativity by filling that empty sheet of paper with something that can be developed (with a bit of editing and a smidge of effort) into a complete song.

Beginning

Of course, writing an entire song is daunting. So just write the title. Easy. Titles can come from anywhere: movies, places, people, objects or events – you can even (if you must) steal lyric fragments from other songs. Write each title quickly and move onto the next. Don't worry about whether they're any good or not. A good title may inspire you – more than that same old G to Em strum – to tell an interesting story.

Some guitar-playing songwriters find lyric writing a chore. And for many of us, creating lyrical ideas, particularly identifying the central theme or meaning, is the most challenging part of the songwriting process. If you concentrate on writing the lyric on its own and add the music later, this problem disappears. People often find the stage that follows (known as 'word setting') to be easier than writing melodies from scratch.

Melody

Now, it's time to lose the guitar. If you try to improvise over backing chords, you can end up pushing your voice into singing static notes that are based around major or minor pentatonic scales. Put your guitar down and sing a melody 'from nowhere' – then, once you've created something you like, pick your guitar up again and work out which chords sound right with the tune. This way, the harmony serves the melody, rather than the other way around.

Another approach is to write a new lyric for a well-known melody. With that task done, the next step is to write a new melody for your new lyric. By replacing both elements one at a time, you've used basic editing techniques to create something completely original.

Rhythm

Now to set the pace. If you don't have an obedient drummer nearby, you can use a drum machine, keyboard or computer to get a beat. Set a tempo of 120bpm or faster, and sing over the top. This has several important effects on your creative brain. First, it forces you to work at a faster tempo than your strumming hand is likely to create on its own, which is great if you're trying to write rock, metal or dance. Second, it encourages you to sing only words that work with the beat. Some words just don't 'sing well', and if you've got a relentless groove going while you're trying out ideas, it will help you identify the rogue syllables.

Loops can be helpful as well, if you're trying to write memorable riffs (most shareware or professional music software now has some kind of built-in looper function). The presence of drums filling up the bar means you're more likely to play a sparser guitar part, which is easier for an audience to remember.

Finally, if you've tried all of the above and you're still stuck, then enlist a songwriting pal. Many a creative idea has been sparked by knocking heads together, and this approach provides an instant audience for every new idea from each songwriter. There's an added psychological benefit to committing to a co-write, too. The very fact that you've agreed to meet will force you to get started and, of equal importance, to get the song finished.

Try writing a title first. A good one may inspire you more than that same old G to Em strum

STAY INSPIRED

Here are 10 simple ways to keep the creativity flowing in your songwriting and to keep you on track

There is no correct way to write a song, but there are many different methods to spark ideas for your next composition. Helping creativity flow to develop your ideas can be as simple as changing basic habits you may have. Try a few of these and you'll notice the difference.

1 GET A ROOM

Playing your guitar in different rooms in your house will affect the way it sounds, and may unlock new songwriting ideas. Take your bathroom as an example. Tiles make for an excellent echo chamber, which can suddenly make your arpeggiated acoustic verses sound even more dramatic – and even give you that push to write the chorus. No wonder Paul Simon wrote the haunting Simon & Garfunkel classic The Sound Of Silence in the loo...

2 USE YOUR PHONE

If you have an idea for a melody, rhythm or a chord progression and you need to capture if fast before you forget, the answer is in your pocket. Most mobile phones have the ability to record audio. You might find it becomes the missing link between inspiration and a finished song, so keep recording all those ideas wherever and whenever they arise.

3 DO THE OPPOSITE

Test your melodies. That 'record every idea you have' rule is all very well, but there's also another school of thought. Let Paul McCartney explain about how he and Mr Lennon worked: "I don't think I had a Dictaphone. I don't think they even had Dictaphones then, but the rule was: if you can't remember them, they're no good – and it's actually a very good rule!"

4 BE ENVIRONMENTAL

The space you play in can either inspire or stifle you. Shut the cat out, turn the TV off and get yourself comfortable. You want to find a place where you won't feel self-conscious or get interrupted. If that means taking your acoustic outside, cranking your amp in the garage or simply playing through headphones, do what you need to.

5 CHANGE GUITARS

Different types of guitar make you play in a certain way. When we pick up our office SG, the first thing we do is start riffing, but if a parlour guitar is around we'll be fingerpicking in no time. One of your guitars may become a long-time writing partner. You've heard the phrase 'this guitar has a lot of songs in it' – let instinct drive you: if you feel like a new instrument will inspire you to write, buy it!

6 LISTEN TO NEW MUSIC
Probably the greatest motivation to create your own music is hearing what other musicians have created. Find new music on Spotify, watch the bands you love and local bands you've never heard before. A great chorus, a tone, a goosebump-raising emotion; every little detail and big impression you take in when hearing a new song can end up sparking your own songwriting and finding a different way to approach your guitar.

7 DON'T SING
It's very easy to get into the habit of writing vocal melodies as you write the guitar music. That's fine, but it can sometimes create melodic and structural ruts in your writing. Try carrying through with an

"GO AND WATCH BANDS YOU LOVE AND LOCAL BANDS YOU'VE NEVER HEARD BEFORE"

instrumental guitar idea and seeing where you can take it musically before coming in with your vocal melody ideas.

8 DON'T REFUSE THE MUSE
Inspiration doesn't work to the clock. Sometimes you'll free up some precious time to write music and nothing will come. Then later, when you're busy with other things and your brain is working overtime, a musical

idea will suddenly pop into your head. It may not be convenient but roll with it. Even if it means humming a chorus into your phone in the office toilets.

9 SOUNDTRACK
Stuck on how to capture atmosphere in your writing? Get some practice by turning your TV to mute and trying to soundtrack what you see when you're channel hopping. You'll be surprised what you're capable of with some imagination.

10 USE YOUR EFFECTS
This is great if you always reach for the same shapes and sounds. Try plugging into your effects pedals or amp software when you're writing. You'll be surprised how you can come up with parts that are directly inspired by time/rhythmic effects such as delay, tremolo or phaser. Using effects to stimulate creativity works for Rage Against The Machine's Tom Morello and U2's The Edge, so try it yourself.

SONG STORIES

Join us as we sit down to hear the fascinating stories behind the making of 14 truly timeless songs, as told to us by the artists who wrote them...

GET LUCKY
DAFT PUNK FEAT PHARRELL WILLIAMS, RANDOM ACCESS MEMORIES (2013)
Written by Thomas Bangalter, Guy-Manuel de Homem-Christo, Pharrell Williams, Nile Rodgers

Nile Rodgers: "I met [Daft Punk] 17 years ago. We had tried to hook up on a couple of earlier occasions, it just never happened. The way that it all worked out, they called me up and said they had a song [Get Lucky], and they thought it'd be cool if I played on it. Well, sure.

"I happened to be in New York, and we recorded it at the same studio where Chic cut their very first single – Jimi Hendrix's place, Electric Lady [Studios]. Total vibe. It couldn't have been more perfect.

"They didn't have any explanation for asking me, other than, 'This is what we've always loved.' But it developed into more than just me playing on a song. They specifically asked me, 'How did you make Chic records?' So I said, 'Well, I'll tell ya how.' I explained to them the layering process that went on, the cleanliness, the tightness. In Chic, we were limited by the capabilities of the technology. Everything we did was a musical work-around. So that meant we had to play this stuff perfectly, because we couldn't move it from one place to the next. We never used click tracks, because we thought click tracks were for musicians that were lame. You've got to remember, this was the spirit of the time, the credo of the music scene. Anybody who needed to use a click track, to us, was somebody who couldn't play."

"Yeah. My vibe with Get Lucky was, 'Well, here's the deal guys, here's how we did it in Chic.' Every Chic record was created with a room full of people, all playing at the same time, but in this particular case, they had already tracked Get Lucky with live musicians, so I couldn't have interplay with the guys because their parts existed already. I thought to myself, 'Well, I can't really play the ultimate guitar part based on what they already have.' So I had them strip it all away, cut everything out except for the live drums. I just listened to the drums, played my ultimate guitar part for that song, and after I did my part, everybody said, 'Wait a minute! He's got his hooky part – let me do my hooky part!' So then everybody went back and cut to me."

TEENAGE KICKS
THE UNDERTONES, TEENAGE KICKS (1978)
Written by John O'Neill

John O'Neill: "I remember coming up with the title," John says. "We used to cover [R&B standard] Route 66, which has the line 'Get your kicks on Route 66', and we also liked Back In The USA by the MC5. One of the songs on that album is called Teenage Lust, so it didn't take a rocket scientist to come up with the title of Teenage Kicks. I can't believe someone didn't come up with it before me.

"We were also big Ramones fans, and it was easy to hear where their influences had come from when you listened to their records – The Shangri-Las and that whole New York R&B sound like The Crystals and The Ronettes. I loved all that, too, and Dion And The Belmonts. A lot of these old rock 'n' roll songs have that same C/Am/F/G chord progression, and I was just messing about, trying to come up with our own riff. It just seemed natural for us to write like that.

"We were getting close to breaking up because we weren't getting anywhere, so we planned to record this EP just to document the fact that a punk band existed in Derry at one point. We never had any expectations that we'd make a living out of it.

"We knew them all backwards. It was all done on first takes. We'd done a show in Belfast the night before, so we just banged the songs out. Teenage Kicks is such an easy song to play, anyway. All those early punk songs are basically just barre chords and Chuck Berry-style riffs.

"I'd been listening to John Peel since 1974, and he was the best thing on radio. I'd never heard him play a record twice in a row and say that it was one of the greatest records he'd ever heard. We couldn't believe it – because we didn't think the song was all that great! It was an amazing compliment that he loved it so much."

MORE THAN WORDS
EXTREME, EXTREME II: PORNOGRAFFITTI (1990)
Written by Nuno Bettencourt, Gary Cherone

Nuno Bettencourt: "It wasn't purposely written, I think I was sitting on a porch somewhere. It might have been at Gary's house. When we were first starting out I was crashing at his place a lot. The song came pretty quick. I was singing and hearing this melody and doing the chord changes. I ran into the house and grabbed a little Fostex four-track recorder and threw the song down as quickly as possible.

"At the time I didn't know if it was good. I knew it was interesting and a different-sounding song. But it wasn't like I was sitting there thinking, 'I just wrote a hit.' The melody was dictating where the chords were going. I remember telling Gary, 'Look, I've got something pretty interesting here.' We quickly attacked it lyrically. It all came together in a half hour period."

"I think when we were recording it I thought it would get bigger with strings and drums. It was really tempting, trust me. But I think that was probably the best decision I ever made, to keep it as naked as possible. It's one of those songs that people don't get too tired of. Maybe the simplicity of it kept it tolerable."

"It's that thing of updating cheesy clichés: I like doing that. The rhythm for 'Coffee + TV' is very old"

COFFEE + TV
BLUR, 13 (1999)
Written by Graham Coxon (lyrics), music (Blur)

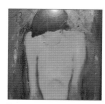

Graham Coxon: "Coffee + TV is about the idea that you feel like a piece of s**t in a crap job, and you want to marry someone and get away from it all. Damon [Albarn] was writing it, and he said, 'I can't get anything together for this', so I said, 'Well, I'll write some lyrics tonight'. So I went home, and had a big row with my girlfriend, because I'd gone through some old sketch books looking for little bits of writing that might help with this lyric, and she thought that I was writing a song about an old girlfriend. So she went off her head at me! I sang the verse, because in Blur it was basically that thing where if you write the words then you sing it, like the 'Oh my baby' bits in Tender."

"It's that thing of updating cheesy clichés: I like doing that. That rhythm is very old. I liked Link Wray and I think it's really a Simon & Garfunkel kinda rhythm. There's a Sonic Youth song called Sunday that has that similar rhythm, too, but I think the biggest influence for me was Stockholm Syndrome by Yo La Tengo, from an amazing album called I Can Hear The Heart Beating As One, which is this almost Neil Young-y thing. The Coffee + TV chord shapes are just ridiculous. They're just unusual. They're not normal. They're sort of minor chords going against major chords. That's another case of me making life very difficult for myself!"

HEY, SOUL SISTER
TRAIN, SAVE ME SAN FRANCISCO (2009)
Written by Patrick Monahan, Espen Lind, Amund Bjørklund

Espen Lind: "We were huge fans of the band and, for me, Drops Of Jupiter [the title track of Train's 2001 sophomore album] is a modern classic. "We were hooked up with the band by the A&R guy on the record, Pete Ganbarg, who asked if we wanted to do something with Pat Monahan, the singer. And we said, 'Yeah, sure!' So we hooked up at our studio in New York and started writing. I think we probably wrote about five or six songs over the course of a couple of months and Hey, Soul Sister was, like, the last song we completed. It was completed around midnight on our very last day!

"Pat came in and said, 'I want to play something completely different today – I want to try to do something more dancey with a backbeat.' He was referencing old 80s records, like INXS, and old sort of four-on-the-floor beats, so we started playing around with something like that. I came up with the music and he ad-libbed over the top of it. He came up with the lyric, 'Hey, soul sister' and the basic outline for the melody, but when we listened back to it with the music I put down, it sounded all right, but it wasn't amazing.

"I just love the ukulele – it's a great instrument for anything from doing simple overdubs to melody lines to just picking up the energy in the control room, and we had Pat lay down a scratch vocal. Then I just stripped away all the music underneath, put down the kick drumbeat, and then I just grabbed the ukulele, started playing around with new chords underneath the stuff that he was singing. And then, all of a sudden, the song was there. I remember, in the control room, me and my partner, Amund, and Pat... we all sort of flipped out, because it sounded so cool and so fresh and so new!

"The A&R and the label actually didn't like it, originally. They were like, 'Yeah, yeah, it's a fun song, but it's never going to get on the radio; it sounds way too weird! It's not going to work!' But I have to hand it to Pat Monahan and Train's manager, Jonathan Daniel, who both loved the song and really fought hard for it. They said, 'No, this is going to be the first single off the album!' And they stood their ground and they got their way. And now the song has sold millions worldwide, and has extended the band's career for many, many years!"

GIMME ALL YOUR LOVIN'
ZZ TOP, ELIMINATOR (1983)
Written by Billy Gibbons, Dusty Hill, Frank Beard

Billy Gibbons: "Gimme All Your Lovin' came together in two parts. The basic track appeared initially, inspired by the guitar riff, which clicked with the rhythm section right off. The words came later, drawing inspiration from Mick [Jagger] and [Keef's] stylistic works. After remaining in exile for a week in room 501 at the Peabody hotel, the pieces were intact. The take-out from Molly's Mexican Cantina kept us going to see it through!

"The solo? Oh, yeah, one take, that! Cutting the rare, one-time take is a bonus, a true reward, falling out of the sky so to speak. That one unfolded in the control room and the up-close proximity with the rhythm track made for a live-like experience. The tail-out solo was tracked during a subsequent session."

Billy Gibbons' writing was powered by Molly's Mexican Cantina...

(DON'T FEAR) THE REAPER
BLUE ÖYSTER CULT, AGENTS OF FORTUNE (1976)
Written by Donald 'Buck Dharma' Roeser

Buck Dharma: "It was one of those things that just sort of fell off my fingers, and I knew I had something there because I liked it the first time I heard it. I was like, 'Wow!' The first two lines of the lyric, again, just sort of came from my head rather unbidden. Then the idea of the song took shape but it took about six weeks to write the rest of it.

"It's a love story that transcends the death of one of the partners and then they get back together again in another plain. It's not about suicide, although I can see how people can think that, but that's not where it's at. It just imagines that there is an afterlife and that lovers will be reunited... Dying is a part of life, so don't fear it, just know that it's there for everybody and it just happens at different times.

"When we were mixing the record and listening to the playback, we knew we had something good, but we had no idea what it was going to do! We were thinking that it was going to be a strong FM radio track, and in those days hit radio was AM and album radio was FM, so we thought we'd have a good album track for FM radio. But beyond that – that it would actually take off and be a hit single? We had no idea!

"I think the song really resonates with people and it doesn't seem to matter how old they are or what generation they come from. And for that I am grateful... it's almost had a life of its own. I don't even think it's mine sometimes – it's just out there! It's unlike the rest of our music and it's unlike the rest of the songs I've written,   too, which is funny."

THE WEIGHT
THE BAND, MUSIC FROM THE BIG PINK (1968)
Written by Robbie Robertson

Robbie Robertson: "I wrote the song in Woodstock, in a house that I had there in a place called Larson Lane. I went upstairs in this house, where I had a table and a guitar, and it was kind of my little workshop area... And when I sat down to try to think of something, I realised I had nothing in mind. I thought, 'Oh s**t!' because some days it comes and some days it doesn't. I sat the guitar on my lap and I was kind of bent over it and I looked inside the sound hole on the guitar and it said 'Nazareth, Pennsylvania' [where Martin guitars are primarily based]. I thought, 'Okay, well let me see,' and I wrote the first line of that song ['I pulled into Nazareth / Was feeling about half past dead'] and I would say, in probably 45 minutes, I had written the skeleton of the whole song."

"I played it for the other guys, to get this thing started. And everybody was like, 'Hell, well that sounds pretty good!' And I said to them, 'Well, it'll just be a back-up song in case some other things don't work out.'

"We didn't really get it that organised until we recorded it," says Robertson. "And it came pretty simply. There was something about it that was so natural that it didn't take a lot of organising... And then this thing at the end of the chorus where the voices stagger for that last line? It was a thing that came to me, like, in the last minute of working on the song. A lot of people say those spontaneous things are the best things and, well, this is one of those cases where that was very true!"

HOTEL CALIFORNIA
THE EAGLES, HOTEL CALIFORNIA (1977)
Written by Don Felder, Glenn Frey, Don Henley

Don Felder: "I had rented a house on the beach in Malibu that summer and we were writing songs for what was going to become the Hotel California album and we'd just come off One Of These Nights, which was a very successful record for us. But we were under the gun to come up with a lot of ideas, so I had put together a reel of say 16 or 17 song sketches – in this little reel-to- reel four-track TEAC tape recorder in my back bedroom. And I was sitting on the couch on a July day – in cutoff shorts, a t-shirt and flip-flops – playing guitar and just goofing around on the couch in this rented beach house in Malibu.

"I looked out at the California sunshine sparkling on the Pacific Ocean and my two little kids were playing in the sand on a swing-set out in front of me, and I just started playing those chords – that introductory progression to Hotel California. I just played it over and over. And I thought to myself, 'I have to go record some of this before I forget it.'

"And so I ran into my back bedroom and turned on the trusty old TEAC and played about five times through the chord progression, then turned it off and went out to join my kids. A few days later, I was looking through this reel of songs I was going to submit to the rest of the band and I thought, I like that, I'm going to finish it. I had a Rhythm Ace drum machine, which was kind of the early stages [of drum machine technology] – I laid down a track on that, put bass on it and tried to envision what Joe Walsh and I could do.

"This was the first album with Joe and I where we could do some harmony guitar stuff and trade off solos, and I wanted to write something that would have some interesting guitar stuff on it. So I pretty much overdubbed everything that you hear on the record now on this little four- track studio, except for a couple of Walsh licks at the end.

"I did a quick mix of it, put it on a cassette along with the other 16 songs, gave a copy of it to everybody in the band and said, If anybody's interested in writing or finishing one of these songs for the record, let me know. I gave a copy to Randy [Meisner, bass], to Joe and to Don Henley. Then a few days later I got a call from Henley and he said, 'I kinda like the one that sounds like a Mexican reggae song – that kind of Spanish thing.' And I knew which track he was talking about instantly. We started talking about it, and Don and Glenn kind of came up with the [lyrical] idea."

MISSISSIPPI QUEEN
MOUNTAIN, CLIMBING! (1970)
Written by Lesley West, Corky Laing, Felix Pappalardi, David Rea

Lesley West: "Corky had maybe half of the lyrics; 'Mississippi Queen / you know what I mean / She taught me everything...' and I soon came up with the guitar riff and the chord changes.

The next thing we knew, we were in the studio. I was surprised how easily it flowed out of us, because usually it takes a while and you've got to take the whole song home, work on it, and you say, 'That's not right, and that's not quite what I was looking for,' but that one really seemed to work. It was very simple to write that song. If only every song was that easy, man!"

"Initially, 'Sweet Child O' Mine' was just a cool, neat riff that I'd come up with"

GOING UNDERGROUND
THE JAM, GOING UNDERGROUND (1980)
Written by Paul Weller

Paul Weller: "It was borne out of the political state we were in at the time. Whether it was youthful paranoia or whatever, I thought we were on the brink of devastation really. We were building up our nuclear missiles.

"I can remember it taking a while to get together. It wasn't one of those tunes where I came in the studio and had it all written. We jammed on it quite a bit. There are good chords in there, without blowing my own trumpet. The chord sequence just lent itself to that key change. It's quite a cyclical chord pattern on that chorus."

"I think the song is still musically and lyrically relevant today. The line, 'You'll see kidney machines replaced by rockets and guns' is still relevant, sadly."

SWEET CHILD O' MINE
GUNS N' ROSES, APPETITE FOR DESTRUCTION (1987)
Written by Axl Rose, Slash, Izzy Stradlin, Duff McKagan, Steven Adler

Slash: "Initially it was just a cool, neat riff that I'd come up with. It was an interesting pattern and it was really melodic, but I don't think I would have presented it to the band and said, 'Hey, I've got this idea!' because I just happened to come up with it while we were all hanging around together. Izzy [Stradlin, GN'R rhythm guitarist] was the first one to start playing behind it, and once that happened Axl [Rose, singer] started making up words, and it took off that way.

"That was a very organic solo that came together simply. When we said, 'Here's the chord changes,' it occurred very spontaneously, and I always looked forward to that part of the song in the live set. It was completely different to the rest of the song."

Morello likes to keep things moving when he's jamming songs in the studio

BULLS ON PARADE
RAGE AGAINST THE MACHINE, EVIL EMPIRE (1996)
Written by Tom Morello, Zack de la Rocha, Tim Commerford, Brad Wilk

Tom Morello: "We didn't know it would be the first single when we started jamming on it," Morello tells us, "but we realised quickly that it was a most potent piece of music. We recorded demos as we wrote and jammed, we didn't want to lose any energy. Our method was pretty much 'jam, roll the cassette, then cut the real track'. Not a lot of time for over-thinking and over-tinkering.

"[Tim Commerford came up with the riff] and then I came up with the wah-wah guitar part. I also came up with the music underneath the verses – I was listening to a lot of Geto Boys back then, so I wanted something dark and sinister. Brad worked up that awesome, artillery marching beat. Hands were definitely on deck.

"When Brendan [O'Brien, producer] heard it, he zeroed right in on it and said, 'Why don't you try beginning the song that way?' It was exactly what the song needed. Zack was still writing lyrics when we cut the main track, but we knew all the changes and what we were doing. The band recorded the rhythm track live, needing only a few takes to nail it. We were pretty much a press-and-play band. We rarely used click tracks. The instinctive speeding up or slowing down of a take can make it much more exciting.

"I improvised the solo in the tracking room with headphones on. That was another toggle-switch workout, the 'scritchy- scratch' DJ part that I had previously worked into the live version of Bullet In The Head. I knew I wanted to find a home for it on record, and Bulls On Parade was the perfect place. You can play the solo with no effects – just turn your amp up to 10. But what I did was I clicked the wah all the way down so it gave me white noise. One pickup was set to 10, the other to zero, then I toggled between them while rubbing my left hand on the strings to create friction.

"The album was a strong piece of work, and I would call Bulls On Parade a real banger. With Timmy's quintessential bass sound booming throughout, it's like the world is exploding. I would also give it up for Brad and his supreme drumming – he shifts on a dime but never loses one iota of power. And Zack's lyrics are so sophisticated and multi-dimensional. As for myself, I just tried to follow the dots on the guitar neck and get some rockin' sounds. Overall, I think I held up my end."

BLACKBIRD
ALTER BRIDGE, BLACKBIRD (2007)
Written by Mark Tremonti, Myles Kennedy

Myles Kennedy (opposite, left): "It was our most collaborative song at that point, and that's one of the things that draws me to it – we were able to capture these moments. The way we were feeding off each other was like lightning in a bottle. As a musician and a writer, those are the moments that keep you going – it's like a drug. It will forever be etched in my memory as a special moment."

Mark Tremonti (opposite, right): I'd been throwing the intro part around for a while and I really loved it – it had such a sad classical feel to it. Then we were all at rehearsals, and me and Myles were trying to come up with a chorus. We've always had trouble with big choruses in a 6/8 feel. So we went into separate rooms at the rehearsal pad, and Myles came running back in with the chorus. We all loved it and ran with it. For the bridge, Myles had a musical part and I had a part. We just stacked them on top of each other and they sounded great!"

Myles Kennedy: As we got to that point musically, I had a friend I'd known for a long time that was passing away. And I remember the lyrics came pretty quick because it was just capturing that moment. I wanted him to find his peace and he did. He passed away within days of completing that song. It's such a universal theme: loss and death. I think that's part of the reason so many people gravitate towards that song; because we've all gone through it, and we're all going to continue to go through it."

Mark Tremonti: "We still think Blackbird's our best song.

Myles Kennedy: "That song is special in many ways. I'm sure in years from now it's something I'll look back on as being a crowning achievement as a writer. We all feel that way in the band."

BEATLEMANIA MASTERCLASS

25 lessons we can learn from the unrivalled songwriting genius of the Fab Four

Between 1963 and 1964, before the chemical-fuelled studio experimentation of their psychedelic 'middle' period, The Beatles were a remarkably well-honed hit-making machine. Their live-in-the-studio performances were tight, and their songwriting chops even tighter – they reeled off hits with remarkable sophistication for songwriters in their early 20s, with a work ethic that puts modern bands to shame.

With John Lennon locking down the rhythm guitar parts, George Harrison's instantly recognisable melodic lead guitar lines drew on a variety of 1950s influences, including Chuck Berry and Carl Perkins, while his early adoption of the Rickenbacker 12-string electric introduced the world to a sound that has now become synonymous with the vocabulary of 1960s pop.

Read on to discover the 25 timeless songwriting lessons we can learn from the undisputed genius of John, Paul and George as they burned their names in the musical history books and gained the adoration of millions.

❶ PARTIAL CHORDS RULE
John Lennon and George Harrison would often play only two or three strings out of each chord they were voicing. Try playing partial chords on electric guitar and full chord shapes on acoustic, like The Beatles do in Can't Buy Me Love.

❷ MASTER THE I-IV-V PROGRESSION
Freshen up the staple rock 'n' roll I-IV-V progression with a brief detour out of the key signature, just as the Fab Four do at the end of each verse in I Saw Her Standing There. Make sure you know the vital progression and experiment with it to include other chords. Try moving to the bVI or bVII instead.

❸ GEORGE'S OCTAVE SHAPES
In songs such as Please Please Me George Harrison would use the octave shapes shown here, instead of the more common shape played on the fifth and third strings. There is no great benefit to this other than comfort. That said, if you transfer these shapes to a 12-string guitar you will find a different arrangement of the notes in various octaves, so it is worth experimenting with it and seeing what you come up with.

E octave

E octave

❹ ADD SOME TEXTURE
The Beatles didn't just use acoustic guitars for their stripped-down ballads. They often used their Gibson J-160Es to add rhythm parts to full band arrangements. In this context, it adds an extra percussive texture that helps songs move.

5 HARMONY HELPS
The Beatles' much-loved and rich vocal arrangements often lend extra depth to the overall harmony. In Ask Me Why, the harmony vocals outline all of the most colourful notes of the guitar chords. You can work out a simple harmony by pitching your backing vocals a 3rd above the lead line's melody.

6 HONE YOUR CRAFT
Hundreds of performances under their belt meant that by the time they came to record Please Please Me, The Beatles were an extremely tight band. As a result, their debut album was recorded in just under 10 hours. The lesson? Put the work in and you'll sound better.

7 WHO NEEDS CHORDS?
Outline chords with root notes, arpeggios and two- or three-note chords instead of just strumming the full chord predictably. The mix of bass guitar arpeggios and two guitars playing partial chords creates a constantly changing rhythm part. Listen to I Saw Her Standing There.

8 FREE THE BASS!
Paul McCartney's basslines are the harmonic glue that holds many Beatles songs together. Encourage your bassist to explore melodic counterpoints rather than staying anchored to the root notes. You can even double these scale-based lines on your guitar to add texture.

MASTER MINOR CHORDS

The Beatles used minor chords to great effect. Here are five ways you can do the same...

9 MAKE YOUR MIDDLE SECTIONS MINOR
A classic Beatles move is to go from a major chord sequence in a verse to one starting on the relative minor for a mood change in a bridge or chorus. Hear it on Misery.

10 IT'S ALL RELATIVE
Listen to All I've Got To Do and you'll hear two chords dominating: E and C#m. These are relative major/minor chords. The verse shifts between each chord as the tonal centre, never settling on either.

11 STRAY FROM THE KEY
Based around E and A chords, the verse in Please Please Me is in E major. However, the break in the middle of the verse 'borrows' a G chord from the key of E minor, so the run is: E-G-A-B. It's a momentary change of harmony and mood.

12 PARALLEL MAJOR/MINOR
Another classic Beatles move is the 'parallel' major to minor change. Try A-Am-E. It's a basic change from A to E, except that the all-important Am leads you chromatically into the E chord.

★ WHEEL OF ★ MINOR FORTUNE

MAJOR KEYS AND THEIR RELATIVE MINORS

13 WORK OUT YOUR RELATIVE MINORS
Learning the relationship between major chords and their relative minors unlocks all kinds of musical possibilities. Use this simple method – start with the major chord of the key that you're in and move down three semitones. Or use our diagram to help you.

Bassists should explore melodic counterpoints rather than staying anchored to the root notes

14 A HARD DAY'S NIGHT INTRO CHORD

The most famous chord in history and certainly the most debated learning this is bound to inspire. The exact way to play this chord has long been the subject of debate and many voicings of the chords have been suggested over the years. The guys from the touring Beatles musical Let It Be Live use an Fadd9 played on a six-string guitar and an Am11 played on the 12-string guitar. This was accompanied by a D note on McCartney's bass. Mixed together, the notes form a Dm7add11, but you can play it as a Dm11/G if you're playing on one guitar.

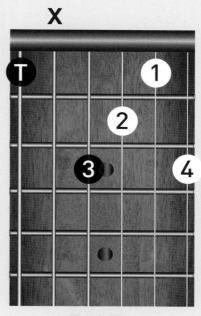

Fadd9
(six-string)

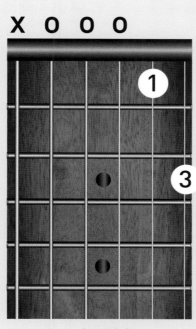

Am11
(12-string)

Dm11/G
(voicing for one guitar)

15 AUGMENT YOUR CHANGES

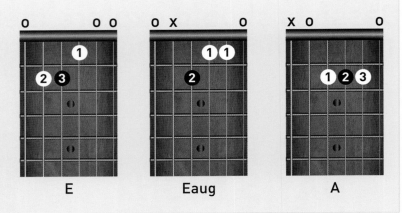

E   Eaug   A

Hang on an augmented chord to emphasise a chord change. Try E-Eaug-A, as a variation on the basic change from E to A. The song Ask Me Why is a great example.

16 TRY VOICE LEADING

Similar to passing bass notes, the idea of voice leading is that you use occasional notes from outside of the key signature to create a melodic line within the notes of a chord progression. The opening to If I Fell is a great example of this.

17 THE I-II-IV-I PROGRESSION

It may or may not be fair to say the Beatles 'pioneered' the I-II-IV-I progression in Eight Days A Week, but the sequence crops up in their later work, too. You Won't See Me and Sgt Pepper's Lonely Hearts Club Band are two prime examples of the band's willingness to return to a musical staple.

18 USING DECEPTIVE CADENCES

In a classic I-IV-V chord progression, there is always a sense that the V chord could be followed by the I chord. The is called 'resolving', and the sense that a musical line is coming to an end is known as a 'cadence'. Just play the open chords D7 (the V), then G (the I) to hear the resolution in action.

The Beatles would often challenge the listener by deliberately heading off to a different chord after the V when writing progressions. For example, in Do You Want To Know A Secret, the VI chord is followed by the V chord, giving a sense that the root chord isn't 'home' for the melody. Try it – start with a I-IV-V progression (E-A-B, for example), and try heading to C#m, F#m or G#m after the B chord.

Try chord inversions where higher notes remain at a constant pitch throughout the progression

19 LEARN YOUR CHORD NUMBERS

We've mentioned using different chords from the key you're in. These are displayed as Roman numerals, meaning they can be used no matter what key the song is in. Working them out isn't as tricky as you might think. The diagrams here give you the notes, intervals and chords in the keys of E major and E minor.

E major	Notes	E	F#	G#	A	B	C#	D#
	Intervals	I	II	III	IV	V	VI	VII
	Chords	E	F#m	G#m	A	B	C#m	D#dim

E minor	Notes	E	F#	G	A	B	C	D
	Intervals	I	II	bIII	IV	V	bVI	bVII
	Chords	Em	F#dim	G	Am	Bm	C	D

The jangly sound of the Vox AC30 is a hallmark of The Beatles' style

25 THE POWER OF 12

On top of the Vox's distinctive sound, The Beatles added extra chime to their tunes by using 12-string guitars. The four lowest strings are tuned in unison pairs – an octave apart – while the two highest strings are tuned to the same register as normal. The result is a huge natural chorusing effect that is brimming with sweet harmonics.

THREE AFFORDABLE 12-STRING ELECTRICS

● Italia Rimini ITR12
With a retro vibe that's verging on Rickydom, Italia's Rimini 12-stringer certainly looks the part. It should sound it, too, thanks to two Wilkinson vintage-voiced soap bar humbuckers, while the unusual six-plus-six tuning key layout eases the pain of tuning a dozen strings.

● Hagstrom Viking DLX 12
By Odin's beard, this is a formidable axe to behold! This 12-string promises tones ranging from vintage cleans to menacing roars, and Hagstrom's Resinator fretboard to wring additional high-end frequencies from the maple body.

● Ibanez Artcore AS7312
The cheapest of our trio, the AS7312 still looks the business. Its pair of Ibanez 'buckers are mounted to a sustain block within the maple body, which reduces feedback and makes the guitar easier to handle on stage.

20 ADD SOME MORE JANGLE
As well as taking over the world with pop guitar, The Beatles gave us the jangly sound that is still used throughout rock music today: the chime of a Vox AC30. The trademark jangle of those EL84 valves is key to sounding fab.

21 CONSTANT CHORDS
The Beatles made this tip their own, but this trick has been employed by loads of people from Oasis (Wonderwall) to Foo Fighters (Best Of You) ever since. When choosing your chords, try to stick to inversions where the higher notes remain at a constant pitch throughout the progression. It works well if these notes are open strings, for some extra resonance.

22 BANJO CHORDS
John Lennon's background as a skiffle player is ingrained in some of his chord shapes – derived from banjo playing. Most notably is this D/F#. It's fretted by playing a standard D shape, and fretting the F# at the 4th fret with your fourth finger. Try moving it around the neck for different sounds!

23 DON'T LIMIT YOURSELF
Their fully experimental period might not have started until later, but even The Beatles' first album draws upon a range of styles including surf, rock 'n' roll, country jazz and soul. Not bad for a simple 'guitar band'!

24 WRITE CONSTANTLY
The Fab Four recorded four albums within a two-year period, taking them from the Star Club in Hamburg to becoming the biggest band in the world. So, the more you write, the better you'll be.

WRITE YOUR FIRST GUITAR SOLO

Kickstart your soloing skills with this five-step approach to lead

If you're starting out playing lead guitar in your songwriting, there are some essentials you should try. We advise beginners learn an essential scale, a few key playing techniques and a handful of creative approaches to keep solo ideas following. You'll find all of that information on these pages.

Learning a common scale is probably the most important step, because it provides you with a set of notes that sound good together, taking some of the guesswork out of choosing notes to play. Sure, you can spend a lifetime finding new note combinations to turn into your solos, but mastering just one basic scale lays solid groundwork to build upon. The A minor pentatonic scale is arguably the best starting point for guitarists.

Once you've practised the scale, you're ready to follow the remaining steps in our lesson. These will help you form your own lead licks.

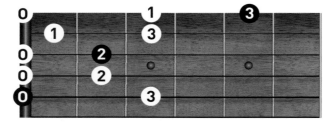

STEP 1. LEARN THE A MINOR PENTATONIC SCALE

The A minor pentatonic scale forms the pool of notes to build your solo from. The black dots are A 'root' notes; the red dots have other names. All you have to do is practise playing from the lowest notes to the highest.

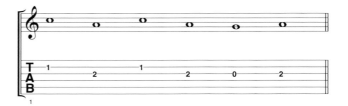

STEP 2. MAKE UP A SHORT, SIMPLE LICK

Take a few random notes from the A minor pentatonic scale to make a lick. Keep things simple at this stage: we've taken just three notes and mixed them up to make a lick. Use notes that are near to each other on the fretboard to make life easy for now.

STEP 3. EXPERIMENT WITH RHYTHM & TIMING

Once you've chosen a few notes to work with, you can start experimenting with the timing. Here, we've made two licks from our initial choice of notes. The symbols underneath the tablature above tell you when to pick with a downstroke (⊓) and when to use an upstroke (V).

TRANSPOSING
Transposing simply means moving any piece of music to a higher or lower pitch. To transpose the A minor pentatonic scale, simply move all the notes one fret higher up the neck (open-string notes move to the 1st fret). This is the Bb minor pentatonic scale. Move the notes up one more fret and you get the B minor pentatonic scale. You can repeat the process to play in other keys.

STEP 4. EXPLORE THE SCALE

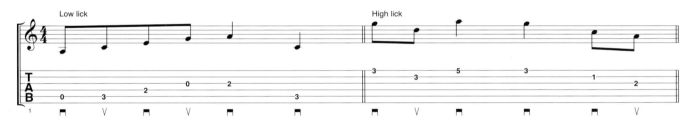

Once you've got the idea, try doing the same thing using notes from other areas of the scale. In the tab are two examples: a low lick and a high lick. After practice you should be able to construct licks using as much of the scale as you like.

STEP 5. LEARN SOME ESSENTIAL LEAD TECHNIQUES

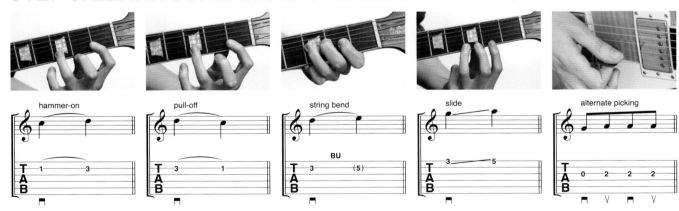

HAMMER-ON
Pick a note and then use a spare finger to 'hammer down' onto the string one or two frets higher up the neck. When combined with pull-offs, this is known as legato.

PULL-OFF
Pick a note, then pull your finger away from the fretboard to sound a lower note on the same string. Pull-offs have a smoother sound than picking every note.

STRING BEND
Fret a note, pick the string, then bend it up with your fretting fingers, keeping the pressure on as you do so. This gives you a smooth and gradual change of pitch.

SLIDE
Fret a note, pick the string and slide your fretting finger to another fret, keeping the pressure on the fretboard as you move. It's not quite as smooth as a string bend.

ALTERNATE PICKING
When several notes fall in rapid succession it can be hard to maintain your down-picking speed. With alternate picking simply swap between down and upstrokes.

BUILDING SONGS

Learn how to effectively structure your songs by studying the classics

Most songs consist of a small number of basic building blocks and the order of these defines the form. Some of the blocks will be familiar to anyone – intro, verse, chorus, bridge and so on – and each has its own characteristics. A verse has the same melody and different lyrics each time it repeats, while a chorus usually has identical lyrics and melody each time you hear it. Intros and outros can have their own original music, but are often just an instrumental version of another section. Intro chords for lots of chart hits are the same as those for the chorus. This is a psychological trick played on the listener so that when the 'real' chorus arrives, we feel we already know it.

Thank AABA for the music

The history of Western pop/rock music is dominated by two classic song forms – AABA and AB. AABA was the most common for the first half of the 20th century, then AB took over during the birth of rock 'n' roll in the 50s and is still used in most songs today.

The 32-bar standard follows a few simple rules: each verse is eight bars long and usually includes the title at the beginning or end; after two verses there's an eight-bar bridge, or 'middle eight', section with different music and a new idea introduced in the lyrics; then there's a concluding verse. After solos, repeat to (good) taste. Thousands of UK and US hit songs from the early 20th century follow

this template, including Ain't Misbehavin', Makin' Whoopee and Over The Rainbow, and the trend continued into early rock 'n' roll (Great Balls Of Fire, All I Have To Do Is Dream). The Beatles were big fans – remember they used to cover a lot of old show tunes in the Hamburg days. A Hard Day's Night and Yesterday are both AABA-form songs with tweaks (Yesterday has seven-bar verses and substitutes the title in verse two, while A Hard Day's Night uses 12-bar verses and adds a solo during one repeated verse).

AABA has been used with adaptations by many successful rock songwriters, including Pete Townshend (Behind Blue Eyes), and Sting (Every Breath You Take). You don't hear AABA much these days, but the occasional singer-songwriter uses it to state their 'timeless' credentials. You may find 32-bar songs can be pleasingly easy to write precisely because the form is so restrictive – and it's surprising how 'authentic' the results can sound if you have a good title and melody.

AB positive

AB form is simpler and more flexible – the term just refers to any song with a repeating chorus (even those with added breakdowns or bridges and so on). But writing really effective choruses is easier said than done. One common difficulty experienced by many new writers is their choruses come out too long, involved, wordy or complicated. Here more than

anywhere, the songwriter can benefit from making use of simple repetition.

Just look at the evidence: Back In Black and Sweet Child O' Mine just repeat the title a few times, as do any number of other well-loved rock standards, including Born In The USA, We Will Rock You and Killing In The Name. Even songs with weirdo lyrics such as Hotel California and Lucy In The Sky With Diamonds save the complicated imagery for the verses and ramp up the title count in the chorus. Some chorus-form songs have an extra section called a pre-chorus, which as the name suggests, arrives immediately before the chorus and often has a chorus-like quality about it (Bon Jovi's Livin' On A Prayer has a pre-chorus that ends with the 'We'll give it a shot' bit).

An honourable mention has to go to the chorus-less AAA (folk song) form, which dates back centuries and is still in occasional use (Squeeze's Cool for Cats, Dylan's All Along The Watchtower). And finally, there's the option of ignoring the rulebook completely. Experimental form has been going on for decades (Genesis, Radiohead, even Girls Aloud have had a crack at it) and there's nothing wrong with bending the song into whatever shape suits your creative vision. But it's amazing how many timeless classics have been written 'inside the box' and won the hearts of millions of music fans. Those Tin Pan Alley guys sure knew what they were doing.

Ever noticed how the intro chords for lots of chart hits are the same as the chorus? This is a psychological trick

SONG STRUCTURE STUDY

The jargon you need to understand to the building blocks of songwriting

Writing a song is like baking: get the balance wrong and nobody will want second helpings. But what are the songwriter's staple ingredients? Here are the core structural terms...

BREAKDOWN

Usually, occurring around two-thirds of the way through a song, prior to the final chorus, a breakdown sees the musical accompaniment stripped back to simpler rhythmic elements, often with a half-time feel, functioning as a dynamic breather before the song's climax.

BRIDGE

A passage that links the verse and chorus and acts as a transition between the two, a bridge is sometimes referred to as a pre-chorus. A great bridge builds anticipation and intensity.

CHORUS

The central focus and theme of a song, its calling card and emotional apex. Usually, based on the repetition of a simple, direct vocal hook, a catchy chorus is the most important part of any commercially minded song. Use your chorus to make your statement, then explore it within the verses.

HOOK

The proverbial ear-worm, a hook is an intentionally repeated musical phrase designed to catch the listener's attention. Although a song's main hook is usually its chorus melody, there's no reason why it can't be a guitar riff or any other musical motif.

MIDDLE EIGHT

A distinct 'B section' of a song, classically but not strictly eight bars in length, the middle eight breaks up the conventional verse/chorus or verse/bridge/chorus pop song structure by shifting gears in terms of the narrative and chord progression. NB: Some people use 'bridge' and 'middle eight' interchangeably, but in pop music it often falls once after the second chorus. Then again, The Beatles reportedly termed anything that wasn't a verse or chorus as a middle eight!

VERSE

Usually, a grouping of two or more lines with a set pattern of meter and rhyme – think stanzas, poetry students! Also, the verse often has a narrative storytelling function.

SONG STOCKPILING

Ever written a catchy chorus but can't come up with anything to do with it? Or a killer riff that you just can't seem to follow with the right verse? You don't have to force things. Store them and call them back up when needed. Prolific songwriter Mark Tremonti has written for the three bands he's in (Alter Bridge, Creed and his own solo band, Tremonti) using his own stockpiling method.

"When I write it's individual ideas," Mark explains. "Sometimes it's two ideas together but most of the time I'll catalogue them and categorise them under bridge, chorus, verse or riff – whatever. So when I have a song that's missing a part I'll go in and check through to see which one fits – whether it's a 6/8 or a 4/4.

"If I write a part, I'll immediately try and write another part that fits with it. But if I lose steam and I'm not coming up with anything else I'll immediately come up with something different. I like to keep going when I'm feeling creative – it's like capturing lighting in a bottle. When you're feeling good about writing, you don't want to stop – you're in that mode. I like to write a great part then write another part later and see if it works; 'This is in 6/8, let's see if it works with the tempo of this verse.' But then you've got two parts that you think are strong instead of forcing something out just to fill a song."

LEARN FROM THE HITS

Stuck with structure? Then look to the classics for some ideas

The order and frequency of the component parts of a song can be the difference between a hit single and a s**t single. However, the good news is that there are no rules other than, 'if it sounds good, it is good.' And that can mean much more than verse/chorus/verse. Consider these three classic hit records and focus on their structural differences, from the remarkable sophistication and brevity of The Beatles, through to Queen's mini rock opera and Kings Of Leon's ultra-efficient, fat-free radio friendly guitar pop.

	THE BEATLES SHE LOVES YOU (LENNON/MCCARTNEY, 1963)	**QUEEN** BOHEMIAN RHAPSODY (MERCURY, 1975)	**KINGS OF LEON** SEX ON FIRE (FOLLOWILL, 2008)
0min	0:00 Drum intro 0:01 Chorus refrain 0:13 Verse one 0:23 Pre-chorus	0:00 A cappella intro 0:15 Piano entry	0:00 Intro riff 0:24 Verse one
0:30	0:38 Verse two 0:51 Pre-chorus	0:49 Ballad section	0:50 Half length chorus
1min	1:02 "Ooooo!" 1:03 Chorus 1:16 Verse three		1:02 Verse two 1:27 Chorus
1:30	1:41 "Ooooo!" 1:42 Chorus		1:51 Verse three
2mins	2:03 Pause ("sho-o-o-uld...") 2:06 "Yeah yeah yeah" outro 2:18 Ends	2:19 Guitar entry proper	2:17 Chorus with rhythmic breakdown
2:30		2:35 Guitar solo	2:56 Chorus
3mins		3:03 Operatic section 3:09 "Scaramouche! Scaramouche!" 3:16 "Galileo! Galileo!"	3:24 Ends
3:30			
4mins		4:07 Hard rock section	
4:30		4:56 Outro	
5mins			
5:30		5:55 Ends	
	DURATION 2:18	**DURATION 5:55**	**DURATION 3:24**

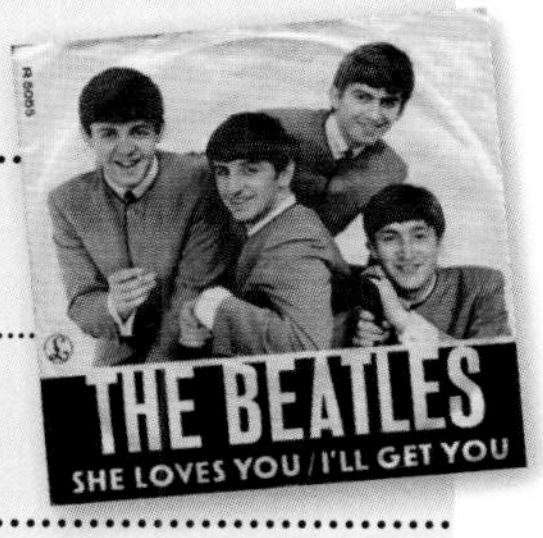

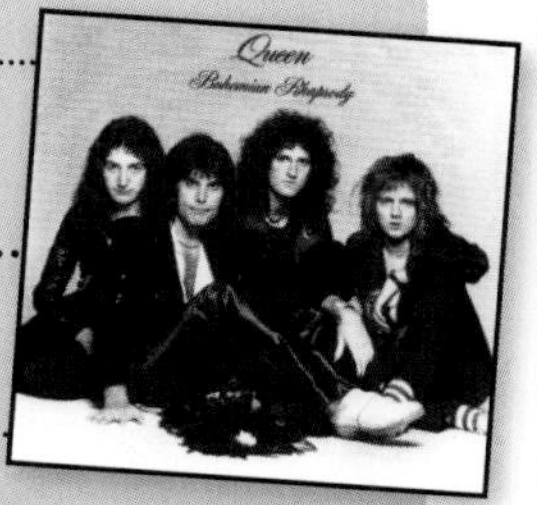

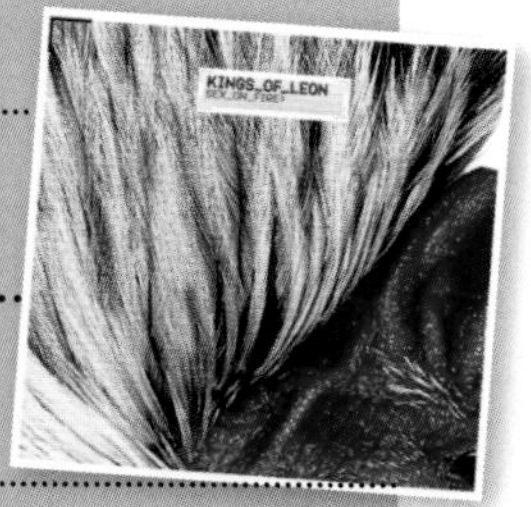

GETTING LYRICAL

With a simple idea and sense of imagery, lyrics needn't be a chore

Guitarists who write songs can be reluctant lyricists. We all find it pretty easy to string some chords together; many of us have no problem humming a melody atop. But sooner or later every songwriter has to ask the question: what is my song about?

There are perhaps two reasons that we find lyric writing a chore: it's not necessarily our first love, compared to the guitar itself; and when we start out as songwriters we often try writing songs 'in the right order', strumming the intro chords and then hoping lyric inspiration will strike us in the fifth or ninth bar of music. The latter seems perfectly logical as a method for writing a song, but in practice it's often just a delaying tactic, avoiding the dreaded moment where you're going to decide what you want to say. Before you know it, you've strummed all four chords (that's G, D, E minor and C) and you've not much to show for it.

Concept and narrative

Classic lyrics generally have one thing in common: a single, clear, concept at the centre of the song. As a songwriter you can help your lyric writing by asking yourself, 'what's the Big Idea?' Let's put a few well-known songs to the test. In each case you can describe the central idea in just a few words. Hendrix's Little Wing = my girlfriend's bonkers and a bit mystical but I think she's great. Adele's Someone Like You = I haven't got over you yet. The Chilis' Under The Bridge = I love Los Angeles, but loneliness sucks (and so does doing drugs under bridges).

Not all song lyrics are purely concept-driven. The 'story song' goes back hundreds of years through the European folk tradition, and has cheerfully survived the birth and growth of rock 'n' roll. Johnny B Goode, All Right Now and Norwegian Wood take a narrative approach to lyric writing, whereby each verse continues the characters' story lines. But even in narrative songs, the plot is almost always very simple. You can't tell a complicated multi-character story very easily in under four minutes.

Visualisation

Of course, for every 'law' in lyric writing you can find a classic hit that breaks it. Stairway To Heaven apparently starts as a simple tale of the 'lady who's sure...' but our girl and narrator soon find themselves being led by the pied piper through a magical world of songbirds, smoke rings and windy echoing forests. Where's your clarity of meaning there, then, eh? Well, this demonstrates the necessary balance that lyricists need to find between being clear and being, well...lyrical. Stairway... is filled with simple lyric phrases that 'sing well', using powerful vowels, easy syllable scansion and, above all, strong visual imagery (interestingly, the song also has lots of lines that don't rhyme). How did they manage to write such an enduring song without being clear about its meaning? Well, it was the 70s...

Adding imagery – by using adjectives or nouns that your listener can visualise – can almost literally paint pictures. And if the images you use also sound great when sung, you may be onto a winner, even if the Big Idea is a little murky. 'Yellow matter custard'. 'Ploughmen dig my earth'. 'We skipped a light fandango'... Well, it was the 60s.

Simplify

Many an inexperienced songwriter tries to defend the right to be impenetrable in lyrics, and some will use examples such as these (and, of course, Oasis) as justification. Is this just hiding an unwillingness to make that commitment to a core meaning? And why would we want to avoid clarity in our lyrics anyway? Perhaps we're worried that keeping things simple will make our lyric cheesy or obvious, or maybe, deep down, we just don't want the hassle of rewriting and editing lyrics until they make sense.

Whatever the reason, it's fair to say that unclear lyrics are the exception rather than the rule. If you can stick to a simple idea, and say something emotionally true that your listeners can relate to, then your lyric will survive, whether you're writing for the mosh pit, the acoustic stage or even a chick-flick soundtrack...

Classic lyrics generally have one thing in common: a single, clear, concept at the centre of the song

WRITING BETTER LYRICS

Ten ways to improve your way with words

Lyrics can be poignant, funny, bizarre, shocking... but they should never just be an afterthought. The world of possibilities is open here, but if you plan to perform your song many times, you need lyrics you won't regret later. Moreover, you need words that will enhance and encapsulate your song. If you're struggling for inspiration, or simply falling into a pattern and need to shake things up, here's some simple methods to improve your world of wordcraft.

1 OPEN UP

Write about what you know – yourself. Don't be afraid to drop your guard because some songs need an emotional honesty and intensity that may feel initially like you're giving too much away to a listener. But if it's your truth, and there can be no more powerful source to pour your lyrics from.
Jason Mraz: "I throw away a lot of ideas and rewrite. Often if I think too narrow – 'here's what I have to do' – it just comes from a place of clever songwriting and not from the heart. It's just a feeling. If I don't have to look at the lyrics I know it's coming from the heart; from the flow."

2 KEEP A JOURNAL

Poetry, musings, rants, titles for songs yet to be written... keep it all in a lyric journal. You never know when a phrase or profound line will occur to you so keep it close. It's old school but it's a brilliant place to draw ideas from, and many successful songwriters depend on theirs.

3 VISUALISE

Before you've written a word, shut your eyes; listen to the music of your song. Does it help you picture a place? A person? A feeling? Write what you see and you'll have achieved a deeper personal connection between your music and lyrics. And if you want to get all cinematic about it, think of that first line as the opening shot in a film.
Brian Fallon, The Gaslight Anthem: "Lately it's more that I'm writing about myself so I already have a picture in my mind because I was there. But I still envision – I try to remember what it felt like; was it raining? What did it smell like? Things like that put me back there."

7 LOOK TO YOUR BOOKSHELF

What do Kate Bush's Wuthering Heights, Pink Floyd's Pigs and Bruce Springsteen's The Ghost Of Tom Joad all have in common? They're just some of the songs that have been directly inspired by well-known literary works. Have you read something that has moved you? Could you retell the story in song or perhaps focus on the experiences of one of the characters? There's a wealth of inspiration just waiting in every literary classic or obscure tome.

4 THINK HOOK

The first lyric you come up with doesn't have to be the first line. It's possible to engineer a whole song around a simple vocal hook. You might have read a punchy headline in a newspaper that would make a great chorus, or something you've overheard and can't forget. Think about the internal rhythm in the phrase based on its syllabic content and try different melodies until you find one you like. Try doing all of this before you pick up a guitar.

5 START STRONG

First lines matter; they can intrigue, provoke or set the scene. Take a look at these classic examples and think about what you want to say at the beginning.

Question: 'If I leave here tomorrow / would you still remember me?'
(*Free Bird*, Lynyrd Skynyrd)

Confession: 'I hurt myself today / to see if I still feel.'
(*Hurt*, Nine Inch Nails)

Statement: 'I am an antichrist / I am an anarchist...'
(*Anarchy In The UK*, Sex Pistols)

Direction: 'Look at the stars / look how they shine for you'
(*Yellow*, Coldplay)

Scene-setting: 'On a dark desert highway / cool wind in my hair'
(*Hotel California*, Eagles)

Emotion: 'I feel good, I knew that I would'
(*I Feel Good*, James Brown)

Time of day: 'When the night has come / and the land is dark / and the moon is the only light we'll see.'
(*Stand By Me*, Ben E. King)

Quote: 'Son, she said, / 'have I got a little story for you'
(*Alive*, Pearl Jam)

Attention-grabber: 'Load up on guns and bring your friends'
(*Smells Like Teen Spirit*, Nirvana)

6 SYNCOPATE

Balancing your vocal and instrumental melodies with what you want to say lyrically involves some give and take, but if you vocal line is more rhythmic, you need to be careful to lose that rhythm with unsuitable words. It's the same if the song may have a very clear guitar melody that you just need to follow. Let that melody take the lead any old words that compliment,

rather than compromise, your rhythmic melody. Now listen to these 10 successful examples of music, melody and lyrics in syncopation in memorable parts, or indeed all, of the song;

1) My Sharona, The Knack
2) Blew, Nirvana
3) Aces High, Iron Maiden
4) On A Rope, Rocket From The Crypt
5) Iron Man, Black Sabbath
6) Here Comes The Sun, The Beatles
7) One, Metallica
8) Night Train, Guns N' Roses
9) All Day & All Of The Night, The Kinks
10) Paint It Black , The Rolling Stones

8 IT'S NOT A CRIME IF YOU DON'T RHYME

Rhyming is good for giving the listener a sense of resolution and security/ predictability. But forced rhymes can be painful to hear. It's very easy to get hung up about the need to rhyme words but it can be limiting and counter productive to the message you're trying to convey. REM's Michael Stipe is a great example of a lyricist who often avoided rhyme but his inventiveness with wordplay and melody in the band meant it was never an issue.

9 DISREGARD YOUR GENDER

Just because you're male or female, it doesn't mean you have to write from that gender perspective. It's the ultimate way to leave your comfort zone. The Gaslight Anthem's Brian Fallon on Here Comes My Man and Billy Bragg's Valentine's Day Is Over are examples of male's taking on the perspective of women wronged at the hands of men. PJ Harvey has taken a male perspective in a number of her songs, including Man-Size and Shaker Aamer. In the song Luka, Suzanne Vega writes tackles the issue of physical abuse from the perspective of a small boy – the poignancy of the dark subject matter offset deceptively by relatively upbeat melodies.
These examples are a rare occurrence from both genders in songwriting and represent a challenge for both writer and listener; which makes it all the more worth trying.

10 GET A THESAURUS

We all have our own vocabulary when we speak and we draw upon it for our lyric writing. This can be wide, but there Is always room for expansion, and if the same words have popped up in a few of your songs so far, a thesaurus (physical book, ebook or free web version) is a great way to find new ways to convey universal themes in your songs. Finding alternative words (synonyms) can change whole lines too, but without changing their meaning at all; 'You shine in the dark' becomes 'You glimmer through the gloom', and 'I'm stuck on my own' becomes 'I'm marooned alone'.

The first lyric you come up with doesn't have to be the first line

PLAYING & SINGING

A beginner's guide to playing the guitar while you're singing

Ever rubbed your belly and patted your head at the same time? The principle of doing two seemingly unrelated things at once can be just as alien and as off-putting for many would-be singer/songwriting guitarists. Don't dismay; it's not rocket science, and you're only going to get better if you follow our guide. Whether you're a guitar player or singer looking to do the other skill simultaneously for writing and performing there are simple ways to start. We'll all be pulling those Springsteen/Tele moves in no time...

YOUR 10-STEP START PLAN

1. GUITAR FIRST
It's all about getting the guitar playing sorted so you can then focus on the singing.

2. KNOW THE SONG
It sounds obvious, but plenty of people rush in without actually knowing the song well. Get familiar with the melody and inflections, and sing over the record to practise.

3. START SIMPLE
Begin by strumming the chords to a song you know and humming the vocal melody over it. When you can do this while staying in time, move on...

4. LEARN THE CHANGES
Focus on the key guitar strumming patterns and what lyrics the chord changes occur on. Simplify strumming to begin with to get comfortable, then build up to a busier rhythm part.

5. USE A VISUAL AID
Write out and read the lyrics and chords in front of you, then tackle things in chunks, singing and playing them over and over.

6. DON'T WATCH YOUR HAND
If you're constantly looking at your strumming hand during chord changes, then you're almost definitely not concentrating on singing and projecting your voice.

7. KEEP IN TIME
Is your strumming rhythm going off? Try using a metronome to help stay in time.

8. RECORD YOURSELF
Be critical – your mobile phone will do for a rough recording. What you hear in your head isn't always accurate and you'll be able to focus on areas to improve on.

9. REPETITION
Don't give up on a song – every time you try, you'll get better.

10. LEARN A REPERTOIRE
Broaden your new multi-tasking skills and even if you're not into becoming a covers act, you can always break these tunes out around a campfire!

TRY THESE SONGS TO START

Oasis – Wonderwall
Green Day – Good Riddance
(Time Of Your Life)
Pink Floyd – Wish You Were Here

RIFFS AND FINGERPICKING

If you're building up to singing and playing your songs in a basic, chordal way, making the leap to single-note parts such as riffs and more intricate fingerpicking can feel like you've hit a significant learning curve.

Again, the guitar part should come first. You need to be able to play the riff part in your sleep so it becomes a muscle memory thing. Play it as you watch TV, while you talk to people, while you eat at the dinner table...

If it's a fingerpicked part, it's vital to start slow. Don't dive in at full speed; it makes everything feel 10 times harder.

NOW START WRITING

Writing parts while playing and singing them as you go along is the best way to get better because you're working on both from the inception rather than trying to add one on to the other later.

So the next time you come up with a chord progression or riff, start thinking what kind of vocal melody could compliment it as soon as possible. Start by humming and then build from there.

TRY THESE SONGS TO START

Nirvana — *Come As You Are*
The White Stripes — *Seven Nation Army*
The Beatles — *Blackbird*

ON SONG THREE SINGER/GUITARISTS SHARE THEIR TIPS

MYLES KENNEDY
ALTER BRIDGE/SLASH

Myles Kennedy has certainly got pipes to rival the best of them, but he also trades riffs with Mark Tremonti in Alter Bridge, so knows a thing or two about the art of rubbing and patting.

"Really, the best thing you can do is just start diving into playing and singing songs you know and like. Try and find songs that aren't too complicated in either realm. Real straightforward. A Tom Petty song would be a good example because it's simple cowboy chords, simple melodies... but brilliant songs.

"Just tackle that first before trying to jump into something a little too difficult, because it really is like patting your head and rubbing your belly at the same time!"

JERRY CANTRELL
ALICE IN CHAINS

The Alice In Chains man has proved how strong vocal harmonies can be, but he needed the confidence to step up to the mic first.

"Anybody can sing – some people are naturals. I don't really consider myself a natural. It's more, just try. I never intended to be a lead singer. At times I have been, and in this band I operate as one as well. William [DuVall] and I kind of work as a tandem, a duo.

"I started off as a backup singer and I got more confidence as I went on. Layne [Staley] particularly gave me a lot of confidence to sing. I didn't particularly think I had much talent at it, but he was always, 'Hey man, you can sing fine – you should sing more.' So I did."

LIAM CROMBY
WE ARE THE OCEAN

When British rockers We Are The Ocean's lead singer Dan Brown quit in 2012, guitarist Liam stepped up into the frontman role – and they've never looked back.

"The first time going on stage as a lead singer is scary and exciting, nothing can prepare you for it. The more shows we played the more comfortable the new role became. We had to adapt to the changes in the band and still put on the best live show possible. Alfie [Scully] took over some guitar parts so I could interact with the crowd. At the same, I found that I focus more on my guitar playing than ever. I try and complement the vocal delivery with the guitar playing, soft in quite parts, hard in the loud. Preparation and practice is key!"

RIFF WRITING

It's time for us to unleash the songwriter's secret weapon...

These 'mini-solos' are easy to play, sound great, and perhaps most importantly, remind everyone that you're the Most Important Person In The Band, of course. Riffs are almost always one, two or four bars in length and are repeated at various points throughout the song. There are three broad types, defined by their function: solo riffs, call-and-response riffs and underscore riffs.

Solo riffs often form the intro of the song and typically reappear between vocal sections. Notable examples include Deep Purple's Smoke On The Water, Thin Lizzy's The Boys are Back In Town and Clapton's Wonderful Tonight. When you're writing a solo riff, you can be as busy or melodic as you like, because anything you play won't get in the way of the voice. Take Steely Dan's Reelin' In The Years: its four-bar riff is filled with fast triplets. It would be near impossible to hear the vocal over such a detailed guitar part, so the band sensibly provides a healthy 16 bars of space to let the riff shine through.

Riff types

Call-and-response riffs are used to fill the gaps between vocal phrases within a section. Examples include John Lee Hooker's Boom Boom and The Rolling Stones' The Last Time, which start exactly one beat after the voice. Again, these riffs give you a lot of freedom to do whatever you want musically, as long as it's the same each time, but you have to get in quick before the next vocal phrase. AC/DC's Whole Lotta Rosie uses call-and-response for the verses, then adapts the

Riffs can be chordal or melodic, but they need to have movement

riff so that it becomes the accompaniment in the chorus.

Underscore riffs are played simultaneously with the vocals. We need to choose notes that are interesting enough to be memorable, while avoiding note clashes with the voice and ensuring that the lyric can still be heard. Here, simplicity is key and this is why songwriters often use chordal riffs (The Kinks' You Really Got Me, Alice In Chains' Them Bones) or very simple note choices (U2's I Still Haven't Found What I'm Looking For, Kings of Leon's Radioactive or the Red Hot Chili Peppers' Californication). And it's still possible to get great countermelodies in there if you choose your notes carefully; the riff from Rage Against The Machine's Killing In The Name supports the vocal without obscuring it.

Fab four

Riffs can be chordal or melodic, but they need to have movement; anything slower than one note/chord every two beats usually sounds closer to a chord pattern than a riff. They also need to be short; anything longer than four bars can sound more like a solo than a riff. Choosing when to repeat your riff is another important factor in getting your audience to remember it, although if in doubt, more is better (playing those two bars from Walk This Way just never gets

old). Riffs can be static, meaning they use the same notes each time they're played, or transposed, meaning that the notes change along with the chords of the song. If you're writing on guitar, try to avoid getting too scalic and busy – most of the killer notes will be found within a single octave.

For the finest examples of the black art of riff writing, we must take the well-trodden songwriting pilgrim's path to The Beatles' front door. Listen to the masterful way the ascending underscore riff from Day Tripper (E-G-G#-B-E- D-B-F# and so on) works against the descending vocal line 'Got a good reason' (A-G#-F#-E). There's not a single note clash in there and you can hear both lines perfectly. The riff gets busier as the vocal gets simpler. The same applies to any number of the band's early hits – Ticket To Ride and You Can't Do That have simple, memorable one-bar verse underscore riffs, while I Feel Fine transposes its riff along with the chords of G, C and D in each verse. What makes the latter even more of an achievement is that it functions as a solo (in the intro), underscore (in the verse) and call-and-response (end of each verse). Yes, these guys show a lot of promise. They should go far.

Great riffs share four characteristics: simplicity, sensitivity to the vocal line, memorability, and finally lots and lots and lots of repetition.

PROMOTING YOUR SONGS ONLINE

You've made music, now you need to get it heard

FIVE WAYS TO PROMOTE

1. COVER
You'll get far more passing trade from searches on YouTube by uploading a cover version. The US band Boyce Avenue launched themselves as a band after having huge success doing this.

2. CROSSOVER
Choose popular artists that have fans who you think might be interested in your music. Post friendly introductions to your music on their forums, YouTube videos and profiles with links to your material.

3. NETWORK
Don't just gig with other bands – promote each other, share fanbases. And don't be shy about tactfully posting a link to your songs on the Facebook pages of venues you're playing because they will rarely do it for you.

4. INCENTIVES
Separate yourself from the pack and keep people coming back – for example, release a new song free every month until you have an album after a year.

5. WATCH
Look at other local artists – how well are they doing? What methods of promoting have they been using and how are they presenting themselves online?

Music doesn't sell itself. Writing songs is only half the journey – you need to get them heard. Even great songs need to be found, and it usually takes a lot of work to get them heard over the din of thousands of other acts trying to do the same. People won't know, and they'll never know about your music unless you tell them all about it. Yes, music is art but it's also a product with consumers.

And like any product, it needs to be sold for a fanbase to be built that wants to have your music in their lives. That doesn't mean it has to be done in a desperate and crass way. You can promote your music in the best way for you, and get the followers for your music that will impress promoters you approach for gigs. But there are basic principals everyone can follow.

It's a big world online, so it's vital you maximise your chances by targeting various channels in the right way.

Build your presence
Your identity online as an artist isn't just about one base (eg a Facebook page or a website), you need to have a presence in as many places as possible to maximise your exposure; Facebook, Twitter, Instagram, YouTube, Soundcloud, Bandcamp, ReverbNation, Spotify... spread your name and tunes far and wide.

GETTING PEOPLE TO LISTEN

FILM YOUR OWN SESSION

Setting up for rehearsal with a couple of well-placed condenser mics going straight into DAW software on a laptop, plus a friend with a video camera/smartphone is a relatively easy way to make a series of 'in session' videos for your songs and promote yourselves as a live band too. It's a given you'll already have good songs that have been well produced, but these videos will be something extra to put out online.

One static camera and a friend moving around getting close-ups is a minimum, and if you can borrow a GoPro camera to clip on a headstock for some fretboard action – even better!

MAINTAINING A PRESENCE

If you're only communicating online when you have a gig or song to plug, your posts are inevitably going to be few and far between. Try to keep updating without spamming the same things over and over every five minutes; people will get tired of that fast. Interesting pics of your gear from band practice, insight into your recording sessions, gigs that you've attended and how they've inspired you; even sharing music by other local artists are all ways to reinforce your identity as an active artist and stay active in the eyes of your existing and new online followers. Making them more receptive when you have a new song or gig date to share.

FACEBOOK FOCUS

If you're a gigging artist the first thing to do is build a local following, but don't confuse your friends with a fanbase. Friends may support you by attending your gigs but you need to reach beyond that to people who will listen without obligation. Though Facebook offers the option for you 'boost' your posts by paying a fee and becoming a sponsored post on an estimated number of peoples' news feeds, the cost/result ratio may not be worth it. This might be because the Facebook prioritises individuals over organisations, and that includes bands. So go back to a grassroots online: any way you can get your posts shared by individuals the better. Do you friends feature in a video you've made? Tag them, then their friends will see too.

BEYOND SOCIAL MEDIA

A Facebook page is easy and cheap to build but don't presume you don't need a website as the home for your music online. It adds a professional touch and offers you greater control and functionality over the way you present your music and online identity. Your social media profiles should link to your site and vice versa. Sidestep the algorithms of social media and send out your own regular updates via a mailing list too. How do you get e-mail addresses? Offering a free song or EP download in exchange for an email is a good way to start.

Resources

TuneCore
If you're an unsigned act, you'll need an online distribution service to get your music on services such as iTunes, AmazonMP3, Google Play Music and Spotify.

Bandzoogle
A website builder for musicians; choose from template designs or use their editor. You can integrate a store, too. Get the free trial, then prices start from $9.95 a month.

Soundcloud
The best service to upload your songs, then embed them on your site and social media. You can gain your own followers through your profile and follow others, too.

A BEGINNER'S GUIDE TO
MUSIC PUBLISHING

When your songs start making money you need to know your rights

A publisher can get your songs heard and make money for you

Wether you're serious about songwriting; recording your songs, trying to get them used on television soundtracks or even writing them for other artists, you need to know about what music publishing means and what it involves. Because if you don't you will leave your songs open to theft and lost earnings.

With the advent of the internet – streaming, sampling and downloading all kinds of music – the business of music publishing companies has never more varied. But it covers three primary areas; valuation, protection and development. Valuation involves registering the works of songwriters with collection agencies – in the UK this means PRS For Music (more on them later). Protection ensures people's work isn't being used without the correct licence and development includes finding and helping new songwriting talent through advice and facilities. Let's discuss this in more detail starting with the whole issue of music copyright...

What does copyright mean in music?

As an upcoming songwriter, it's very likely that you'll start off by giving away your music for free online to get attention and build a fanbase – you won't get far without doing this. But it's important you know that once your song has been documented in writing (eg sheet music) or in a format such as a sound or video recording, it is automatically copyrighted and that copyright is owned by the composer/s.

You hold this copyright for 70 years, after which it becomes public domain and can be sampled, used for synching (more later) or covered without clearance permission or royalty payment. Until that time, publishing can be involved with the registration, exploitation and collection of this song.

What does my song copyright apply to?

Just the musical melody, the lyrics of a song are covered by a separate literary copyright (automatically applied when the song is written). Because you hold the copyright after writing it, you can play, sell and distribute the song as you like.

What if I was signed to a label?

When a signed artist's record is sold there are two areas of rights and resulting royalties involved; one is the physical recording and the artist who performs on it, the other is for the songwriter/s who penned the song. They may not necessarily be the same person. The artist is paid by the record company; they get a royalty cut of the wholesale price of the record. The songwriter gets what is

termed as a mechanical royalty (the right to mechanically reproduce the writer's song on, say, a CD or download) and this can vary between countries in how it's paid; a fee every time the song is sold or a cut of the wholesale record price. Music publishing is only concerned with this second area; the rights and royalties of the songwriter.

What if a writer's songs are used somewhere other than a record?

Songwriters can receive royalties from other areas besides mechanical; performance, synchronisation, special use (eg karaoke, phone ringtone) and in print (ie the guitar tablature of the song).

What is synchronisation?

This is the use of any piece of music alongside a piece of visual media; film, television, advertising, computer games and apps. You will be paid by the producer of the visual media for the right to use your music, should you grant them permission.

How is this money collected?

In the UK, the Performing Rights Society (PRS) represents over 100,000 composers, songwriters and music publishers who make up its membership. PRS collects royalties for members when their music is publicly performed, synchronised and used online. PRS are also affiliated with MCPS (Mechanical-Copyright Protection Society Limited) that collects royalties for its members whose music is reproduced.

So what does a publisher do?

For starters, a songwriter's publisher may be an MCPS member and collect royalties MCPS has secured on behalf of the writer to pass them on. But the publisher's role goes much further than that. The major record labels have their own publishing divisions, others are independent companies but major affiliated – dealing closely with the majors when it comes to licencing deals – while some publishing companies are completely independent and self-funded. Which means they may deal with the labels closely when it comes to licencing. A publisher may find a songwriter online, and then choose to

investigate them further live. Once a publishing company has signed a deal with a songwriter, they take on a role of promoting their work. This might be to labels who may need songs for an artist, or approaching radio, television and film with their writer's songs for possible use.

Some publishing companies are more hands-on than others with regards to promotion, feedback, arranging collaborative writing sessions and creative support (eg finding the artist a suitable space and gear for songwriting). However, some writers handle most of the publisher role themselves, sometimes hiring someone to help with the admin of licencing.

What's their cut in terms of songs?

Often 50 percent of the profits generated by the songs. The writer hands over half of their copyright for a song they have written to the publisher. This is commonly held for a set amount of time before full rights for back to the original owner, but it used to be for life.

That's a significant cut...

Indeed it is. A publishing deal can mean everything in terms of a songwriter's earning potential. A publisher can get your songs heard and make money for you. But a bad deal can have financial implications that could be seriously harmful. It's vital to get legal advice and representation before signing any publishing deal.

Always get legal advice before you sign on the line

COPYING ©

Know where you stand before making a potentially costly mistake

It's a common feeling. You write a line and it immediately sounds just right. Timeless. Familiar. Too familiar. You play the song to your friends and someone notices – you've copied an existing track. Gutted, you delete that great-sounding line and spend hours trying to write something as good.

This sort of copying happens to every writer from time to time. Most of us just exhale sadly and wait for inspiration to flow again, following the tracks of our tears. But some take the darker path, keeping the copied section and hoping that no-one will notice. Leading us to the inevitable question: how much of someone else's song can actually be copied?

The law

The answer, frustratingly, is 'none at all'. Contrary to popular myth, there's no maximum number of notes you can copy 'legally'. If your song sounds recognisably like part of another song, and the other side can demonstrate in court that copying has occurred, you could end up owing someone a lot of money, or even lose ownership of your own work.

Many songwriters say that's unfair. There are only 12 notes to the octave, and surely you're bound to copy a song accidentally sooner or later – infinite monkeys and all that? Well, this argument doesn't stack up when you apply some simple maths. It's actually quite easy to write a unique melody because there are hundreds of billions of possible combinations of pitches and rhythms over just a few bars. Notes themselves cannot be owned, just as a painter cannot own a colour nor a poet copyright a word. It's the arrangement of notes in order that creates melody, and therefore the longer the melody, the greater the odds against it being coincidentally similar to another. The numbers multiply up very quickly.

Shared ownership

However, popular music, and particularly rock, likes parts of its musical palette to be fairly restricted. And sometimes a musical idea becomes so common that it enters shared ownership. An obvious example is the 12-bar blues chord sequence. Presumably someone, back in the day, thought this combination of chords was 'original' and wrote a song around it. This inspirational bluesman may be long gone but his musical idea remains, endlessly recycled by all of us in many a jam session, and cheerfully copyright-free forever.

Which brings us to Deep Purple's Black Night. The very mention of that title has probably already started the riff playing in your head. You would be forgiven for thinking that if you used the first bar of this riff in a song you'd be stealing from Ritchie Blackmore et al. Not so. They got it from Ricky Nelson's 1962 hit Summertime, a rock reworking of the old George Gershwin standard, where the two-bar pentatonic riff was played, and presumably invented, by guitarist James Burton. In fact, by 1970 Deep Purple were the third band to have used the Summertime riff in a single, the others being The Liverpool Five in 1966 and Blues Magoos in 1967. The reason that this particular riff could be so easily traded is that it was not written by George Gershwin so wasn't technically considered part of the copyright in Summertime. Therefore the Black Night riff isn't owned by anyone. Although if you do put it in your own song it's a dead cert that everyone will think you've ripped off Deep Purple...

Respect

But Black Night is an exception, and in most cases such blatant copying would land the songwriter in very hot water indeed. These are some rules of thumb to keep your songs from harm. Use whatever chords you like – it's almost impossible to copyright a chord sequence. Don't steal any melody knowingly – it's just not worth the risk, and this certainly includes riffs. Re-use someone else's title if you really have to – although it's unnecessary to do it. And avoid stealing lyrics at all costs – it's a dead giveaway.

For songwriters, the question is a moral one. Why would we want to copy someone else's ideas when the art of songwriting is all about an expression of our own creativity? Surely it's better for us all to respect each other? Or, to put it another way: imagine all the people, living life in peace... Oops.

IF YOUR SONG SOUNDS LIKE PART OF ANOTHER SONG, YOU COULD END UP OWING SOMEONE A LOT OF CASH

ED SHEERAN ON SONGWRITING

We spoke to Ed early in his career to get the lowdown
on guitars, songwriting and gigging

Photography By Jesse Wild

Meet the biggest UK singer/songwriter success story in years. When he's not having hits of his own he's penning them with One Direction and Taylor Swift. But Ivor Novello and Brit winner Ed Sheeran's hybrid of urban and confessional folk music is not an overnight sensation; it's built on years of relentless touring, sleeping on sofas around the country with his trusty Martin Mini, and putting out self-funded releases through a work ethic that saw him play 300 gigs in one year alone. With three huge-selling albums, Ed's songs have connected with the masses worldwide. He's also someone with experience all singer/songwriters can learn from, as we'll find out...

Who are the main songwriters that influenced you when you first started out writing your own material?
"I would say, from Damien Rice to Van Morrison to Bob Dylan to Luke Concannon – he's in a band called Nizlopi – all the way down to people like Eminem, lyrically. I listen to a lot of rap music and a lot of folk music and everything in between. But those are the two main spectrums."

Looking back, when you first started out as a guitar player, how long did it take you to go from first learning the basic steps of playing the guitar to actually sitting down and writing your own songs? Was it something that came early for you?
"Yes, it was. Starting off playing the guitar, you learn other people's songs, and then when you start writing your own songs, you just use, for the first songs you

write, you use other people's chords, and their melodies. You are 11 years old; you are allowed to plagiarise. The first song I wrote was basically a Green Day chord sequence that was quite a simple thing to play.

"The first song that I ever learnt to play on the guitar was Eric Clapton's Layla. And I used to be really into guitar-driven music, only play the electric guitar and know all the solos for Guns N' Roses and stuff such as that. And then I got into Damien Rice and realised that you could do singing and guitar and do it without a band – you wouldn't have to have a band behind you. You could, technically, just do that on your own. So I got an acoustic and I haven't really looked back since."

The Martin LX1E signature model that you use onstage is a bijou, parlour-sized instrument.
Do you use that because of its obvious convenience, or because you prefer the sound you get from a smaller-bodied guitar?
"Well, it helps that it sounds good. Martin don't make bad guitars, so of course it helps that it sounds really good. But, to be honest with you, I lived without a home for quite a while, just going on trains, sleeping on people's sofas; playing all around the country. So all you have is a guitar and a case that is, technically, a backpack. And you can fit a lot of clothes in that case, if you stuff it in. And in the little pouch you have your toothbrush and toothpaste, and phone chargers and stuff like that. So, it was basically my suitcase that also happened to have an acoustic guitar in it, and that was very convenient."

"I think it's important to remember that you are not at an open mic night to showcase your songs, you are there to entertain."

"But I started off with a smaller guitar, I had a backpacking guitar first, the teardrop-shaped one [Martin's ultra-portable Backpacker model]. And I had two of them, one broke from overuse, and then the other one I still have now. And then later I got that small mini Martin. I've actually got four of them now, but the first two I got were a little bit better, because they are not lacquered, they are just plain wood. I think they sound a bit better."

What sort of advice could you give a singer/songwriter who wants to play out, in terms of quickly getting a good sound?
"A good sound for acoustic live, if I'm giving advice for my kind of sound, is I like my sound to be really fat and warm. I know some people that have humbuckers on their acoustics and they like a very jagged, trebly sound. But I'm into the warmth. So, usually, if you have a bit of bottom end and a lot of mid on a guitar and just a tiny bit of top end, that will give you a warmish sound. And the way I test it is, on the bridge, I beat it like a drum and it makes a kick drum sound. That's because I do a lot of percussion on the guitar, that's usually when I know that the sound is good."

Do you do anything to stop it feeding back?
"The guitar only feeds back when the monitors are too loud. So I guess, don't have the monitors too loud. For me, that's the only time it feeds back, and with the guitar I use I don't really get that."

Doing original material on an acoustic can make it difficult to hold people's attentions sometimes. How did you go about it in the early days?
"That's the thing I had to realise over a lot of gigs; that no one goes to gigs – be it your friends or family or strangers – no one actually goes to those gigs to hear your songs. They go to be entertained, they want to have a good night out. So the trick, for me, was to not just play my songs, but to give them a show and entertain. And anything I could throw in that would make them go, 'Oh, okay!'

"I play a song, one of my tunes called, You Need Me, I Don't Need You. And it's got a laid-back verse in it and a 50 Cent verse [from the 50 Cent track In Da Club], and I do a long rap in it. Even stuff like that where people will just be, 'Okay, I recognise that a little bit'. But then you go back into your own song, and you have tricked them a little bit to catch their attention.

"Or by splitting the crowd into two, and getting one half of the crowd singing one bit, and one half singing the other bit, and make them in competition with each other. And that gets them to sing, which in turn gets them to watch. I think it's important to remember that you are not, at an open mic anyway, you are not there to showcase your songs, you are there to entertain.

"And I know people go into it as if they are going to showcase their songs, but what I realised over the years is, people don't give a s**t. They really just go to smile and be entertained, that's why people go on nights out. So, you know, you still get to play your songs, but just make it a little more interesting and entertaining.

"That's what I have done anyway, because I was playing slow songs. And the way to spice up slow songs is to have a bit of banter with the crowd, and get them involved a bit."

So, what's the toughest crowd that you've had to play to, in terms of getting them onside?
"Really, the toughest crowd I've had for going on stage was a gig in Inglewood in LA, at a place called The Savoy Entertainment Center. And Inglewood is in, for want of a better word, the hood. And it's quite a rough area. It was my first gig in LA, [from] my only contact, so if I did a s**t gig then my month would be s**t.

"So I got there, and it was around 400 people all seated, and me and the promoter were the only white people in the venue. And it was a comedy and poetry night. No music, and certainly no decent music.

"So you have a whole crowd that are there to watch comedy and poetry. And the guy before me was a comedian and I had to set up my stuff on stage before him. And he thought I was the stagehand, like just a guy helping out. So he was ripping into me, and being like, 'Who the f**k are you man?' And yes, going on a bit. Then I got up to play, and suddenly it was like, okay, what's going to happen here?

"I opened up with You Need Me, I Don't Need You, and instead of dropping a 50 Cent verse into it, I dropped one by Snoop Dogg, who is from [LA]. So I dropped in a verse of his, and seeing a slightly chubby ginger white kid drop a verse with the right kind of timing and the right stuff, I guess, that's what won people onside.

"But that was quite a tough gig, because it just wasn't my crowd. But that's what you learn from, you learn to make them your crowd."

THE STORY BEHIND ED'S BREAKTHROUGH SONG AND MASSIVE HIT, 'THE A TEAM'

HIT-MAKING

"A few years ago at Christmas, I did a gig in a place called Camden Proud Galleries in London. And I finished up my show and my friend, Cave, who also played that day, he came up to me and said, 'Ed, what are you doing after this, tomorrow? Do you want to come down and play a gig for me?" And I said, "Yes. Where is it? What is it?"

"He explained that this homeless charity called Crisis do this thing every year where they get given big warehouses in lots of different areas around the country. But this particular one was in east London. And they sweep the streets of east London, basically, and house homeless people over the Christmas period for a week. They give them healthcare, shoes, food, dental, cinemas, beds and house them. And Cave asked me if I wanted to be the entertainment.

"So I go down the next day, I got a little badge that said, 'I'm here to help.' I was instantly put into the main room while they were setting up the gig downstairs and they said, 'Ed, just play. Just go out to people and play covers.' So I spent the first hour walking around meeting everyone, playing different covers. And all around the room there were these posters that said, 'Angel's Rules' with what you could and couldn't do. And Cave explained, that there was this woman called Angel, who was part of the shelter, who had been breaking all the rules from day one. And they told her if she stopped breaking the rules, she could be the sheriff and make her own rules.

"So they printed up and laminated these papers. And we met Angel and sat down and had a talk to her. She was a big Guns N' Roses fan, so I played Sweet Child O' Mine four times for her. And then I was brought downstairs to the main gig, and just jammed for two hours, just every song. Going from Let it Be into No Woman, No Cry, sticking on one chord sequence and just jamming a song for half an hour in different tunes, and then going onto the next one."

"And as I was packing up my stuff, Cave said to me that his job on the last day was to take everyone from inside the shelter and put them back out on the street again. And he was saying where someone like Angel had come from and where she was going back to. And how she made her money and how she spent her money.

"And me being 18 at the time, and I had lived in London for a couple of years, but I had never really seen the dark underbelly of it. And that really affected me and I got home that day, I was on the train, just thinking... thinking, thinking, thinking. And I got home and started off, started off the tune, the first line I wrote actually was, 'She's just under the upper hand'. Because I felt that half the people in that shelter were just not quite able to get out, but all they needed was a push. But yes, that's how the song was written."

You once did over 300 gigs in a year. How did you manage to keep yourself motivated?

"Well, it's a lot easier being on your own than it is in a band. Me being solo, I could book the gigs myself and not have to ask someone else if they were free on that date, like I would if I was in a band. And I could find places to stay quite easily, because it is just me, and I'm quite a small person, I'll fit anywhere.

"In the same sense, it's a lot easier to not have those moments where you feel like giving up because there's no one else to tell you that they think it's a bad idea. I mean, no one ever said anything to me, it's only recently that I have had certain family members coming up and saying, 'Yes, I thought it was meant to be, dropping out and doing all of that'. But, you know, it was very much my own self determination.

"So, if I said I was going to do something, I would do it. Whereas, with a band, one person can be like that and then another person could be like, 'Actually, I would prefer to go back to school and get a degree', kind of thing. So it's a lot easier being solo."

You've integrated percussive playing and a looper pedal into your sound, how did that develop?

"The looper came from a guy called Gary Dunne who I saw supporting Nizlopi. And the strumming thing came from, I think, I had lessons for the first three years and then I didn't have lessons anymore. Because, learning Damien Rice and stuff like that, you can generally work out the chords yourself, so then I stopped having lessons. And then I started learning other people's songs on my own, and developed this kind of percussive strumming technique, I guess. So that's where that's coming from."

Have you ever got into any difficulty using the looper live?

"Of course, yes. One of the first gigs I did in London, the batteries cut out halfway through a song. And obviously, you can plug it back in, but your loop has gone. So there's always times that it doesn't work. But that's when you learn the beauty of unplugging and sitting on a stool in the middle of the room. So when it f**k up, you are just like, 'Yes, sure, f**k it.'"

It's just about having a back up plan, isn't it? Because if an artist just freezes onstage then that's the end of the gig, everyone is going to walk away disappointed...

"The key thing is to not think about it. So, if it cuts out, it will be like, 'Cool, unplug, go [into the crowd],' instead of being, 'S**t, s**t, s**t, s**t. What do I do?' kind of thing. Even if you do end up going a bit, just act confident. The crowd likes confidence."

When it comes to sitting down to write songs, how do you put the chord progressions together? Do you just play and stumble over something or do you think about it in a calculated way?

"No, if it sounds nice and it goes along with the sentiment of the song, then it usually works. I'm not too scientific when it comes to writing songs. I don't

"I got an acoustic and I haven't really looked back since"

"If you are a singer/songwriter trying to build up a fanbase, the best thing to do is just release as much music as possible"

write songs like Radiohead, I write songs like Damien Rice. They are not too complicated, you know, C/G/D/Em, that kind of thing."

When it comes to recording those songs, how do you know where to draw the line in terms of adding extra instrumentation?
"I think, less is more. Always. Always in the studio. I saw an interview, Dan Wilson who wrote Someone Like You with Adele, talking about Rick Rubin, when he produces. And he said, when you record a song you have ideas for drums and the bassline. You need to strip it down, so the bassline is literally one note in four bars, instead of going through the whole thing. Having just minimal stuff that will go together well. So I guess, less is more in that sense. And I only perform on my own with an acoustic guitar, so I don't want it to be too overblown, without a band."

Do you have any advice for artists who are trying to break through?
"Yes. Just try to be original, try and do new things. For me, it was doing the five EPs. Like the first one was the You Need Me EP, and it was a full band and it was indie. And the second one was Loose Change, which was more singer/songwriter. The third one was Songs I Wrote With Amy, which was more folk. The fourth one was the live EP and DVD [Live At The Bedford], which I funded from the first three. And then I did the collaborations EP.

"There's a singer/songwriter called Frank Hamilton, who is he writing a song a week, and then releases a full track EP every month. His first EP was called January, the second was called February, and by the end of the year, he'll have 12 EPs.

"Now some people might think that's pointless, but if I'm a fan and every month I have got new music to listen to, it doesn't matter whoever it is, I'm going to become more of a fan, just because there's more music to listen to. And it is like, some people are very precious with their songs, and they release one EP a year if they are an independent artist. But what I found, by releasing lots of EPs was that, with my album going out in September, for instance, and it has sold 1.2 million copies up to today, there are still new people finding [my music] today. But people that heard it at the beginning already want the new album, it has only been eight months, but they already want the new album."

"But that's because music is so quick nowadays; Rhianna releases a new album every year. There is no kind of wait. So if you are a singer/songwriter trying to build up a fanbase, the best thing to do is just release as much music as possible. So I think Frank releasing an new EP every month is absolute genius. And I think the key is stuff like that; doing original things that no one else is doing, and doing them well and using them a lot."

Who are the people that you use as a sounding board when you write new songs? Or do you just operate alone?
"I operate alone, probably 80 per cent of the time, and the other 20 per cent of the time I'm in the studio and I've got half an idea for a song. And my producer, Jake [Gosling], will flesh it out. That's kind of what happened with Lego House. I had the verse and the chorus written, and that was it. And we fleshed it out and made the song.

"Whereas, with The A Team, it was very much that I sat on my bed and wrote that and thought, 'I like that song'. So it just differs."

Is there anyone you play finished songs to for an opinion early on?
"My manager is good for opinions, and so is my dad. But my dad is very honest with me, so I never really want to play him too much, just because, if he tells me it's s**t, and I think it's good, then it is going to be very conflicting!"

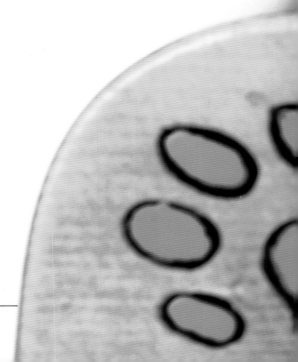

CHOOSING YOUR ACOUSTIC

Every songwriter needs a trusty acoustic at their side – but which factors affect your guitar's tone?

The humble acoustic guitar is an essential part of every guitarist's arsenal, but how many of us can actually explain the tonal differences between, say, mahogany and Engelmann spruce? And how much impact do nut and saddle materials really have on a guitar's tone? We shine a light into the soundhole of acoustic myth and tells you what you should be looking (and listening) for in a steel-strung companion.

❶ Soundboard

Think of this as the guitar's speaker cone – the soundboard responds to the vibration of the strings and air movement. In general, the thinner the wood, the more responsive the soundboard is with these vibrations. But it needs to be thick enough to be strong.

❷ Back and sides

These play a key part in your acoustic's tone. Laminate guitars are made from multiple thin layers of wood bonded together with adhesive, while solid wood parts are made from a single ply. Laminate construction enhances the guitar's strength, but may not transfer the resonance as well as solid construction.

❸ Nut

These can be made from various materials but all need to be hard enough to stop the strings wearing them through. The material choice has an influence on the tone – see the opposite page for more on that.

❹ Truss rod

Just like an electric guitar, the truss rod's job on an acoustic is to counteract the tension of the strings on the neck – adjustment is made from either the headstock end or through the soundhole. The golden rule is to adjust with caution, and make small-increment turns.

❺ Neck

The most common woods used for neck construction are mahogany and, more recently, Spanish cedar. The neck's properties have an impact on tone because when you play, as much energy as possible needs to travel to the bridge to get those soundboard vibrations cooking. A very thin neck may be easier to play but your notes won't sustain as strongly compared to a thicker neck. It's a matter of compromise.

❻ Fingerboard

The radius of a typical acoustic fingerboard usually measures between 15 and 18 inches (381-457mm) – significantly flatter than most electrics. Most acoustic 'boards are made from rosewood or ebony: the latter wood is denser and tends to sound brighter.

❼ Frets

The frets on an acoustic guitar tend to be thinner than those on an electric guitar, because acoustic playing technique usually involves far fewer string bends.

❽ Bridge saddle

Like the nut, these tend to be made from plastic, bone or synthetic ivory (see the opposite page for more on the differences between them) and have an impact on string vibrations and therefore sound of the guitar.

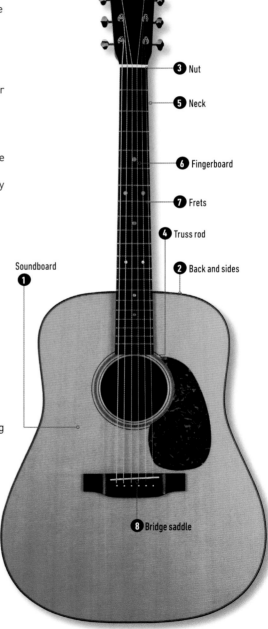

❸ Nut

❺ Neck

❻ Fingerboard

❼ Frets

❹ Truss rod

❷ Back and sides

Soundboard ❶

❽ Bridge saddle

Acoustic FAQ

What shape of guitar is best for me?
Characteristics related to acoustic shapes make them better for some players than others. A dreadnought is a good all-rounder; it's the classic acoustic shape that's suitable for flat-picking or strumming. Ditto the grand auditorium, with its wider lower body bout – a Martin signature model of this shape was used on Eric Clapton's Unplugged performance and many other brands' examples sport a cutaway. The bigger-bodied super jumbo is better for strummers who want a big, booming rhythm sound, whereas the smaller-bodied parlour shape has been favoured by traditional blues and folk players who want midrange punch for fingerpicking styles.

Is it worth paying the extra for a guitar with a solid back and sides?
Usually, but it doesn't cost a lot extra. Guitars with solid backs and sides take some time to mature but often end up having a warmer, more resonant sound than the laminated variety. One of the greatest things about an acoustic guitar that you bond with as a player is that it could become a friend for life – whether as a songwriting tool, essential studio muse or just an accessible strummer for the living room. And the more inspiring it sounds for you, the better. The advances in manufacturing in countries such as China mean solid-construction acoustics are nowhere near as expensive as they used to be.

With unplugged acoustic tone, we're talking about the way that the air is being pushed around and the vibrations that movement creates. You want your guitar to enable rather than stifle the vibrations, and solid wood back and sides are going to help push the sound out the soundhole.

Different tonewoods have different characteristics, too. Rosewood tends to be warmer sounding for back and sides with more tonal colour in the lower mids. Trebles also tend to have more presence compared to the main solid alternative, mahogany. But mahogany has its own attractions. The best mahogany guitars have strong trebles with an almost chimey string separation when combined with a spruce top. With fewer midrange overtones, notes sound more direct than with rosewood.

Dreadnought | **Grand Auditorium** | **Super Jumbo**

There are other options available, including sapele – an African wood that's similar to mahogany – and koa, which sits somewhere between the warmth of rosewood and the bright, punchy attack of maple.

A lot of acoustic guitar tops seem to be made from spruce – why's that?
Spruce is ideal for tops because it has a good mix of strength, clarity and dynamics, and it looks good. There are a few different types. Sitka spruce is the most common, found in the US and Canada. The lighter Engelmann spruce is found in the same part of the world and is seen as an upgrade from Sitka. German spruce is often used for classical guitars and is similar to Engelmann, while Adirondack is the most expensive – it responds well to hard playing while delivering balanced dynamics.

I heard a nut and bridge saddle made from bone is best... is it?
Bone and synthetic bone (Graph Tech's Tusq is an example of a man-made bone-replica) are good for transferring the sound of your strings. Cheap plastics won't contribute much at all in comparison. On the whole, synthetic bone helps the tone sound a little brighter than the real bone. It's also more resilient so will need replacing less often.

Some acoustics have the neck joining the body at a different fret – either the 12th or the 14th. Does it really matter?
Yes, it does. Most acoustics you'll come across will be the 14-fret join variety and 12-fret acoustics tend to be smaller-bodied guitars. The difference is about more than just how far down the dusty end of the neck you want to play.

The point where the neck heel is joined to the guitar's body differs between them, and this affects how rigid the neck is, as well the position of the bridge on the guitar's soundboard.

These are two factors, among all the others, that affect the tone of an acoustic guitar. Which leads us to a final point we can't stress enough: with all these variables, you need to get your paws on as many different acoustics as possible and get a feel for them. Take a guitar-playing friend to the music shop with you and play the guitars together for a live appreciation of their differences. Sooner or later, you'll find your steel-strung soulmate.

FIX YOUR GUITAR

This is my guitar this is my axe. There may be others like it but this one is mine..." if that's your mantra when it comes to your guitar then taking care of it should come as second nature. In the following pages, we show you the basic of restringing and retuning your guitar to getting the soldering iron out and fixing major issues. Be warned though – if you are unsure of ANY of the techniques here then take it to a professional.

RESTRINGING YOUR GUITAR

Changing your strings isn't difficult, but by following this guide, you'll make sure you get it right quickly and easily every time

Learning how to change your strings is an essential part of playing the guitar. You should aim to change your guitar strings every month or so, or as soon as the sound starts to dull/the strings start to oxidise.

The good news is that this is one of the easiest running 'repairs' you can make to your guitar, and the more you do it, the easier it gets!

Here, we're using a steel-string acoustic guitar to demonstrate but you can apply a similar principle (minus the bridge pins) to an electric guitar too. It'll become second nature in no time!

1 When you're removing bridge pins, always use the right tool for the job. Most string winders have a built-in notch for removing pins. Never use pliers or snips – you could damage the bridge or pins.

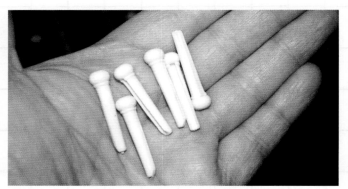

2 If the bridge pins in your guitar are worn out or look like they've been got at by a hungry critter, replace them. Plain plastic pins cost from around 50p each. Right, on with the restringing...

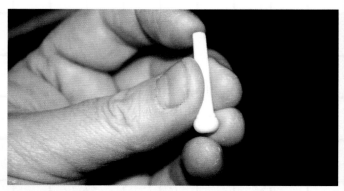

3 The ball end of each string has to secure itself against the underside of the guitar's bridge. If you allow it to sit on the tip of the pin (see above), the pin will work itself loose.

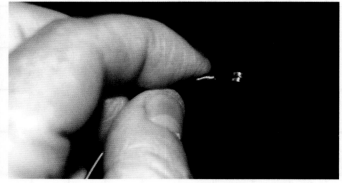

4 Putting a curve in the string's winding will help the ball end avoid the tip of the bridge pin and go where it's supposed to. Gently bend the winding as we've shown above.

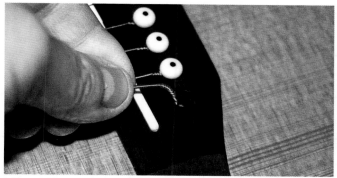

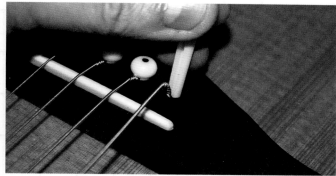

5 The ball end of your string should look like the one in the picture. Next, slip the string into its hole in the bridge. Then grab a bridge pin and slide that into the hole.

6 Make sure the groove in the bridge pin is facing the soundhole of the guitar. If you don't, the pin and string won't lock together and the pin will pop out when you tune the guitar.

7 Push the pin into place while simultaneously pulling on the string with your other hand. You should feel the string and pin snap into place. Right, let's move on up to the headstock end of the guitar...

8 It's time to wind the string around its corresponding machinehead post. First, snip the string about two inches past the machinehead. Next, poke the end of the string through the hole in the 'head.

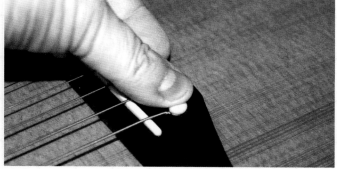

9 Start winding the string on the machinehead post with your string winder. You want to end up with four or five neat windings on the post. The windings shouldn't overlap.

10 As you're winding the string up to tension, keep an eye on the bridge pin. You might find that it pops up a bit as the string tension increases. If it does, just push it back down.

11 Repeat the restringing process with the rest of the strings. When you have them all up to pitch, give them a good tug one by one and retune. The tuning will eventually settle.

12 We've seen bridge pins wrapped in tape and jammed into their holes, held in place by Plasticine, and even entombed in superglue. Don't cut corners; get it right and your pins will stay put.

ADJUSTING YOUR GUITAR'S NECK

Getting your neck's 'relief' right will improve playability, tone and tuning. Here's how to get ahead of the curve...

Steel-string guitars put a lot of tension on the neck of your guitar. To counteract this and to strengthen the neck, your guitar is fitted with something called a truss rod. If your truss rod is too loose, it won't be working hard enough to offset the tension from the strings when they're up to pitch. This can result in a high action (the distance between the strings and the fretboard) and poor intonation (your guitar's tuning across the scale of the neck). You can adjust your truss rod with an Allen key (usually supplied with your guitar) to sort out a dip in the neck.

While adjusting the truss rod is a simple task, you do have to treat it with a certain amount of respect – overzealous tightening can break the rod in two – so pay close attention to our step-by-step guide.

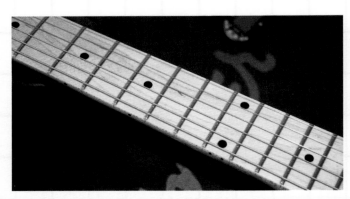

1 Just to make sure we're all on the same page here, a truss rod is a metal bar that runs through the centre of a guitar neck. Adjusting the truss influences the 'straightness' of the neck.

2 Before you eyeball the neck, confirm that your guitar is tuned up to pitch, or your preferred alternate tuning, with fresh strings. If the tuning isn't right, it can affect the straightness of the neck.

3 Hold your guitar's body. If you hold the guitar by the headstock, you'll put slight pressure on the neck and this will give you a false reading of the neck's straightness. You have been warned!

4 Look down the bass side of the fingerboard. Try closing one eye as you do so. You'll look like Popeye, but it helps you focus. You should now be able to tell if the neck is straight or warped.

5 If the neck needs adjustment, find the truss rod adjuster bolt. On most modern guitars, you'll find the bolt in a hole or under a plastic plate next to the top nut on the headstock.

6 Most modern guitars have an Allen bolt that's adjusted with, you guessed it, an Allen key. Some guitars, such as Gibson Les Paul and SG models, have a nut that's adjusted with a box wrench.

7 Some guitars and basses, like our Tokai Hard Puncher, have a truss rod bolt at the body end of the neck. You may have to remove the scratchplate, or the neck itself, to access this bolt.

8 If, when you've eyeballed the neck, it's 'over-bent' (higher in the middle than it is at the headstock and body ends), use the Allen key, wrench or screwdriver to adjust the truss rod bolt anticlockwise.

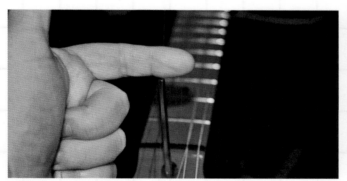

9 When you're faced with a neck that's 'dipped' (lower in the middle of the fingerboard than at either end), simply increase the tension on the truss rod by using your tool to adjust it clockwise.

10 The Allen key, wrench or screwdriver should be seated firmly in or over the truss rod bolt or nut to avoid damage. Chewing up the nut or bolt creates a big problem for future adjustments.

11 Even small adjustments of the truss rod can make a big difference to the straightness of the neck. With every small turn, retune the guitar and peer down both sides of the neck to check your progress.

12 Now that the neck has been adjusted correctly, you should find your choking notes are just a bad memory. The truss rod isn't really intimidating at all – you just have to treat it with respect.

FIX YOUR GUITAR

ADJUSTING YOUR GUITAR'S INTONATION

All you need is a screwdriver and your tuner and off you go!

If your guitar sounds out of tune the further you play up the neck, or open chords sound out of tune with each other, then you need to check your guitar's intonation. Let's be honest here, this job frightens most guitarists – but as you'll find out, it's really easy to do yourself. All you need is a screwdriver and a guitar tuner. And, importantly, make sure that your guitar has fresh strings. If your strings sound dull then they may not intonate properly. Okay? Deep breath.

1 Connect your guitar to your tuner and strike the first string. That's the thinnest one, naturally. Make sure the string is in tune. Next, fret the string at the 12th fret.

2 The fretted E note should register the same as the open first string. Your tuner will show you if the fretted note is intonated properly. If the note is flat or sharp move to step three.

3 If the fretted note is sharp use your screwdriver to move the bridge saddle away from the guitar's pickups. If the note is flat, move the saddle towards the pickups.

4 Each time you move the saddle check the string's tuning before testing the intonation. You should have the guitar in the playing position when checking the tuning, not on its back.

5 When the string is properly intonated repeat the process from the rest of the strings. Then you can congratulate yourself on a job well done. You'll never have to pay someone to intonate your guitar ever again!

If your jack socket breaks, your gig or rehearsal is over – so take care of it!

FIX YOUR GUITAR

BROKEN JACK SOCKET

Here we will help you make the gear you already have sound and play better than ever!

Words: Ed Mitchell

Of all the perishable items bolted to our guitars, the jack socket is the one we all forget about until it goes wrong. We can just about survive a broken string, even a faulty pickup switch providing it still works in one position. But when a jack socket snuffs it, the rehearsal is over. Worse still, imagine you're at a gig and you're suddenly the silent partner in the band. It doesn't matter how cool your guitar looks if you can't make a noise.

The good news – and the reason why we're here today – is that a dodgy jack socket can often be fixed. And better still, it can usually be mended by you, with some simple tools, for nothing! You can even prevent it breaking bad in the first place by following our advice.

Before we crack on with this easy guide we should point out that pulling bits out of your guitar can invalidate your warranty. So check your warranty and all the fine print before you get stuck in. Right, let's fix your guitar!

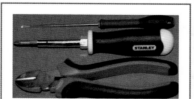

WHAT YOU NEED
Screwdriver
Pliers
Guitar cable
Your amp
Sandpaper/Emery board

SKILL LEVEL
Beginner

What's The Deal With...
TRUSS RODS

The chances are your guitar has have a metal bar running inside the length of its neck. This bar, what we guitar geeks like to call the 'truss rod'. It counters the enormous tension exerted by the strings on your guitar's neck to stop it bending over time.

It wasn't always thus. Despite the fact that brilliantly-named Gibson employee Thaddeus McHugh patented the first true truss rod in 1921, as late as 1950, Fender Esquires [the single-pickup version that would become the Telecaster] were rolling out of Fullerton, California, without a truss rod fitted. By '51, Leo Fender had a change of heart and an adjustable truss rod soon became the standard.

1 Like most of the sticky situations we find ourselves in throughout our lives, in guitar maintenance, prevention is always the best cure. So, keep an eye on your guitar's jack socket. If it starts to work loose, don't ignore the problem until it's too late. Grab some pliers and tighten the nut.

2 Your jack socket stands a better chance of a long life if you take the strain of the weight of your guitar cable off it. Run the cable between your guitar's strap and its body. Now, if you accidentally tread on your cable you won't pull it out of the jack socket or cause any damage.

3 Classic scenario. You signal is cutting out. Must be the socket, right? Well put the tools down – it's more likely that your cable is to blame. Imagine stripping down a car engine and realising you just ran out of petrol. So, test with another cable to see if the problem is still there.

4 So your cable is fine but the guitar is still cutting out or dead. Let's eliminate other potentials: you could have a dirty pickup switch. To test it, run the switch back and forth quickly to see if the guitar springs t life. If so, then clean or replace your switch. If not, the socket needs to come out...

5 Most guitars have a jackplate – a piece of square, oblong or rugby ball-shaped plastic or metal that anchors the socket where it needs to be. Grab your screwdriver and remove the plate's mounting screws. Now, put them somewhere safe where they can't get lost or scratch your guitar's finish.

6 Hopefully, when you remove the Jack socket what you have looks the same as the little guy in our photo. Old school sockets such as these can usually be repaired if they aren't badly corroded or missing parts. If your socket is the long enclosed barrel type then it will have to be replaced.

7 As long as there are no loose wires, the first thing to do is make sure the socket holds your jack plug securely. That is the job of long metal clip above. Test fit your cable and see how secure the plug is in the socket. If the plug wiggles around then that long metal clip will need to be adjusted.

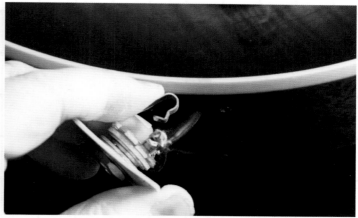

8 Gently push the long metal clip towards the hole in the centre of the jack socket. Bend it a little (don't break it!) then test fit the jack plug. When it fits firmly in place and doesn't move around test the guitar through your amp. You should be back in business but don't screw it back in place just yet...

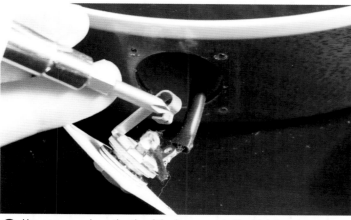

9 You can now clean the tip of the long metal clip. Metal parts can attract dust and develop corrosion that causes your guitar to crackle. Just scratch the surface of the clip where it mates with the tip of the jack plug. You can use light sandpaper, Emery board or a screwdriver tip.

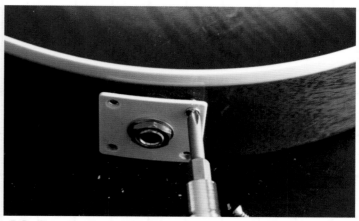

10 To protect your sanity, always test the guitar before you put it back together. You don't want to do guitar maintenance while angry! Take your time and ensure that you don't trap any wires under the jackplate, strip the screws that hold the plate in place, or damage the guitar's finish.

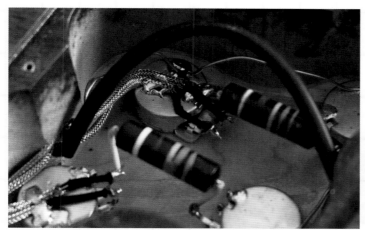

11 Get used to thinking about the health of your guitar's inner workings. When a control feels loose get on it right away. If you hear a buzz or crackle don't wait until it ruins a gig. The volume and tone pots (aka potentiometers) and the pickup selector switch can usually be cleaned.

12 You may have pulled out the jack socket to find the ultimate horror: a loose wire. This can occur when the socket is loose and spins around in its jackplate. To fix the problem you'll need to become proficient in the noble art of soldering – an essential guitar maintenance skill.

Soldering can help you do many basic fixes on your guitar

THE ART OF SOLDERING

Get to grips with a skill that will open up a whole new world of guitar fixing for you

Words: Ed Mitchell

Of all the basic guitar repair skills that you can learn to do yourself, soldering is the one that will just keep on giving. Master the noble art of soldering, and you can do all sorts of cool stuff – from installing a set of new pickups, to repairing those pesky broken wires and also replacing faulty components like switches, pots and jack sockets. You can even custom-build your own guitar cables if you want to! And all this is possible with equipment that costs about the same as it would to pay an expert to fit a set of pickups to your guitar.

However, remember: we are dealing with serious heat here – a bad burn from a soldering iron will probably land you in A&E, so you have to know what you're doing and be careful. That's where our step-by-step guide comes in. It's actually in two parts (alongside Switching Pickups on page 195). In this first installment, we'll take you through the essential equipment and techniques, plus the safety stuff you need to get started.

WHAT YOU NEED
Soldering iron with stand and cleaning sponge
60/40 rosin core solder
Helping Hands
Solder sucker
Solder mat
Safety glasses
Snips

SKILL LEVEL
Intermediate

What's The Deal With...
FINGERBOARDS?

A fingerboard isn't just the place for your frets, what it's made from makes a real difference to your tone. Pre-1950, most 'boards were made from rosewood and ebony. Rosewood is a softwood, that provides a warm tone. Ebony is a hardwood often used on more expensive guitars, which offers up a snappy tone with great sustain.

In 1950, Leo Fender came up with an new concept, a solid body guitar with a detachable maple neck. The Esquire and Broadcaster had maple 'boards, which like those earlier ebony jobs, possessed a bright tone which would hook generations of country pickers. So remember, fingerboard wood is an essential part of your tone palette.

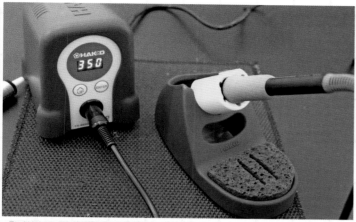

1 We're using a pro soldering iron, but cheaper models are easily available. Go for 40-watts so you can generate decent heat, and make sure it has a pointed tip, not a flat blade. Get one with a stand [with a solder sponge for cleaning the iron's tip] so you have somewhere to rest the hot iron safely.

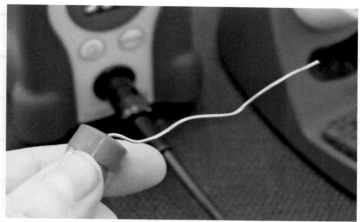

2 You're also going to need some solder. Get a roll of the 60/40 rosin core stuff. It's the best for guitar maintenance jobs. We'd also recommend buying a solder mat to protect the surface you're working on. Hot solder will happily burn holes in your shiny dining room table, so be careful!

3 Get yourself a 'Helping Hands'. These useful little stands have crocodile clips to hold small components in place for soldering, and a magnifying glass so you can see what you're getting yourself into.

4 Other essentials? We couldn't live without our 'solder sucker' – a spring-loaded gadget that sucks hot solder off of a component. So if you put too much solder on a component, dropped it in the wrong place, or there's old solder you want to replace, you can use this handy little tool to get rid of it.

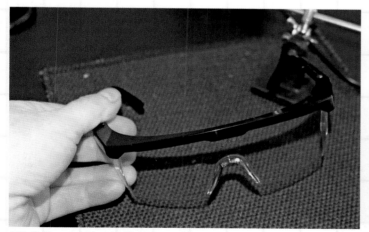

5 Before you heat stuff up, get a pair of safety glasses. Don't skip this step! Hot solder can spit and you really don't want that in your eyes. Also, only solder in a well-ventilated room [hot solder gives off fumes] and keep the iron away from your guitar's finish, relatives, pets and body!

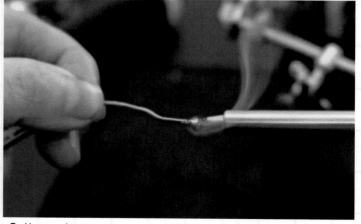

6 You need to prepare a new soldering iron by 'tinning' its tip: plug in the iron and allow it to heat up. Apply solder to the tip of the iron until it's coated in the shiny stuff. Leave it for a few seconds then wipe it on the solder sponge. Repeat this process a few times...

7 When possible work on new components away from the guitar with your Helping Hand. New components have a protective coating to prevent corrosion that make it difficult to solder onto. So scratch the coating with a file or the tip of a screwdriver to give the solder something to grab onto.

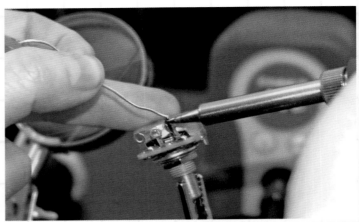

8 If you want to solder a wire to a tab on a potentiometer, you have to prepare both parts first. The secret is to apply heat with the tip of your iron to the component first, then introduce the solder and allow it to flow onto the tab as shown above.

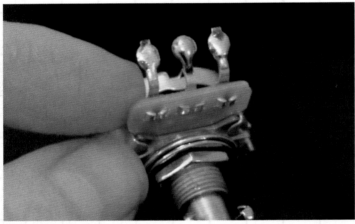

9 If you've got this far, you're doing great – but now it's time for a little quality control. A good solder joint will look shiny. A dull solder joint is bad news. It might hold for a while but will eventually break from its component. So, if it's dull, do the job again until you get a shiny silver finish.

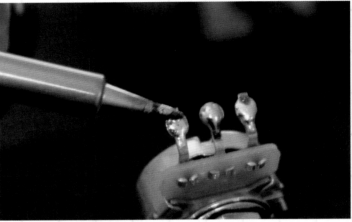

10 Always allow solder to cool naturally. We've seen countless solderers blow on hot solder to cool it down. This isn't helpful though – no matter how tempting. There's moisture in your breath and that can wreck the integrity of the joint. Solder cools down and toughens fairly quickly, so leave it alone.

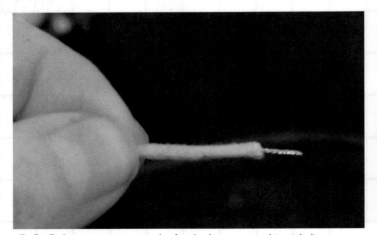

11 Before you prepare a wire for tinning, you need to strip it. Vintage-style wire has a cloth covering that you pull back to expose the metal core inside, as shown above. Modern plastic-coated wiring needs to be stripped with a pair of snips. Be gentle and ensure you strip the coating and not the wire.

12 With the wires exposed, apply heat with your iron and flow solder on. Now connect to the tab in the pot. Introduce the wire to the tab and melt the solder in both with your iron. Take the iron away, hold the wire in place and allow the joint to cool. You have now mastered basic soldering!

Fitting new pickups can really enhance your guitar's tone

SWITCHING PICKUPS

Want to give your guitar a tonal overhaul? We'll show you how to swap out your old coils for some shiny new pups!

Words: Ed Mitchell

In the previous pages, we showed you the basics of how to solder stuff together, and also promised we'd talk you through the process of retrofitting a set of new pickups to your electric guitar – well, now that time has come! Learning to fit new components to your guitar is a real time- and money-saver. It saves time, because you don't have to drag your gear all the to your local music shop or luthier's holdout and then wait a few days or whatever to get the stuff back. Money? Well, you fix it, you don't pay a repair bill, of course! Buying a set of new pickups that will offer a noticeable boost in your guitar's tone can cost a couple of hundred quid or more. Having them fitted by a tech will add upwards of £50.

It can also help you better understand how your guitar works, so there really are many reasons why doing the job yourself makes sense! So, stick on your safety goggles, plug in your soldering iron and let's get stuck in!

WHAT YOU NEED
Soldering iron with stand and cleaning sponge
60/40 rosin core solder
Helping Hands
Solder sucker
Solder mat
Safety glasses
Snips

SKILL LEVEL
Intermediate

What's The Deal With... COIL TAPS?

For years, guitar players have taken to describing any device that turns a humbucker into a single coil as a 'coil tap'. Nope. Some guitars do indeed have coil-taps, but many others have a coil-splitter. And there's a difference.

The coil-splitter, a switch, generally a push/pull function on a tone knob, switches one coil of a humbucker (which has two coils) off. A humbucker with one coil down is now a single coil...

In a coil tap, the control dials out a chunk of the pickup's copper winding to reduce output which gives more of a single-coil voice..

The bottom line is you're getting two sounds from a single pickup but hey, it's good to know the difference...

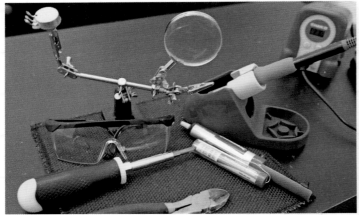

1 Gather all your kit together on your work bench – it's also listed opposite for quick reference. Before we start, make sure your work surface is protected by your solder mat, open a window for ventilation and put on your safety glasses – yes we mean it!

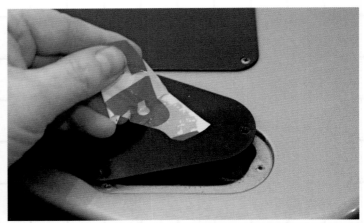

2 Find the control plate. On a Strat or Tele that plate will be on the front, but our guitar has it on the back. Remove the plate – carefully storing the screws – then have a good look around inside. If the plate won't pop out, try sticking some tape on it and pulling.

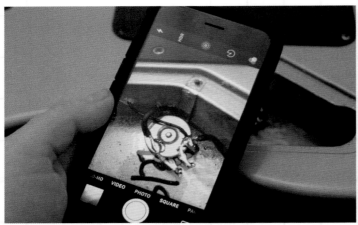

3 Take a good look at the wiring inside the guitar. Before you do anything else, make a note of where the pickup wires are. You can follow them with your fingers. Either make a diagram or, more simply, just take a few snaps of the details on your phone.

4 Look at the wiring diagram that came with the pickups. If you didn't get one – say the pickups are second hand – a Google search help. Hopefully, the pickup wiring in your old and new pups will be the same. If not, you'll have to work out which are the hot and earth wires before you proceed.

5 It makes the most sense to remove the strings before you fit new pickups and replace them with new strings when you're done. However, you can complete the task (with a little more annoyance) by just loosening the strings and keeping them out of your way.

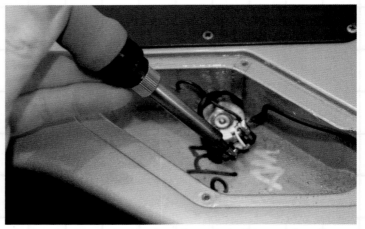

6 First desolder their wiring from the controls. Take your time. You don't want to scorch the guitar's finish or any other wiring. Heat the spot where the wire is soldered to the pot or switch. When the solder melts, gently pull the wire to free it. Don't yank it, as hot solder can splash back on you!

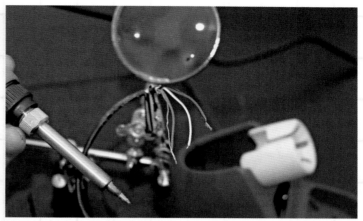

7 With the pickup wires removed, you can unscrew the old pickups. Start with the bridge unit. Carefully remove the screws, use the right size screwdriver, then pull the pickup from the guitar. Repeat the process for the neck pickup – if you're replacing that too – then prepare the new pickups.

8 Apply the tip of the soldering iron to the end of the wire and allow the solder to flow onto it – a pair of Helping Hands (like those pictured) would help here. Remember, a good coating of solder should be shiny, not dull so keep your eye on the quality at all times.

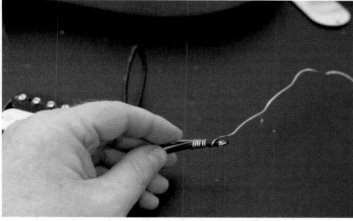

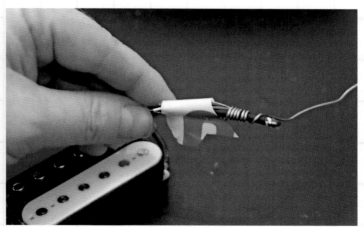

9 It's time to install the pickup wires. Threading the wiring through the body and into the control cavity can be a pain, so instead thread some solder through the body until one end is in the pickup rout and the other is in the control cavity, wrap it securely around the new wire and then slowly pull it through.

10 Install the new neck pickup first. Once it's screwed in place, fit the bridge unit. If you fit the bridge pickup first you make it harder to thread the neck pup's wiring through the body as it has to pass through the bridge pickup rout. Place tape on the wires to remember which is which.

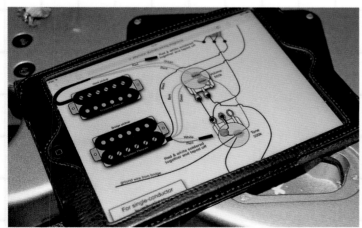

11 Heat your iron and don safety goggles. With your wiring diagram establish which wires are to be connected to ground and which are hot. Apply heat to the tabs with your iron. When the area is hot introduce the solder. Next, reheat the solder and dip the end of the wire into it and hold...

12 Allow the hot solder joint to cool naturally before giving the wire a gentle tug to make sure it's secure. Once done, you can test the new pickups by connecting to your amp and tapping the pups with a screwdriver – now to rock!

REPLACING YOUR POTS

Snap, crackle and pop is for breakfast cereal, not guitars – sort out those annoying noisy controls with this guide

Words: Stu Williams

Your guitar's controls are a low-cost, yet integral part of your tone, yet they're often overlooked. There are three main things that can go wrong with your control pots. The first (and easiest) is when the pot has come loose, so if you turn your volume or tone control to 10 it continues to turn, because you're actually spinning the entire pot around inside your guitar. Not only is it annoying, but leave it long enough and you'll snap the connecting wires inside –

which is a much bigger problem! Next up is a scratching or popping sound when you turn the control. It's usually intermittent, but it's up there with microphone feedback on the list of 'Things your audience will hate'. It's also a simple fix, which we'll get to in a moment. Finally, you may discover that your pot is simply worn out, not connected or even physically broken – it might be creating some extreme noise, or not operating at all. Let's take control and sort this out...

WHAT YOU NEED
Soldering iron with stand and cleaning sponge
Control pot
Helping Hands
Solder sucker
Screwdriver
Safety glasses
Electrical cleaner

SKILL LEVEL
Intermediate

DOFF YOUR CAPS

Your tone pots will have a capacitor attached to them. This component is the bit that actually rolls off your high frequencies when you turn it down. Capacitors used in guitar circuits aren't polarised, so it doesn't matter which way round you fit the legs – we normally go with the printed side facing out from the pot. They're measured in microfarads (uF) and will be marked with a number. You can experiment with different values and materials for different results.

1 The process of working on volume or tone controls is similar, but there are differences. Volume pots often use a logarithmic (B) or 'audio' taper, while tone controls are often linear (A), but can also be logarithmic. They will be stamped with the relevant letters, so go like-for-like when replacing them.

2 When replacing a volume or tone pot, you need to make sure that you get the right value for your guitar. As with most things, it's not set in stone, but as a rule of thumb, single-coil pickup guitars use 250k pots, while humbucker-equipped ones use 500k pots.

3 Before you remove your pot, you'll have to take the control knob off. This can vary between 'simple' and 'why won't this budge?!' in difficulty, depending on your guitar. Don't use a screwdriver to prise it out: instead, grab yourself a thin cloth or duster and head to the next step.

4 If you find that your knob just won't budge no matter how much you pull, get the edge of your cloth underneath. Next, fold the cloth up and pull straight up – the fiddly piece of plastic should come straight off. Go slowly – you don't want to break it.

5 Next, you need to determine how to get to your guitar's innards. On a Strat-type guitar with scratchplate-mounted electronics, you'll need to take the strings off and unscrew the scratchplate. If your controls are mounted through the body (like on our Les Paul), getting to them is easier.

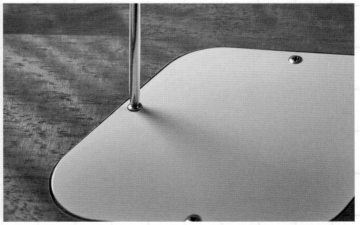

6 This is the guitar's control cavity cover. Take out the screws and lift it out – you should be able to do this with your fingernails, if not, turn it upside down and let gravity do it's thing. Again, don't try to prise it out with a screwdriver you could damage the surrounding wood.

7 You're in! Our Les Paul is pretty neatly wired, but if your guitar has had previous after-market work, it may not be. Arrange the wires neatly and take a photo on your phone. This way you'll be able to see where everything goes if you accidentally dislodge a wire.

8 If your controls are turning past the point of their usual travel, you need to fix them down properly. Arm yourself with the correct sized spanner or socket. Push the bottom of the pot so it's firmly in place, then tighten that sucker up. It's one of the easiest fixes you can make.

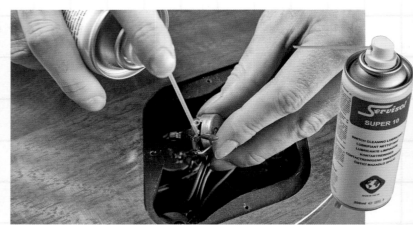

9 Let's look at the problem of crackles. The back of your pots are pretty much sealed, but that doesn't stop dust and causing noise when you turn the control. You can see inside the pot by looking along the edge near the contacts, which allows for cleaning the inside track of your pot.

10 Get some cleaning solution (we're using Servisol Super 10, which both cleans and lubricates), attach the straw to the nozzle and blast it in the gap. Don't go mad, or you'll end up with a flood inside the control cavity. Whatever you do, don't use oil, it's not the same thing!

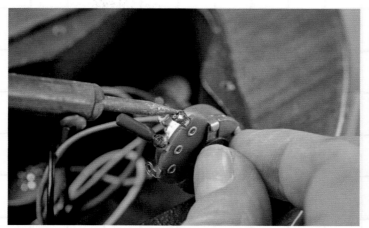

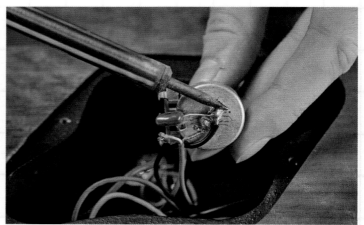

11 Next, quickly turn the pot up and down a dozen or so times to help dislodge the crud. If that doesn't fix it, it's time to replace the pot. Make a note of where the wires are connected, then desolder the connections. Undo the nut we talked about earlier and put your replacement pot in.

12 With your new pot safely back in the body of your guitar, refer back to the photos, notes or pieces of masking tape that you used to determine what goes where, and connect the wires back up. There you go – noise free operation for thousands more turns!

Making your own leads lets you customise them to fit your 'board

MAKING YOUR OWN GUITAR LEADS

With a few simple tools you can mend and make your own custom guitar and pedalboard cables, learn how below!

Words: Jack Ellis

TOP TIP

Guitar cables use mono jacks with two terminals inside. You can tell if a plug is mono or stereo by the black ring around the plug – if there's one, it's mono!

Making your own cables can save you money and offer up some new options to you, What if you need a 45cm right-angle patch lead that's straight on the other end? Got a suspicious crackly lead? Give it a new lease of life or even take your friends' dud leads and repurpose them... sneaky you!

There are basically two types of quarter-inch jack plug (6.35mm if you're metrically inclined): the sealed unit and the type you can take apart. The sealed type usually found on cheaper cables are unfortunately non-serviceable - that doesn't mean you can't liberate the wire though. Brands such as Neutrik or Rean make decent quality jack plugs and you can get quality screened cable from high street electrical stores. If you're making a fresh lead, a good screen will cut down on cable noise and hum in your signal chain, which cheap cables really do not help...

Get your goggles on, and fire up your soldering iron: it's time to lead the way!

WHAT YOU NEED
- ▶ 40-watt soldering iron
- ▶ 60/40 solder
- ▶ Safety glasses
- ▶ Heat shrink tubing
- ▶ Multimeter
- ▶ Helping Hands
- ▶ Scissors
- ▶ Lighter
- ▶ Pliers
- ▶ Wire cutters
- ▶ Wire strippers
- ▶ New mono jack plugs
- ▶ Screened instrument cable

SKILL LEVEL
Intermediate

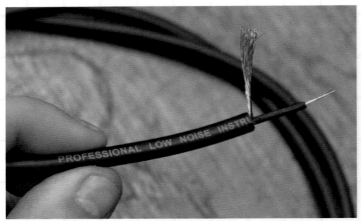

1 Screened cable is a type of audio cable that has an outer wire (screen) that shields the inner wire from electromagnetic hum. We need two wires within this cable – one for the tip of the plug (this carries your signal) and one for the sleeve (to earth). Snip off the length of wire you need.

2 The screened cable needs stripping back and we have to do this in two stages. Let's take off the outer jacket first; this is a delicate scissors job. Slowly roll the cable in the scissors to cut it. Try to cut it 80 percent through then pull the rest off. It's important not to slice through the copper screen!

3 With the outer jacket of the cable gone all of those copper strands of the screen need a twist. Now get your wire stripper and strip the inner wire – this is the wire we will attach to the tip of the lead. Twist those little copper strands a twist, too.

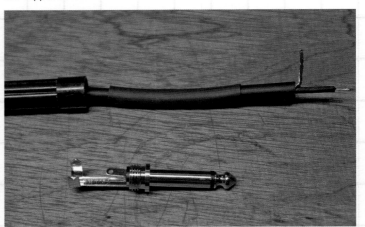

4 Before we get any further into our DIY cable build, slide on the socket's outer screw-on case followed by your shrink tubing that's been cut to length. The tubing will cover over the solder joints and also will hang out of the back, acting as a strain relief for the jack plug, too, so it's doubly useful!

5 Tinning is the ancient art of adding a little solder to the two parts that are bound by fate for each other. Pop the jack plugs into your helping hands and put a decent blob of solder on each terminal. Don't over do it and try not to heat it up too much. Tin the ends of the cable while you're at it, too.

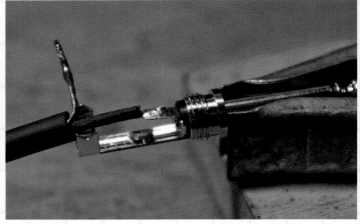

6 With the jack plug still in the helping hands, solder the inner wire to the middle solder tab of the jack lead. If your stripped centre wire is too long trim it down first. We've purposely stripped a little too much outer jacket, and you will see why we've done that just over the page...

7 Now we'll solder the screen cable onto the plug. On some plugs it's not obvious where to attach it. As we have a little excess cable here, the screen will bunch up the centre wire a little. This is a good thing as it means if the lead gets yanked it's less likely to pull off the delicate solder joint.

8 The testing phase. Set your multimeter 20 kOhms and place one probe at the different places of each end of the jack socket. Tip-to-tip should read 0 ohms (no resistance), sleeve-to-sleeve should read as 0 ohms. If you get no reading or "1" you have a break in the wire or a dodgy solder joint.

9 Next up we're going to connect one end of the multimeter to the tip and the other to the sleeve. The reading we're looking for here is 1 kOhms – that's your multimeter's way of saying infinite resistance, or in other words, "the wires are fine."

10 Finally, you can try plugging the cable in and testing it. Check it's not humming or cracking when you wiggle the lead, too. If all is well, gently squish the jacket clamp down with your pliers so it grips it tightly. Not too hard, however, as you may puncture the jacket and cause a short circuit.

11 Slide the shrink tubing in place and heat it with a lighter on a medium flame. Be careful not to melt the shrink tubing (or burn your thumb). You can re-soften the heat shrink tubing later if needed.

12 Finally, slide the outer tube up and screw into place to protect your wiring. Make it tight to ensure they don't unscrew by accident. If you have a second larger gauge of heat shrink tubing, you can encase the screw-on cover with this to make it even sturdier.

Aluminium foil is good for more than just cooking your baked potatoes...

HOW TO SHIELD YOUR GUITAR

This technique for fighting earth noise upgrades any guitar

Words: Jack Ellis

In the world of audio, hum and interference are the enemy – the extraneous sound that you hear in your chain is known as noise.

Guitar pickups are actually thousands of turns or tiny wire wrapped around a magnet and they are an antenna for picking up accidental noise alongside the actual string's signal. Single-coil pickups are completely unprotected with the P-90 being the "noisiest" type, whereas humbucking double-coil pickups are cleverly designed to "buck the hum" hence the name. Single coils have no such protection, and so they need all the help they can get!

It's not just the pickups either – the rest of your guitar's circuit can let in noise, too. To combat this we apply foil to the rear of the pickguard and the walls of the electronics cavity will create a closed aluminium box to block out all of that nastiness and keep the signal clean.

With this upgrade your guitar's hum will be reduced, as any noise creeping in through the main circuit will quite literally be foiled!

WHAT YOU NEED

▸ Aluminium foil shielding tape
▸ Electrical insulation tape
▸ Scissors
▸ Philips screwdriver
▸ Wire cutters
▸ Wiring diagram for you guitar
▸ Jiffy bag or soft cloth
▸ 60/40 solder
▸ 40w soldering iron
▸ Safety goggles
▸ Multimeter set to 20k ohms

SKILL LEVEL

Intermediate

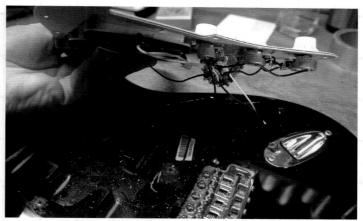

1 We're going to shield a Strat-type guitar today. Conveniently, the Strat has all of its innards mounted to the pickguard, so servicing it can be pretty easy. Take off the strings and the scratchplate screws, and make sure you store the screws in a pot so you don't lose them.

2 Gently lift the pickguard up. Depending on the type of Strat you may have there will be some wires attached. Ours has three that we need to disconnect: two wires to the jack socket (the signal and earth wires) and a string earth wire connected to the chrome bridge.

3 Get yourself something soft to rest the scratchplate on to reduce the risk of a scratched paint job. You should be able to find a wiring diagram for your guitar online, but it's a good idea to make notes on where the wires we're about to remove go – take some pictures on your phone if that helps.

4 Time to cut the wires. By leaving a millimetre or two of the cable attached to the pot, you can use it as a breadcrumb trail when it comes to re-soldering later. If your wires are the same colour, you can label them with masking tape. Make life easier by also removing the jack socket.

5 This is the foil tape, it costs about a five pounds and has an adhesive back to make application easier. Before you stick it down give the electronics cavity a clean and clear out any dust. Luckily this scratchplate is already shielded. If yours isn't, it's definitely worth doing that, too.

6 Foil it! Cover each nook and cranny to minimise interference getting to the wiring. We're going to cover the walls and bottom of the electrics cavity and the pickup routs, too – walls included. Try to be as neat as you can, but more importantly make sure it's firmly stuck to the walls.

7 With the cavities covered, cut an extra piece of foil tape. This is going to be used as a tab to make sure the rear of the pickguard (which is already foil shielded) makes contact with the cavity shielding when the screws are done up. Stick this over the screw hole next to the pickup selector switch.

8 Using the guide you made earlier, reconnect all the wires you cut with a soldering iron. Tin your connections and take care not to melt the plastic shielding on your wires. Take it steady, and enlist an extra hand from someone if you need to steady the scratchplate while you handle the iron.

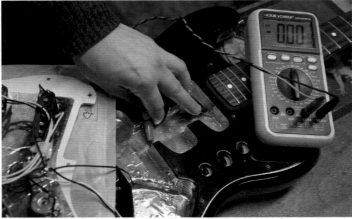

9 With the wires soldered, we're nearly ready. Before we screw the scratchplate down, let's do a couple of tests. The two prongs of your multimeter should read "0" when you attach it to each part of the shielding. This means you have no resistance between each piece.

10 Flip over the scratchplate and put it in place. Before screwing, ensure you haven't trapped any wires and plug the jack lead into an amp. Strike your tuning fork and test each pickup, switch position and pot. Investigate any crackles – the downside to foil is that it is conductive...

11 As a result of this conductivity, if any terminal or wire other than an earth connection makes contact with the foil you'll get a short circuit, and kill your output. If you find that this is happening, move the wire so it can't touch the foil or insulate the offending wire with electrical tape.

12 Once you're sure it's working properly, you can screw down your scratchplate – this seals the lid on your newly shielded electronics cavity. If you have it plugged into the amp at this point you will hear the hum disappear as the pickguard drops on. Voilà, electrical hum can now buzz off.

INDEX

INDEX